Charlie Connelly is a travel and sports writer and the author of six books. *Attention All Shipping* was a Radio 4 Book of the Week and *Stamping Grounds* was selected as one of the sports books of the year by the *Independent* and the *Irish Times*. Charlie is a former rock 'n' roll tour manager, mortuary assistant, operating-theatre orderly and marketing manager for the *Complete Works of Lenin*. He has written for a range of publications including *Arena*, *Time Out* and the *Glasgow Herald*. His media appearances include BBC Radio 4, the World Service and *The Big Breakfast*, and he has been a presenter for BBC1's *The Holiday Programme*.

D1047927

Stamping Grounds

Exploring Liechtenstein and its World Cup Dream

Charlie Connelly

ABACUS

First published in Great Britain in May 2002 by Little, Brown
This paperback edition published in November 2005 by Abacus

The author gratefully acknowledges permission to quote from
the following:
Valley of Peace: The Story of Liechtenstein by Barbara Greene. Copyright ©
Barbara Greene, 1947. Reprinted by permission of Liechtenstein Verlag AG.
Extracts from the *Liechtensteiner Vaterland* newspaper.
Extracts from the *Liechtensteiner Volksblatt* newspaper.

Every effort has been made to trace the copyright holders
and to clear reprint permission for the following:
*The Little Tour: A Journey to Europe's Four Miniature States – Andorra,
Monaco, Leichtenstein* (sic)*, San Marino* by Giles Playfair and
Constantine Fitzgibbon.
Principality of Liechtenstein by Baron Edward von Falz-Fein.
Extract from the *Kurier* newspaper.
If notified, the publisher will be pleased to rectify any
omission in future editions.

A CIP catalogue record for this book
is available from the British Library.

ISBN 0 349 11488 9

Typeset in Sabon
by Palimpsest Book Production Limited,
Polmont, Stirlingshire
Printed and bound in Great Britain by
Clays Ltd, St Ives plc

Abacus
An imprint of
Time Warner Book Group UK
Brettenham House
Lancaster Place
London WC2E 7EN

www.twbg.co.uk

Acknowledgements

I am greatly indebted to the following people for their assistance in the preparation of this book.

Martina Michel-Hoch and Roland Büchel at the Liechtenstein Tourist Office (www.tourismus.li) were most accommodating to my requests for information and assistance and I am very grateful to them both.

Thanks also to Elisabeth Haddow at Austrian Airlines for her help in arranging my travel.

I am hugely grateful to Ralf Wenaweser, Ernst Hasler and Patrik Hefti for their assistance during my time in Liechtenstein. I couldn't have done it without them.

Thanks also to Lola Brown, Martin Frommelt, Peter Rutz, Alan Samson, Sarah Shrubb, Stefanie Leibfried, Chris Stephenson at the Swiss Travel Centre, Matt Wright, Werner Koisser, Robert Diermair, Doug Chapman, Markus Schaper, Lapo Novellini, Thomas Banzer, Tim Bennett, Otto Biedermann, Heinz Zöchbauer, Donald Cowey and Tim Glynne-Jones.

The *Liechtensteiner Fussball-Verband* website can be found at www.lfv.li, while you can read the work of the Greatest Football Journalist in the World, Ernst Hasler, at www.vaterland.li. To catch up with the latest movements of Liechtenstein's star player, see his website at www.mario-frick.li.

Finally, and most importantly, all my love and thanks to Katie.

Stamping Grounds

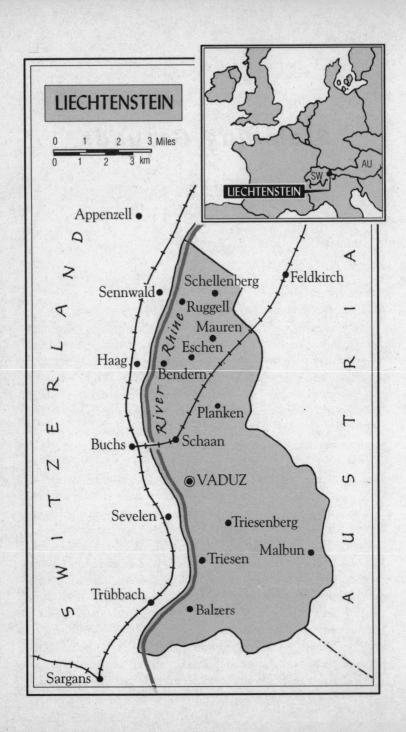

Preface

Liechtenstein, a tear-shaped speck wedged almost unnoticeably between Switzerland and Austria, is really very small.

Just sixteen miles long and less than four wide, there are probably bigger British industrial estates than Liechtenstein. The country's 32,000 residents would not even half fill Old Trafford, and if the population of the Isle of Wight came to stay and was shared out between the Liechtensteiners they'd have four people each. Local bed-linen retailers would be whooping and high-fiving each other for years to come.

Liechtenstein is the fourth smallest nation in the world. Only San Marino, Nauru and Tuvalu can boast shorter borders than Liechtenstein, which could fit itself into Ireland 437 times and into that behemoth of Europe Luxembourg sixteen times. Liechtenstein is so small that the centre pages of its most popular tourist brochure show a map of the entire country and its alpine environs. To give you an idea of the scale, this map of a nation has children's playgrounds marked on it. Liechtenstein has no airport, probably because by the time any planes had landed and skidded to a halt they'd be in Switzerland. When Swissair named one of their aeroplanes *Fürstentum Liechtenstein* (Principality of Liechtenstein) recently, the royal family had to drive to Zurich to cut the ribbon and fly over the principality because there was nowhere to land.

Most of the residents of Liechtenstein's eleven village

communities busy themselves with the country's three main occupations: high finance, the production of postage stamps and the manufacture of some of the world's most finely crafted dentures. Liechtenstein is also a tax haven, and hence is home to three times as many registered companies as people. But amid the principality's snow-capped peaks, quirky industry and bulging bank vaults Liechtenstein's national football team enters every World Cup and European Championship qualifying competition. And in football it's not just in size that Liechtenstein is disadvantaged. The country has no league and only seven football clubs, all of whom play in the lower divisions across the border in Switzerland. Of Liechtenstein's population of around 32,000, over one third are foreign nationals and thus ineligible for the national side.

Indeed, the pool of international talent in the principality can be measured reasonably accurately: there are approximately 3,000 Liechtenstein men in total between the ages of fifteen and thirty-five. Not all of them will play football, and of those who do only a percentage will be capable of kicking a ball in a straight line. So it's probably a reasonable guess that coach Ralf Loose has around four or five hundred basically competent Liechtenstein footballers from whom to select a national team.

Until recently Liechtenstein had just one professional footballer. The same player, Mario Frick, is Liechtenstein's all-time leading international goalscorer. With three. And one of those was a penalty.

Liechtenstein's national team thus faces odds as insurmountable as the alpine peaks within its borders if the climb were to be attempted in flip-flops. It's not surprising then that Liechtenstein's international record consists largely of heavy defeats. Before the start of the 2002 qualifiers Liechtenstein had played thirty World Cup and European Championship qualifiers and lost twenty-seven of them. They had achieved two draws and a solitary victory, 2–1 over Azerbaijan in Vaduz in 1998.

In those thirty matches Liechtenstein had scored just six goals and conceded one hundred and thirty-two. Yet despite a record as unenviable as that of the record company executive who said yes to Marillion, Liechtenstein keep coming back for more. And, surprising as it may sound, they are no longer the pushovers they once were. Drubbings such as the 1–11 home defeat to Macedonia in 1996 and regular 0–7 and 0–8 scorelines are a thing of the past.

When, in the qualifying round for the 2002 World Cup, the principality was drawn with Bosnia-Herzegovina, Israel, Spain and neighbouring Austria, it was hard to see where Liechtenstein was going to add to its derisory points total. Spain had been one of the most impressive teams at an outstanding Euro 2000 and boasted players of the quality of Raul and Gaizka Mendieta. Austria had had a lean spell but a 5–1 spanking of recent World Cup finalists Iran just prior to the start of the qualifying matches gave notice that they were back on an even keel. Israel had made the play-offs for the Euro 2000 finals and could field players such as Haim Revivo and Eyal Berkovic, whilst Bosnia-Herzegovina were finally getting their international act together after years of ethnic divide, and players like Elvir Bolic, Elvir Baljic and Sergej Barbarez were establishing themselves at some of Europe's top clubs.

Liechtenstein conceded the first goal of the 2002 World Cup. Just sixteen seconds of their opening match against Israel in Tel Aviv had passed when Alon Mizrahi buried the ball past eighteen-year-old Peter Jehle in the Liechtenstein goal.

However, the avalanche of goals expected by the home crowd did not materialise as Jehle played the game of his life. The youngster's goal was breached only once more and Liechtenstein came away with a respectable 0–2 defeat. The Israeli fans broke off temporarily from their abuse of the home side to applaud the Liechtensteiners from the field. It was a respectable first step on their latest World Cup odyssey, a journey into perpetual defeat on which I decided to become a fellow traveller.

There is no particular mission behind this book. No tracing the steps of a Victorian explorer, no drunken bet, no desire to play tennis with anyone, nothing like that at all. I have no blood ties to Liechtenstein and had never even been there before arriving in Vaduz for the first home match with Austria.

I knew virtually nothing of Liechtenstein beyond its smallness and its stamps. Most history books bypass the nation altogether, while a few note that it is little more than an anachronistic relic of the Holy Roman Empire. Norman Davies' awesome 1,400-page *Europe: A History* devotes two sentences to Liechtenstein. But then again, Liechtenstein probably has as much right to a mention in a book on European history as Sidcup.

So why did I elect to follow the eleven representatives of this tiny principality through their World Cup campaign and hang out for long periods in a place where, due to its size, strangers tend to stand out?

In the UK, we are weaned on the expectation of victory. At international level, English football in particular is measured in terms of victories and goals, nothing else. But as football becomes sucked further into the success = money = success equation, I wanted to show that the spirit of the game still lurked somewhere beneath the glitz, and that success can be measured in other ways than points and silverware.

In addition, the use of international football as a tool of nationality is a subject that has long fascinated me. If any country has determined a nationality against the odds it is Liechtenstein. Liechtenstein has no real physical or linguistic difference from its neighbours. Swiss customs officials staff the border with Austria, the Swiss franc is the national currency and there is no standing army. Even the Liechtenstein national anthem is sung to the tune of 'God Save The Queen'.

So, other than the princely family and postage stamps, football is one of the few ways the nation can express any real sense of 'Liechtenstein-ness' on the world stage.

Given the nation's size and population, however, Liechtenstein's football team is condemned to almost perennial defeat. And being a fan of the underdog, that was good enough for me. I've always had a leaning towards the obscure. For me the Milan derby holds less appeal than the Torshavn equivalent between HB and B36 in the Faroe Islands. I've always been more Inter Bratislava than Inter Milan; more Skonto Riga than Primera Liga.

For example, one Easter in the early nineties I was ecstatic to discover that Latvia would be playing its first ever international outside the Baltic as an independent nation in Bucharest against Romania. By coincidence my friend Paul and I would be chugging around the continent dossing on trains and giving off foul smells at the same time as the match.

Yet despite this rare opportunity to be a part of football history, somehow I couldn't persuade my travelling companion to forsake the Uffizi Gallery and the Brandenburg Gate in favour of a four-day round trip to watch Romania against Latvia in front of 6,000 people in Bucharest. Latvia lost 2–0 and fielded a player called Shitiks; surely reason enough for a pan-postcommunist European odyssey in itself.

For a few years now I have managed to eke out a living writing about travel and football. This is something that still surprises me with a barely controlled yelp when I wake up in the morning, not least because I am a terrible traveller.

Situations I can cope with perfectly well at home suddenly become unavoidable sources of slapstick comedy with me as the butt of the joke. If there's a wrong side of a train to get out of I'll find it and end up on the track. A jug of something to knock over in a quiet hotel breakfast room, it's my elbow that will oblige and my 'Aaaah, fuck!' that will further disturb the peace. If there's an airport arrivals and departures board to mix up, I'll be the one looking from board to boarding pass with an expression of increasing panic, a lamp-post to walk into, it'll be my nose meeting the ironwork. All these have happened. People could probably write a medical paper about it, these normally rational people oozing with common sense who descend into buffoonery the moment they cross water and leave Britain.

Liechtenstein, I thought, was a safe enough bet. No wars, nor the threat of them. I even had a smattering of the language, but would be incredibly fortunate enough to find that many Liechtensteiners speak almost flawless English. There were even lots of nice mountains to look at, visible from every window.

So no pilgrimage, no mission, nothing, just a fascination with the small and an interest in the perpetually vanquished.

There could have been more taxing nations to follow: Iraq, El Salvador, Yugoslavia or even England. But I was fascinated to know what, if anything, makes Liechtenstein unique. What is it about the people, history and culture that separates this tiny nation of no more than a couple of mountains and a riverbank from its neighbours beyond the quirks of the long defunct Holy Roman Empire?

Why does the football team keep turning up with their kitbags over their shoulders and an eager-to-please smile in the full knowledge that they will more than likely be given a football rodgering over the next ninety minutes?

Having grown up in England, it's difficult for me to imagine a sense of pathos attaching itself to a national football team. Years of failure and mediocrity do not appear to have dampened the ardour of those who think that England should be the best in the world bar none, and nothing less will do.

It's quite the opposite in Liechtenstein. When I suggested to Markus Schaper, Chief Executive of the *Liechtensteiner Fussball-Verband* that there might be the chance of an upset in the Liechtensteiners' first home game against Austria he all but laughed in my face. The very thought of the national team pulling off a result against anyone other than a minor football power was ridiculous, yet he still dreams of success. And having been weaned on the Charlton Athletic teams of the late seventies and early eighties, that was something I could identify with.

For it is in nations like Liechtenstein that the heart of the game still beats healthily within the bloated obesity of modern football. Not once did I see a Manchester United shirt, for example, nor was David Beckham's vacant expression peering from any posters or shop windows. Players still tend to stick with their local teams, save for those fortunate enough to pursue a professional career outside Liechtenstein, and football remains a sport, not a means of making vast fortunes (the Liechtensteiners have that sewn up elsewhere).

At the *Jahrmarkt* funfair that took place during my first

trip to Vaduz the teenagers were clad not in the paraphernalia of Manchester United, Bayern Munich or any other pan-national football corporation but in the tracksuits of their local teams.

Young lads in FC Schaan and FC Balzers tracksuits stood around smoking self-consciously in the flashing lights of the dodgem cars, whilst boys in FC Vaduz and FC Triesenberg tops tried in vain to conceal their erections by fanning their fingers in their trouser pockets whenever a group of local girls happened to glance their way. When your nation consists of villages of no more than 5,000 people it's more or less inevitable that you will become attached to your local team in some form or other.

In this respect, Liechtenstein made a refreshing change. No razzmatazz and no superleagues. In fact, er, no leagues at all. No domestic professionals, no *ultras*, no hooliganism. No club superstores, no executive boxes. A relaxed alpine retreat in a football world spinning rapidly out of control.

This is a national team that has to fit in its training sessions around the players' working week. A team whose manager (a 'foreigner', incidentally) also runs the junior teams and whose selection headaches have included telephoning personal appeals to employers to release players for World Cup duty, and losing his captain for an away World Cup qualifier because the wine he makes for a living was at a crucial stage and couldn't be left.

It's a team destined inevitably for the role of David against Goliath in every match. But in addition to the plucky performances on the field I found behind-the-scenes intrigue. I found a team that combines the glamour of Serie A with matches attended by four men and a bratwurst. A team that combines professional footballers at famous European clubs with, for example, a schoolteacher whose headmaster begrudges him the time off to play a match against Spain. I even found a man who claimed to be married to an eagle.

No one's written at such length about Liechtenstein before. Maybe that's because there's not much to say. But I hope that I've dug up enough people, history and culture to provide a worthwhile portrait of this tiny country and its extraordinary football team.

The Fixture List:

2 September 2000	Israel v Liechtenstein
7 October 2000	Liechtenstein v Austria
24 March 2001	Spain v Liechtenstein
28 March 2001	Liechtenstein v Bosnia-Herzegovina
25 April 2001	Austria v Liechtenstein
2 June 2001	Liechtenstein v Israel
5 September 2001	Liechtenstein v Spain
6 October 2001	Bosnia-Herzegovina v Liechtenstein

One

A pint, a paper and a perusal of the bookshops was all I had in mind that rainy afternoon in Charing Cross Road.

I had just finished writing a lengthy book and was having to come to terms with an immediate future without this career crutch. It had been a four-year project, one that had come to dominate my working life like nothing else before. The deadline had provided the chronological yardstick for my work, and now it had been and gone I felt rootless and panicky. I was in a similar position to Wile E Coyote when, duped by Road Runner, he'd run straight off the edge of a canyon. I was at the point where he was hanging in the air and turning to camera just prior to plummeting earthwards. Most of my other work had been hung around the book, so I had now ground to a literary and, perhaps more importantly, financial halt. The puff of dust was about to rise from the canyon floor.

Hence I found myself idling away days in the pubs and bookshops of central London pondering my next career move. Pondering, in fact, whether there would be a next career move. I'd just turned thirty, we'd had an offer accepted on a wreck of a house and I had begun to notice my girlfriend dropping hints about my future. Newspapers would appear open at the jobs section. Subtle questions would be weaved expertly into conversation, like, 'We've got a mortgage – how are you going to pay your half, skint boy?'

The big three-oh arrived and smacked me around the face with a herring emblazoned with the words 'responsibilities' and 'the future' (it was a big herring). But, terrified of coming to terms with anything sensible, I sought solace in pubs and, most of all, second-hand bookshops. I am a sucker for these places, and Charing Cross Road is full of them.

Old football and travel volumes are my major weaknesses. I have boxes and boxes of obscure dusty tomes lurking around the house ready to bruise unsuspecting shins.

Wandering into a favourite shop I made for the travel section, which housed a large selection of ancient volumes. The shelves stretched up to the ceiling, a wall of faint gold lettering on sun-faded spines all fronting thousands upon thousands of miles of experience dating back over a century. We tend to forget what a small world it is today; how relatively easy it is to gain access to other territories and cultures. Before the widespread use of television, armchair travellers had to rely on books to slake their thirst for other nations.

These were accounts from the days of 'real' travel: of steamers and cutters, huge heavy trunks with gold-embossed initials, panama hats, pith helmets and Port Said.

Most of the travel books here seemed to be typical of the genre: memoirs of heroic imperial explorers called things like *My Time Amongst the Zulus* with the unwritten subtitle Which I Cut As Short As Possible By Shooting Most of the Buggers, and *In Search of Inca Treasure*, unwritten subtitle In Order That I Might Steal It.

But among these paeans to blunderbuss tourism I found an old hardback called *The Little Tour: Andorra, Monaco, Leichtenstein* (sic) *and San Marino*, by Giles Playfair and Constantine Fitzgibbon. With names like that you could almost see the brightly coloured handkerchiefs sticking out of their blazer pockets, hear the swish of their flannel trousers and smell the linseed oil on their tennis rackets. Leafing through the yellowing opening pages, I was delighted to discover that *The Little Tour* had been published in the early fifties by the Travel Book Club of 121 Charing Cross Road – the book had come full circle.

Having had a mild fascination for the mini-states of Europe for some time *The Little Tour* seemed to me like the ideal accompaniment for an afternoon out of the rain in the warmth of a pub, and it turned out to be eight quid well spent. I adjourned to a quiet, dingy hostelry to the rear of 121 Charing Cross Road, gave an Australian an outrageous sum of money in return for about four-fifths of a pint of lager and sat down to read.

I find that most second-hand books come with an easily discernible story attached, whether it is an inscription written on the frontispiece or something concealed within the pages. Tucked inside *The Little Tour* was an invoice from the Travel Book Club to the book's original owner, a Mrs Brown of Ruislip. It was dated November 1955. Presumably Mrs Brown never paid it because 'it is imperative that members return this invoice with their remittance'. Maybe the bailiffs went round, gave Mrs Brown a good slapping and flogged the book to a second-hand shop. Maybe Mrs Brown had been tragically killed in an unfortunate accident involving a trip to the post office, some carelessly spilled motor oil and a hansom cab. Maybe Mrs Brown had skipped the country, unable to pay the four shillings (including sixpence postage and packing) she owed for the book. Who knows? There's a story attached to every second-hand book and Mrs Brown's could conceivably involve forged papers and furtive exchanges with men in raincoats amid the steam at border railway stations. Or maybe she just decided that she didn't want the book and sent it back.

Flicking through the pages I found a slim brochure called *Foyle's Christmas Book Guide 1955* containing a selection of now long-forgotten volumes ripe for festive purchase in the mid-fifties.

'A new edition of the great children's classic *Struwwelpeter*', for example, comes with the recommendation that it is 'a book for the unusual child'. Two volumes of *Novelty Goldfish Books* are marketed with 'a plastic goldfish bowl with real water and a model goldfish'. *Katy No-Pocket* is the moving story of a kangaroo without a pouch, whilst *Growing Up Gracefully* is 'a grand book for girls. A delightful book on etiquette and good manners for teen-agers'. Boys aged eight to fourteen meanwhile will apparently enjoy *The Young Winston Churchill*, 'the story of the adventurous youth of our great warrior-statesman'. Stirring stuff. And what do boys read nowadays? Their older brother's well-thumbed *Loaded* and Harry Potter. These days the character-building adventurous youths of our great warrior-statesmen can't get a look in between Gail Porter's knockers and a dysfunctional boy who dabbles in the occult. Tut, what has society come to?

Things were a bit better for grown-ups. Their consumption of the adventurous youths of politicians presumably behind them, sturdy chaps could turn to 'recommended books for men' for addition to their Christmas lists. Prominent under this heading was the ill-disguised porn of *The Girl With the Swansdown Seat*: 'an informal and highly entertaining report on some aspects of mid-Victorian morality providing a candid and rather racy picture of high and low life'. Informal? Candid? Rather racy? Can only mean one thing, eh fellas? Phwooarr!

It's hard to believe that it's less than fifty years since young children could still be given 'delightful little books that have remained a popular favourite with all small children' called *Little Black Sambo* and *Ten Little Nigger Boys*. Yet there they were, a couple of pages before *The Man-Eaters of Kumaon*, 'Colonel Corbett's remarkable experiences and adventures among the jungle folk of India'.

So it was amongst these literary and cultural high spots that Messrs Playfair and Fitzgibbon had set off for the mini-states of Europe. The blurb inside the front flap opened with a sentence perhaps best read in the voice of Terry Thomas:

> One fine day in April, the two collaborators and a lady photographer set sail from Southampton on a wine ship bound for Bordeaux with the comforting knowledge that the discoveries they intended to make in the Lilliputian states of Europe were assured in advance of such immortality as publication could afford.

Okay, Terry, you can breathe now. From this single cumbersome sentence I knew at once that these two gay chaps were those classically upper-class products of the Empire: verbose, wine-soaked and with that unshakeable confidence that only an English public school education could provide. The sort of people for whom the outbreak of war would cause concern only if it meant difficulty in obtaining a good claret.

The text was wincingly parochial at times. Take this description of the most powerful nation in the world: 'America is of course plentifully supplied with hell-raising alcoholics and more or less tiresome species of neurotics.' If only these dunderheads had spent more of their childhoods reading about the adventurous youths of great warrior-statesmen, eh?

I turned to Liechtenstein first. By coincidence I had just read in the newspaper how the Liechtenstein football team had conceded the first and fastest goal of the 2002 World Cup competition. I had almost gone to Liechtenstein whilst interrailing in the early nineties. However, my companion and I had crossed it off the list having spent a thoroughly boring day in Luxembourg and concluded that Liechtenstein would probably be about the same. They did both begin with L after all.

It turned out that Playfair had been to Liechtenstein before, in the late twenties, and had taken his father with him. 'You'd better bring your dinner jacket,' said Playfair Senior, 'as I may get an introduction to the Prince.'

They stayed in the capital Vaduz at the Hotel Adler, one of three hotels in the village, which had only recently had its first bathroom installed – something of which the owner was so proud he'd call people in from the street to look at it.

Once there, the authors struggled to entertain themselves. What could possibly match the entertainment they found advertised in Vaduz, such as 'Mister Harry, the man with two stomachs, the despair of doctors and the wonder of both hemispheres'? Unfortunately they had missed the show so we will perhaps never know how you make entertainment out of having two stomachs.

I can only think that Mister Harry's act went something like this: an enormous silver platter is brought on to the stage. A glamorous assistant removes the lid with a flourish to reveal two Scotch eggs. A frisson of anticipation shimmers through the audience. Mister Harry picks up one Scotch egg and eats it, kissing the tips of his fingers and pronouncing it excellent to thunderous applause.

'That Scotch egg,' he would say, 'made from the finest sausage meat and the produce of chickens belonging to the Crown Prince of this fine principality, is now stewing in the gastric juices of ONE of my two famous stomachs.' More thunderous applause and then awestruck silence as Mister Harry picks up the other Scotch egg delicately between thumb and forefinger. A blur of white gloves, a couple of chews and it's gone, the glamorous assistant mopping the crumbs from his immaculately curled moustache with a lacy napkin.

'That Scotch egg,' says Mister Harry, 'was as fine as the first and now, ladies and gentlemen, rests in my other stomach awaiting digestion. I thank you.' An elaborate bow, a slight belch and the assistant throws a velvet cape around Mister Harry's shoulders, hands him a top hat and cane and escorts him from the stage to a standing ovation.

Well, it beats *Stars In Their Eyes*, anyway.

Whilst in Liechtenstein the author's father worked on his autobiography. 'He could not have chosen, perhaps, a lovelier or more peaceful place for this purpose but he could have found places elsewhere as lovely and as beautiful,' said Playfair.

This was something that I had wondered about these mini-states. How could somewhere as small and as geologically indistinguishable from its neighbouring countries as Liechtenstein work as an independent nation? Switzerland looks after most of Liechtenstein's diplomatic affairs and Swiss customs officials staff Liechtenstein's border with Austria. Even the Swiss franc is used as currency in Liechtenstein. What then made Liechtenstein Liechtenstein?

Just as there was nothing ethnical so there was nothing scenic that really gave Liechtenstein a distinctive character of its own [Playfair continued]. It might have been a mere extension of either Austria or Switzerland. Its highlands were beautiful, but not uniquely beautiful. There were other highlands, no less green, other highlands with the same profusion of wild flowers, other highlands where you could hear the whisper of the mountain streams and the lonely tintinnabulation of the cowbells.

Even the name Liechtenstein is nothing more than the name of the family that bought up the counties of Vaduz and neighbouring Schellenberg in the early eighteenth century to get a seat at the ruling council of the Holy Roman Empire. After that a ruling monarch never even set foot in the place for more than 150 years. If the people who owned the place couldn't be arsed for a century and a half to nip over from Vienna to have a look at the country they'd bought, then what hope did it have of asserting an identity of its own?

So, where I should have been turning my attention to my future, I was instead ruminating on what distinguished a Liechtensteiner from a Swiss. Football soon came to mind. Liechtenstein have played competitive international football since 1994. They could play against the Swiss and the Austrians. They could sing their national anthem alongside those of their larger neighbours before the matches. Eleven Liechtensteiners could line up with their nation's flag on their chests and battle for their country in a less fatal way than their ancestors would have done in the European wars of history.

I turned back to the newspaper that had reported briefly on Liechtenstein's gallant defeat in Tel Aviv. Just as I'd thought – Liechtenstein were in the same qualifying group as Austria. Indeed they'd be playing them in Vaduz a couple of months hence.

If I'd been a cartoon character, a light bulb would have appeared above my head. Thoughts of a proper job evaporated quicker than Mister Harry's showbiz career as I was consumed with the sudden urge to discover Liechtenstein.

I drained my glass, pulled on my coat, turned up the collar around my ears and swept out into the rain, trying to impress upon the Antipodean barman with my slightly squinting eyes and tight-lipped expression that I was a man taken with a sudden and mysterious sense of purpose. I think he was impressed as I plunged out of the door to throw myself upon the mercy of the elements and a tiny mountainous principality. He was probably still impressed when I returned two minutes later to retrieve my copy of *The Little Tour*, which I'd left on the table.

Suddenly Charing Cross Road opened up before me like Jacob's Ladder, at the top rung of which I could make out a distant alpine landscape and almost hear the far off tinkle of cowbells. I dived in and out of the bookshops looking for Liechtenstein like a Tasmanian devil in search of a self-help guide to relaxation techniques.

Books on Liechtenstein are few and far between, especially those written in English. Even the established travel guides give the country short shrift. Rough Guides, for example, gives over just six pages to Liechtenstein in their Switzerland edition, and even then it concludes that Liechtenstein is only worth visiting for its 'novelty value'. The snort of derision I emitted whilst reading this in Foyle's was the first tangible piece of evidence that I was becoming a Liechtensteinophile. There's probably no such word, but then there has probably been no need for one until I came along.

In another shop I found *Valley of Peace: The Story of Liechtenstein* by Barbara Greene, a slim, charming-looking volume published in 1947. The top half of the cover was blue, the bottom red in a representation of the Liechtenstein flag. A pencil drawing of an alpine church amongst the meadows adorned the front. Within seconds it was mine, hard cash now helping to affirm my determination to immerse myself. The opening paragraph was enough to convince me of the suitability of my mission:

In the very centre of a storm-tossed and weary Europe lies the Principality of Liechtenstein – a little island of peace. Life is unhurried there: it flows like a slow-moving river on which hardly a ripple can be seen. The people are courteous and friendly and an atmosphere of quiet calm lies over the country. There are flowers everywhere, in every garden and carpeting the mountainside right up to where the rocky crags stand guard over the green valley through which the Rhine winds its sparkling way. For a hundred years now, fate has been kind to the little land. Even during the last terrible war Liechtenstein was left alone – too small to be of interest to anyone. And so, among the ruins of Europe, there still remains a small corner to remind us all what peace is really like.

The Balkans it ain't. I arrived home and threw myself on to the World Wide Web, desperate for more knowledge of this tiny country.

Before long I'd found the website of *Liechtensteiner Vaterland*, one of the principality's two (!) national daily newspapers. Turning to the sport section I found the lead story intriguingly titled Wolfgang Matt: Vice European Champion. Not realising there was a Europe-wide competition for prostitutes, let alone that Liechtenstein's were apparently the most accomplished in the whole of Europe at the nocturnal arts, I read on. Alas, the truth was less scurrilous:

Following a successful participation in the European Championships, Wolfgang and Norbert Matt were welcomed back home with a big celebration. At the championships in Belgium they had shown model aircraft flying at its best. Norbert and Wolfgang Matt, the two Liechtenstein participants in this year's European Championships in Model Aircraft Flying, had reason to celebrate: Norbert Matt finished in a good 25th position. His elder brother even reached the final and won his fourth silver medal behind reigning world champion Christophe Paysant-le-Roux of France.

Knighthoods have been given for less. A back edition reported another Liechtensteiner success – this time in the European woodworking championships. As someone whose sole school woodwork achievement was gluing sandpaper to a piece of wood and calling it a pencil sharpener I was impressed. I had only recently successfully sawn my first piece of timber in half.

I found Liechtenstein's only webcam. Strangely it focussed on neither the alpine scenery nor the centre of Vaduz. Instead, the nation's one webcam was trained upon the drive-thru queue for its only branch of McDonald's. And by the looks of things the nation's only McDonald's wasn't doing great business: the image showed nothing more than an empty expanse of red tarmac. Perhaps it's a cow thing – they like their bovines alive and wearing bells in Liechtenstein, not sliced thinly within a sesame seed bun.

Next I tracked down the *Liechtensteiner Fussball-Verband*. It's an austere site, short of thigh-slapping gags. A picture of the LFV staff, however, taken at a function that appeared to have been held in a dungeon, revealed a smiling, amiable-looking group of about half a dozen people.

Within minutes I had dashed off an e-mail to the LFV mooting the possibility of a book about the principality hung around the football team's World Cup 2002 campaign.

Barely an hour had passed before the reply came back from Vaduz.

Dear Mr Connelly,
    Thanks for your great idea and your intention to write a book about the football here in Liechtenstein. I'm sure that we can help you. In order to organise the help in the best way I beg you to give us concrete information about the matter of subjects as soon as possible.
    Waiting for your answer we remain with kind regards,
    Markus Schaper.

Within seconds, another mail had arrived, from the Liechtenstein Tourist Office.

Dear Mr Connelly,
    Thank you for your mail regarding your planned book about the Liechtenstein national football team and a portrait of life in Liechtenstein [I hadn't sent them an e-mail: maybe everyone in Liechtenstein shares an e-mail

address?]. We will be glad to assist you in regard to the part about life in Liechtenstein. Please let us know how you plan to proceed. Regarding the part about the football team you have already received an answer from Mr Markus Schaper.

Wishing you much success with the project, we remain expecting your reply, sincerely yours,

Roland Büchel.

The game was afoot. I was already falling headlong for a country about which I knew little beyond a couple of books half a century old and the fact that Liechtensteiners sign their e-mails with astonishing politeness. It was time to commence some proper research.

Two

In my first year of secondary school a man called Mr Galliver taught me history. Being obsessed with football at a school that inexplicably found the greatest route to personal development to be in rugby union, I was dead impressed that Mr Galliver would ruminate at length during lessons about the fortunes of Portsmouth Football Club. Although I wasn't a Portsmouth fan myself, when he would start recalling the great days of Jimmy Dickinson I would be bolt upright in my seat giving him my undivided attention. I also remember clearly Mr Galliver confessing his astonishment during an end-of-term general knowledge quiz that I knew the nickname of Bury Football Club to be the Shakers. To me that kudos was worth half a dozen glowing parents' evenings.

Unfortunately, that's about all I do remember of Mr Galliver's history lessons. Which is a shame, because the nuggets of knowledge I missed about Charlemagne and the Holy Roman Empire would have been an immense help to my understanding of why Liechtenstein exists.

Barbara Greene's 1947 book *Valley of Peace* ruminated dreamily about 'a little island of peace', where 'life is unhurried' and 'the people are courteous and friendly and an atmosphere of quiet calm lies over the country'.

I think she meant it was dull. However, despite this paean to pacifism, Liechtenstein is not the sort of utopia to which

Captain Kirk used to beam down, snog a couple of local lovelies ('On Earth we call this . . . kissing') before discovering that the planet was actually populated by cannibalistic psychopaths and hotfooting it back to Bones.

Idyllic as Liechtenstein is, its history is dominated by famine, war, greed, disease and a healthy dose of witch-hunting. In fact possibly the only thing missing from the history of the area is the presence of an amorous Captain Kirk.

Even the cannibalistic psychopaths are there. The first recorded people to occupy what is now Liechtenstein were the Rhaetians. According to the Greek historian Poseidonios writing in 100 BC, the Rhaetians:

> have unkempt hair smeared thickly with soap and combed back in long strands from their foreheads. Mouths are covered with hanging moustaches that serve as a sieve when drinking.
>
> Always thirsty and quarrelsome they sit in their round huts on the bare ground, drinking and boasting of their deeds, falling into sudden tempers which end in bloody fights. Terrible are their rough war cries and their disdain for death.

The Romans arrived, threw their weight around and built some straight roads. By the end of the fifth century, however, Roman power was on the wane and a miserable three hundred years ensued. As the centuries passed the region became the site of a number of long-forgotten territorial wars as the Holy Roman Empire's central power weakened. Centuries of battles trampled all over what is now Liechtenstein.

Around 1300 there arrived in the mountains overlooking the Rhine Valley a number of families from the Wallis area of southern Switzerland, escaping a terrible famine and settling at Triesenberg, which still overlooks the modern communities of Vaduz and Triesen. They reared cattle, built homes and called themselves 'Free Walsers', a community that still exists in Triesenberg to this day with their own dialect and customs.

Meanwhile, by the middle of the fourteenth century, Count

Hartmann de Montfort had inherited the county of Vaduz and taken up residence in the newly constructed castle overlooking the village. He awarded himself the title Count of Vaduz and in 1396 established his estate as a fief of the Empire. This act asserted Hartmann's independence from the nearby Dukes of Swabia and sowed the seeds for modern Liechtenstein.

The Montforts ruled for another twenty reasonably peaceful years before losing their family fortune backing losers in German civil wars, as well as falling out with the powerful local bishops of Chur and abbots of St Gallen. By 1416, the last de Montfort was forced to pledge Vaduz and its environs to the Brandis family.

While all this was going on there were similar shenanigans in the neighbouring county of Schellenberg. The Knights of Schellenberg ensured safe passage between Swabia and Italy for the German emperor and had become loyal to the Habsburgs, accumulating considerable wealth from their faithful service.

In 1317, however, Schellenberg was suddenly sold to the Count of Werdenberg who kept the locals so destitute that they stormed his castle. According to legend, the count saw the lynch mob coming up the hill and hot-footed it from the scene on a black charger. Somewhere up in the mountains near Gamprin, both horse and rider plunged from a rocky crag. Apparently on dark nights you can see and hear the final deathly plunge.

Whilst the caddish count was making his rapid descent the people of Schellenberg were busying themselves plundering and burning down the castle. The estate was eventually sold to the Brandis family of Vaduz, and with the unification of the counties of Schellenberg and Vaduz the territory of modern Liechtenstein had been established.

The fifteenth century was another period of war and destitution for the put-upon people of what is now Liechtenstein. The region became a popular battlefield for the endless skirmishes between the Dukes of Austria and the Swiss, who demanded freedom from Austrian rule. The Brandis family sided with the Austrians. In 1499 local bishops, fed up with having blood spilled on their doorsteps for the entire previous century, called both sides together at Feldkirch, now just over the Liechtenstein border in Austria, and knocked a few heads together. Remarkably they managed to broker some kind of agreement and it looked as though peace might finally settle over the valley.

Unfortunately the Swiss army's return journey meant that they passed the castle of Gutenberg which still overlooks Balzers in Liechtenstein. Set atop a steep hill in the middle of a flat piece of ground, Gutenberg had since prehistoric times been a strategically important place, standing as it did on one of the main alpine crossings between Germany, Switzerland and Italy.

The Habsburgs had taken control of Gutenberg in 1308 having ousted Heinrich of Frauenberg, a well-known troubadour, from his home. A harmless, cheerful chap, Heinrich was renowned for his happy rural ditties, and there he was, suddenly deposited amongst the nymphs and shepherds of whom he sang. Turfed out of his hilltop castle for no apparent reason, and finding that shepherds and nymphs actually all smell of dung, as Heinrich sat amongst his belongings at the foot of the hill it's quite conceivable that, predating the likes of Robert Johnson and Blind Lemon Jefferson by about seven hundred years, he invented the blues. You can get a half-decent twelve bar out of a lute, you know.

Having taken the previously impregnable castle whilst Heinrich was looking the other way, the Habsburgs installed an Austrian garrison at Gutenberg that was independent of the lords of Vaduz. The castle was to stay in Habsburg hands for five hundred years.

So as the weary Swiss army wandered back from the peace talks planning what they would do now they didn't have to fight Austrians any more ('Well, I'm hoping to develop this idea I've had for a useful multi-purpose knife with, you know, a can opener on it and everything'), the Austrians felt safe in indulging in a bit of banter from the battlements.

From the castle the Austrians taunted the Swiss with 'moo moo' and 'baa baa' noises. Not the most inventive abuse they could have come up with but enough to cross the linguistic barrier and rile the Swiss into retaliation. Unable to storm the castle the Swiss instead burned down a house nearby and kicked off a battle in which over a hundred people were killed. The Swiss, peace negotiations forgotten, laid siege to the castle but couldn't remove the Austrians.

Their credibility was kneecapped finally when a specially designed gun was brought from France with which they intended to pound the castle walls. Unfortunately for the Swiss, as they lined up the monster machine it promptly fell to pieces, much to the amusement of the Austrian garrison who were able to let rip with some more farmyard noises (they'd been practising).

Eventually peace was again restored, albeit with the Habsburg garrison still happily ensconced at Gutenberg. Indeed, a relatively quiet sixteenth century ensued with Count Rudolf of Sulz taking over at Vaduz castle after the last Brandis died with no heir.

Rudolf was a popular, kind ruler, fiercely Catholic even amongst the spread of Lutheranism, and Liechtenstein remains staunchly Catholic to this day.

In the early seventeenth century war returned to the area. By this time, Vaduz and Schellenberg had passed into the hands of Count Kaspar of Hohenems (weren't they the ones who nailed Gulliver to the floor?) only for Austria and the nearby canton of Graubünden to start fighting each other. Vaduz and Schellenberg were caught right in the middle. With all the looting and burning that accompanied the armies as they marched backwards and forwards the region was plunged into desperate poverty. And then along came the Black Death. This was tailed closely by the outbreak of the Thirty Years War between the fading Holy Roman Empire and the resurgent German Protestant states. Just think what all this did to property prices.

By the time peace broke out in 1648 Vaduz and Schellenberg were in ruins and their people starving.

As usually happens in times of hardship a scapegoat emerged. Thus began the merciless witch-hunts that swept across Europe in the seventeenth century. Given the terrible conditions in the Rhine Valley it's no surprise that Vaduz was a popular area for witch-hunters. Indeed, in Vaduz alone in August 1648 fourteen women were burnt as witches. The orchestrators of the lynchings were the powerful, ruthless and self-appointed *Brenner* (burners). This notorious band were finally tricked by the priest of Triesen and put to death. However, such were the *Brenners*' misdemeanours that even hell was deemed too good for them. Hence their souls were banished to a deep gorge at Tobel where they are obliged to sit in silence until a day of judgement to be known as *Tobelhocher*.

The departure of the *Brenner* should have seen an upturn in fortunes for the beleaguered folk of Vaduz and Schellenberg. Alas, they had Count Franz Wilhelm to contend with. The Count enjoyed the high life and levied enormous taxes from his subjects in order to finance the lifestyle to which he had been accustomed. When his son succeeded him, things became even worse.

Eventually even his own family grew sick of the latest Hohenems to mess up the district. In 1696 Adam Müssner from Schellenberg and the not inappropriately named Christoph Anger presented a lengthy list of grievances to the Holy Roman Emperor who deprived the Counts of Hohenems of their authority and imposed imperial administration on the district. Schellenberg was put up for sale to clear the Hohenems' debts.

Enter the Liechtenstein family. A wealthy bunch based in Austria, Styria and Moravia, the family seat was at Castle Liechtenstein in Vienna. The Liechtensteins were famous for their impressive collection of art and for owning huge tracts of land that included 24 towns, 46 castles and 800 villages. For all their wealth and land, however, their princely rank was meaningless as none of their properties was under the immediate authority of the Emperor and this meant they couldn't take their seat at the prestigious Imperial Diet at Regensburg.

Schellenberg was an imperial fief, however, and offered the princes of Liechtenstein the opportunity of buying their way into power. The purchase was finally completed in January

1699 for 115,000 Dutch guilders. Twelve years later, Prince Johann Adam secured Vaduz as well for 290,000 guilders. And finally, on 23 January 1719 Emperor Charles VI officially united the counties of Vaduz and Schellenberg as the Principality of Liechtenstein, the 343rd state of the Holy Roman Empire.

Despite the principality's new standing and its role in elevating their familial status above the riff-raff, its owners chose not to visit for a hundred and fifty years. The aim had been to gain a seat at the Imperial Diet. This had been achieved, so why bother going to a poor, muddy riverbank when you could be swanking around Viennese palaces looking important?

Neglected by their new landlords, the Liechtensteiners continued to suffer. The Austrian wars of the mid-eighteenth century meant the usual procession of pillaging troops of various nationalities passing through the valley as Liechtenstein adopted the demeanour of a hedgehog on a dual carriageway. The wars didn't concern the country directly but as they were caught slap in the middle of it all, the Liechtensteiners once again found themselves robbed, looted and plundered.

On the resignation of the German Emperor Franz I in 1806 Liechtenstein became a sovereign state in its own right, thus earning the official right to object to other people tramping onto their land and beating the living daylights out of each other. Looting and pillaging could now be met with a stern finger-wagging in the knowledge that the combatants were now officially trespassing.

As peace broke out in the valley for the first time in centuries, it was still 1842 before Prince Alois II made the short hop across from Vienna to have a squint at the land which bore his family name and which had secured his seat at the Imperial Diet a century and a half earlier.

You might have expected the population to be a little cynical when the royal party swept along the Rhine in all their pomp. The Liechtensteiners might have been forgiven for standing there tapping imaginary watches, but instead Alois II's arrival was the cue for great celebration and hospitality. A national holiday was declared, with bread and wine being distributed freely by the royal party. The Prince had such a good time in fact, that he visited the principality on two further occasions before his death in 1858.

It was all a bit too good to be true, of course, and when the Austro-Prussian War broke out in 1866 the eighty-strong Liechtenstein army was called into service. Posted to a mountain pass between the Tyrol and Italy, the Liechtenstein battalion did not even see any fighting, let alone fire a gun. In fact the only remarkable thing about their month away was a freak snowstorm (it was August).

The Prince laid on a huge reception for the soldiers on their return. Not only had the Liechtensteiners lost no one in action, they actually came back with one more soldier than had left Vaduz – they'd made a friend on the way home.

Shortly afterwards the Liechtenstein army was disbanded altogether. The last surviving soldier stood guard outside Vaduz castle until his death in 1939. His image can still be found on postcards today – a dishevelled Spike Milliganesque old man with a white beard. His apparent bewilderment in the photograph is probably accounted for by the fact that the camera was the most dangerous thing pointed at him in his seventy-year military career.

As well as removing the possibility of sending male Liechtensteiners to their deaths in wars that didn't concern them, Prince Johann, who had succeeded his father Alois II, also built churches, commenced the restoration of the castle at Vaduz and instigated other lovely things to earn himself the nickname of Johann the Good. In actual fact, given the turbulent and troublesome history of the region, Johann could probably have earned his sobriquet just by not punching, stabbing or robbing anyone. At least, not in public.

As the First World War decimated Europe, for the first time in the history of European conflict the whole thing passed Liechtenstein by. The only way the Great War affected the principality was the destruction of the Austrian Empire, which prompted them to turn to their other neighbour Switzerland for their customs union. Liechtenstein had suffered heavy financial losses as a result of the Austrian collapse. Wars in which they took no part had stopped ravaging the landscape, but now battered the economy instead.

In 1924, four years before Johann died after over seventy years as Crown Prince, Liechtenstein signed a customs, monetary and postal union with the Swiss, the finer points of which had taken three years to finalise. This meant that although Liechtenstein maintained its sovereignty, the Swiss franc became its legal currency and Swiss customs officers patrolled the Liechtenstein border with Austria.

Franz I took over in 1928 following Johann's death, but such had been Johann's longevity that he was already an old man. In 1938 he handed over to his son Franz Josef II.

The new prince went by the catchy full name of Franz Josef Maria Alois Alfred Karl Johannes Heinrich Michael Gorg Ignatius Benediktus Gerhardus Majella of Liechtenstein. An autograph hunter's dream. Franz Josef deserves most of the credit for transforming Liechtenstein from a poor rural farming community into its current status as one of the most economically advanced nations in the world. He is also believed to be the only monarch in history to have been a fully qualified expert in forestry.

Franz Josef also managed to keep Liechtenstein out of the Second World War. Conscious of Liechtenstein's history of being caught up in wars that didn't concern them, in 1938 the Prince went to visit Hitler in Berlin. The two leaders disappeared into a room for several hours before emerging with Liechtenstein's neutrality assured. No one knows what exactly Franz Josef arranged with the Führer, but whatever it was (compromising photographs with farmyard animals perhaps?) it worked, and another global conflict passed the principality by.

Franz Josef also won favour at home by becoming the first Liechtenstein prince to take up residence in the castle at Vaduz. When he sent his son Hans Adam to the local primary school, his place in the hearts of the people was assured.

In the last fifty years Liechtenstein has changed beyond recognition. It has one of the highest standards of living in the world, is a member of most European political and economic bodies short of the European Union itself and has a banking system the envy of most of the world. Thankfully, the locals have stopped using their moustaches as a strainer for eating soup.

Three

As the date of my first visit approached I searched largely in vain for Liechtenstein related information. I had to improvise.

Given the faintly gothic sound of the name and the fact it had a castle, I had watched James Whale's 1931 film *Frankenstein* on video. Pushing the cassette into the player and retiring behind the settee, I peered between my fingers as Boris Karloff lumbered around the Tyrolean countryside pursued by bearded men in lederhosen carrying flaming torches. They all appeared to be called Hans. Suspiciously well-scrubbed peasants, none of whom appeared to be malnourished or disease-ridden, strolled gaily through the villages. The twinkle in their eyes deflected attention from the steely coldness that emerged when someone a teensy bit different turned up in their midst. Like a seven-foot monster constructed from dead people's body parts, for example. After an unfortunate incident in which Boris's monster mistook a little girl for a flower and threw her into the river (and come on, we've all made that mistake at least once), he came to a sticky end in a burning windmill as a slavering lynch mob stood around cheering and waving pitch-forks and torches. As they barbecued Boris, there was violence in their eyes and the smell of blood in their nostrils. I hoped that I wasn't getting a true sense of Liechtenstein here.

I'd also purchased a volume of gothic novels. Most of them seemed to be set in European castles, so I surmised they might be a good bet. Hence I would not have been surprised to find Liechtenstein chock full of vengeful knights, ghosts, giants and noblemen heading inevitably for a grisly end.

A lovely lady called Martina at the Liechtenstein Tourist Office was helping me via e-mail to secure accommodation, presumably typing with one hand to allow for the flaming torch in the other. A week or so before my first visit a room was booked for me at the Gasthof Grünesholz in Vaduz. I leafed through the *Where to Stay in Liechtenstein* brochure (cynical answer – Switzerland) and found a picture of the Grünesholz. It was one of those typically Swiss, chalet-style buildings, simultaneously cuckoo clock and austere, with the words *Gasthof Grünesholz* painted on the fascia in elaborate thick gothic lettering.

On the day I set off for Liechtenstein for the first time, to watch their opening home game with Austria, I stood on a suburban London rail platform with a mixture of anticipation and trepidation. It was 7 a.m., it was raining, and for the first time I asked myself what the bloody hell I thought I was doing. In about six hours I would be arriving in a country where I knew nobody beyond the e-mails of the saintly Martina, and which would play a rather large part in my life for the coming year. The rain dripped from my chin on to the holdall between my feet and I was filled with a sudden urge to bolt for home. Fortunately, the train arrived at that point and I squeezed on.

It was the early-morning rush hour and the train was packed. I'd carefully positioned myself by the doors in order to facilitate my escape at Peckham Rye where I had to change trains and I was not about to budge.

As stations came and went, a succession of commuters tutted and harrumphed at me as they attempted to circumnavigate my luggage to get into the train. Being British, I ignored them, fixing my attention on the safety warning above the doors and praising myself for my steely diligence. Naturally, when the train reached Peckham Rye, the platform was on the other side of the train for the first time on the entire journey. As I made to heave myself and my stuff across the packed corridor, the man next to me muttered 'no chance'. This served only to harden my resolve as I battered my way through the crowd, bashing ankles and pushing newspapers into faces before spilling out on to the platform.

I resisted the temptation to turn around and raise my middle finger to my unhelpful fellow passengers. It would have been pointless anyway as it's well known that British commuters loftily ignore anything that occurs between the home and work-place. So as I turned around to gloat, I saw only that the people in the doorway had assumed the glassy-eyed vacant stare into the middle distance that only the experienced commuter can master. Not even the hijacking of the train by Mexican rebels in huge sombreros would have garnered a reaction beyond a tut. And only then if one of them had inadvertently trodden on somebody's shoe whilst passing through the carriages firing bullets into the ceiling with triumphant 'arribas'.

Naturally my connection to Luton Airport was cancelled, and the next train hopelessly late. Fortunately, being a nervous traveller, I leave ridiculous amounts of time to get to airports. Mid-afternoon flight departures see me skulking out of the house under cover of moonlight. Journeys that take barely half an hour have me leaving home or hotel about three hours in advance of even the flight check-in opening. So despite the hold ups I still arrived at Luton in plenty of time to really appreciate what a horrendous airport it is. A huge cavern of a place with a couple of apologetically shabby shops and a singular lack of anything useful, attractive or appetising.

Now Stansted, that's another matter. I could go to Stansted and just hang out, not even fly anywhere. Public transport takes you right to where you need to be, the check-ins are easily negotiable, the food and drink outlets are palatable and not ridiculously overpriced, the shops have stuff in that you actually want to buy and you get to ride on those groovy driverless trains to your departure gate. If you're lucky enough to be right at the front you can pretend you're driving. Yes, Stansted Airport is just a nice place to be.

It wasn't until I started writing about travel that I learned to appreciate airports for what they are. Family holidays had always begun from Heathrow or Gatwick, airports so vast as to be towns in themselves. It wasn't until I went elsewhere, reporting on places off the beaten track in an attempt to gain a foothold in the close-knit travel writing clique that I began to distinguish airports from each other and regard them as individual entities rather than just a stepping stone en route to wherever.

Vagar in the Faroe Islands for example. Constructed on the only piece of land flat enough and long enough to accommodate a runway (and even then it's the shortest in Europe) the approach to the Faroes by air is breathtaking. A distant speck in the North Atlantic becomes a series of specks, then you see the runway on a tiny patch of green between two huge rocky promontories. The aircraft aims between them and barrels out of the sky heading for what looks from a distance like a child's school ruler dropped into a garden rockery. I'm sure that above the engine noise I heard the pilot shout, 'Geronimo!'

Sarajevo is another memorable landing. As your plane touches down on the runway you see the shattered, burnt-out hulks of military transporter planes to either side and view the burnt-out shells of nearby houses.

Luton has none of that charm or historical significance. That it found fame thanks to a cockney woman in a seventies drinks advertisement is wholly fitting to its dated, hostile ambience.

Thankfully I was soon in the air and heading for Zurich. Zurich Airport is the Stansted of Switzerland, wonderfully compact and well organised. I almost skipped to the carousel and retrieved my bag which, and this is a first, was there waiting for me. Descending to the rail station, I bought my ticket to the Swiss border town of Sargans without a hitch. It did involve a change of trains at Zurich's main station, however, which allowed eighteen platforms' worth of wrong train opportunities. I had in the past developed a remarkable talent for confusing *Abfahrt* (departures) and *Ankunft* (arrivals), and many's the time I have missed connections by looking at the arrivals board when I wanted departures and vice versa. Waiting on a lonely platform for a train to arrive and watching hundreds of people disembark when it does can be a sobering experience, particularly when you get on the train and start to wonder why a) no one else has joined you and b) it's twenty minutes late leaving. The penny usually drops just when the train jolts into movement, destined not for a distant European capital but some grimy suburban engine shed half an hour away.

This time I was ready and waiting at the correct platform at the correct time. And imagine my delight when the train pulled in in all its sleek, double-decker, smoked-glass glory. Now I'm no trainspotter, but this was a truly impressive piece of machinery. The destination was displayed on an LCD screen by each of the doors, which opened with a barely perceptible hiss of refined hydraulics. The coolness of the air-conditioning tumbled out on to the platform and wrapped itself around my legs in an almost visible cloud of luxury. I felt too scruffy to board.

But board I did, settling into a comfy chair at the top of the stairs. When you're forced to use British railways it's easy to forget that train travel can be not only pleasurable but exhilarating. And it doesn't necessarily require remortgaging your house either. As we glided soundlessly through the Zurich suburbs and into the countryside I began to realise why people get excited about train journeys. The route to Sargans passes alongside the southern shore of Lake Zurich, a breathtaking ride whose beauty was enhanced by my lofty position on the top deck where the windows curved overhead and into the roof. Snow-sugared peaks provided the backdrop to the deep blue of the water as we passed through storybook towns and villages with whitewashed chapels and verandahed lakeside restaurants with gaily coloured parasols. The names of the stations at which we paused might have sounded like a sneezing fit – Thalwil, Wädenswil, Pfäffikon, Ziegelbrücke – but I was filled with relaxed contentment, possibly a first for a British person on a train.

Naturally, locals take the view for granted. On the other side of the carriage two middle-aged women gossiped their way towards the border, blissfully unaware of the beauty flashing past the window. I was astonished that they could regard this awesome alpine vista in the same way that I would, say, Deptford or New Cross. An angry-looking young man with lots of hair sat opposite me, sulkily immersed in a book. Evidently, it wasn't a comedy. I almost had to restrain myself from whipping it out of his hands, tossing it down the carriage and pointing out of the window whilst gibbering, 'Look . . . just look, all right?'

After an hour of my relentless gawping (even when the train passed through tunnels), we eased into Sargans and I was forced to disembark, mopping the dribble I'd left on the table through my open-mouthed astonishment with a skilfully disguised swipe of the sleeve.

Here I had to connect with the bus to Vaduz. As well as having no airport, Liechtenstein has only one railway station. Realising that their own rail service would be impractical (you could board in one village, walk through the carriages and get off in the next without the train even moving), the Liechtensteiners noticed that Austrian and Swiss railways could take a handy shortcut between each other by crossing Liechtenstein territory. Thanks very much, said the Austrians and Swiss when this was pointed out to them, that's awfully nice of you. Once the track had been laid and the workmen had gone for their *Schnitzel*, the Liechtensteiners hastily built a station at Schaan before anyone noticed. As far as I could gather, however, the subterfuge had evaded the timetablers and trains only stop there in leap years on 29 February. And then only if it's a full moon, or something.

Either way the bus was by far the easiest and best way in which to reach Vaduz. Having read some more gothic tales on the plane I was half expecting an open horse-drawn cart full of straw driven by a cackling maniac with a hump and a flailing whip.

I bought my ticket and found the bus throbbing away outside the station. It was long, yellow and had VADUZ written on the front. Excitement began to mount. Until now Vaduz had been a name, a place overlooked by a picturesque castle in photographs. When I disembarked from this bus I'd actually be there. As I boarded butterflies whizzed around my stomach and my face broke into a grin. It was obviously the right thing to do. A couple of old women resting shopping baskets on their laps greeted me with a smiling '*grüss Gott*' and a slight nod of the head. These were my first Liechtensteiners and, by crikey, I liked them already. I only just resisted the urge to take their faces in my hands and plant slobbery kisses on their mouths.

A plump driver in a light blue shirt climbed aboard, '*grüss Gotted*' his passengers, revved the engine and set the bus into motion with a grinding of gears and hiss of hydraulics. He had no whip and didn't cackle.

Early roadsigns did not look promising. One invited me to 'Wang' (I declined), another pointed towards the grim sounding 'Bad Ragaz'. Fortunately we went in the opposite direction to both.

Again I immersed myself in the scenery and hence completely missed crossing the border into Liechtenstein for the first time. This is probably because there is no real border between Liechtenstein and Switzerland – you cross a bridge over the Rhine at the village of Trübbach, which Martina Hingis calls home, and hey presto, you're in another country before you know it. The Swiss flag is at one end, the Liechtenstein flag at the other and there's a small lollipop sign halfway across saying 'Fürstentum Liechtenstein' to provide the only clues that you've crossed the border into a new country.

Hence it wasn't until the silhouette of Castle Gutenberg loomed ahead that I realised we must be in Balzers and there-fore in Liechtenstein.

My disappointment at missing this spiritual *rite de passage* was tempered, however, by my first sight of the Gutenberg castle. It stands amid a large flat plain on a strange, almost perfectly conical hill, a bit like the bump that rises out of Tom's head when Jerry hits him with an anvil. The Alps rise in the background, their peaks shrouded in mist, the bluey haze of the view making the castle in the foreground stand out even more as the sun hits the beige stone walls. Lines of vines stretch up the hillside. It truly is fairytale stuff.

As we drove further into the country I began to grow nervous. I have always had a mortal fear on public transport of missing my intended stop. It's almost as if I'd topple off the edge of the world if I were to pass the correct alighting point.

It's bizarre, I would rather get off half an hour's walk early than go just one stop further on and walk back.

I was on a train in Hungary once, going from Budapest to Szeged, a town in the deep south of the country. It was a stiflingly hot, airless day as we travelled across the flat, blasted landscape of the Great Plain. I had no idea how long the journey would take and so took to jumping up every time the train began to slow and saying 'Szeged?' to the man opposite me, commencing this routine around half an hour into the journey. '*Nem*,' he replied the first time with a chuckle and a shake of the head. Three hours later he had gone from pleasantry to a sharper, '*Nem!*' and in the end a look that said, 'Listen, if you ask me once more whether this is Szeged I will break your bulbous, rosy English nose.' As it turned out, Szeged was the last stop. I couldn't have missed it if I'd tried.

So as the bus stopped at place after place my anxiety grew. The saintly Martina had told me that the Grünesholz had its own stop, I couldn't miss it. I saw a building that looked a bit like the Grünesholz and jumped off the bus. It was then I realised that almost every building looks like the Grünesholz and I was in the wrong village. I looked at my map. I'd alighted four stops too early and was in Triesen rather than Vaduz and found that I was about one sixth the length of the country short of my destination. I could walk it in no time.

I heaved my bag on to my shoulder and set off. After ten minutes I spotted something familiar – a huge pair of golden arches. In this alpine valley of beauty and peace my first familiar point of reference was McDonald's. There it was with its own roundabout and, of course, Liechtenstein's only webcam pointing at the tarmac. Had I not been so keen to see Vaduz I might have passed a pleasant few minutes pulling faces at the camera.

There is no visible break between Triesen and Vaduz other than blue signs with the respective village names picked out in white on each side. Indeed on one side of the road an office building straddles the boundary. You can imagine the hilarity that punctuates the office routine when someone says something like, 'Hey, I'm just going to Vaduz for some paperclips,' and walks to a cupboard on the other side of the room.

As I passed into Vaduz I came upon a juxtaposition that, though I didn't know it at the time, sums up this most unlikely of European capitals succinctly. To my left was a small, roped-off field. Within it three cows chewed lazily on the grass and regarded me with absolutely no interest whatsoever. One welcomed me to Liechtenstein by unleashing a steaming torrent of urine. To my right was a near-completed building destined to be a bank, all mirrored glass and steel. Either side of one road, barely thirty feet apart, were the two sides of Liechtenstein: the traditional and the modern.

Eventually the familiar façade of the Gasthof Grünesholz hove into view. It had taken me twenty minutes to walk one sixth of the country – by that token I could do the lot in well under two hours. I walked up the steps of the Grünesholz and pushed the door open. A rush of warm air and bonhomie flew around me and I went inside. To my left was a dining room of dark wood filled with Liechtensteiners. Ruddy-faced men with moustaches tucked into steaming plates of meat and potatoes, accompanied by their wives, who all had their hair tied up in neat buns. Above the clatter of cutlery, loud conversation and laughter boomed around the room. Sturdy wooden chairs scraped on the stone floor as girls in crisp white blouses and black skirts dodged between them and placed enormous glasses of beer on the tables.

A large middle-aged man with fantastically shiny red cheeks who looked not unlike Jimmy Edwards saw me through the doorway, raised a frothing glass of beer and bade me, '*grüss Gott!*' I nodded in kind, and he returned to his steaming pile of food. To my right was a bar area, behind which stood a young woman polishing glasses with impressive meticulousness, holding each one up to the light before placing it on a large tray. She must have done about a dozen, all flawless and glinting. I made my way to the bar, heaved my bag from my shoulder and waited for her to look at me. I was about to have my first conversation with a Liechtensteiner.

Should I attempt the language? I learned German at school but haven't had much call for it since. Indeed, about all I could remember at that particular moment was the phrase '*Ach! Mein Bein ist gebrochen! Haben Sie Hansaplast?*' which translates roughly as 'Curses! I appear to have broken my leg. Do you have a sticking plaster?' The only other phrase I could call to mind was one gleaned from childhood war comics, and I figured that the German equivalent of 'Hands up! Quickly, quickly, pig-dog!' wouldn't really be an appropriate opening gambit. Nope, I would chicken out and stick with the Queen's English in this land of the Prince.

She continued to polish, apparently unaware of my presence. 'Hello,' I said, eventually. She turned her gaze to me. I smiled my friendliest smile and ventured, 'Do you speak English?' Why somebody in an alpine retreat rarely visited by people from these shores should speak English is, of course, a stupid question, but it's one that's always worth a try. It's also one that meets with success in the most unlikely places. A sleazy underground drinking den in Slovakia is probably my record, where I had a long drunken conversation about Brazilian football in perfect English with a sloshed Slovak taxi driver and a Ukrainian alcoholic.

She stopped polishing for a moment and looked at me. 'Shhpeeeeak Englissshhhhh,' she intoned slowly, echoing my question and looking at the counter. Then she put the glass she was holding on to the tray with all the others. 'Today,' she announced, 'I don't want to.' And with that she disappeared through a back door leaving me standing there with my mouth opening and closing, looking like a fish that has just received some startling news.

From the unpromising beginnings at a rainy Peckham Rye, this was my journey's end. And one my first Liechtensteiners had snubbed me. I felt a mixture of anger and the creeping melancholy of loneliness rising up my spine. After a minute or so during which I heard a loud disagreement from the back room between the ungracious glass-cleaner and another female voice, a chubby middle-aged woman with a fierce expression came through the bar with a huge desk diary, slapped it on to the counter and *grüss Gotted* me tersely. I explained that I had a reservation; she ran a finger down her list and nodded affirmation, shutting the diary with a whump that made the glasses all clink together. Taking a key from a Tupperware box she beckoned me to follow. As I picked up my bag the young woman who'd greeted me so enthusiastically walked back behind the bar. I wondered how long it would take her to notice the thumbprint with which I had carefully embossed every glass on her tray.

The older woman led me upstairs and pushed open the door to a room. She stood in the doorway, motioned inside and said, 'Toilet.' Once I'd passed and entered the room she was gone.

I closed the door. It was a big, bright, airy room with a friendly ambience. I shouldn't have my impressions tainted by the exchange downstairs, I thought. I wondered whether the place was called the Grünesholz after the noise guests made shortly after trying to engage the woman behind the bar in conversation. Walking to the window I marvelled at the wonderful alpine vista I would have seen had there not been a building site twenty feet away. I sat on the bed, relaxed a little and listened to the silence that was broken only by the distant tinkle of cowbells, the splashy passage of the Rhine and the two pneumatic drills running off a large generator outside.

I did the usual new hotel room routine: flushed the toilet, had a look in the shower ('Why, professor! Fancy meeting you here!'), opened and closed the wardrobe door and made sure the TV worked. I bounced on the bed a couple of times, opened and closed the window, and did all the human equivalents of a dog marking its territory short of urinating in each corner of the room.

It was late afternoon, still time to have a wander around Vaduz before dark. Martina had furnished me with a map of the place, so I picked it up, walked back through the bar, avoiding the gaze of the glass-polisher, and out into the street. The Grünesholz is on the main road through Vaduz. In fact it's the only road through Vaduz. For such a small place the traffic was extraordinarily busy. Expensive cars vroomed past with 'FL' number plates. Indeed, in all my time in the principality I wouldn't see a car any older than about three years. I walked towards the centre past a couple of closed restaurants and an enormous Georgian-style building that housed the Liechtenstein government. Farther along was a vast church before the banks commenced.

Dominating the village is the sheer, tree-covered rock face that rises to the east, against the foot of which Vaduz is pressed. Its top was shrouded in mist, and stray wisps snaked through the trees at lower levels. Overlooking the centre of town, about halfway up the hillside, is the Castle of Vaduz, home of Prince Hans Adam II and his family. Picked out against the dark greenery of the trees that cover the entire mountainside, the castle managed to look at the same time charming and eerie. Although I'd seen pictures of the ancient building, with its rounded walls, painted shutters and fourteenth-century tower it was still an inspiring sight. The red-and-blue Liechtenstein flag flew above the wall.

My first impression of Vaduz was tinted with disappointment. Having expected a charming mixture of old chalet-style buildings, welcoming bars and the odd bank, the mishmash Vaduz town centre came as a bit of a shock. Much of it is characterless concrete, the bus station and post office complex being one of the most monstrous crimes against architecture I've ever seen. There's no focus, the buildings are generally featureless, unimaginative and constructed without a thought to their surroundings. Liechtenstein has been converted from a poor, agrarian nation to a fiendishly rich nub of the banking industry in around fifty years and Vaduz has struggled to keep up. Its charmless nature deflated me a little.

Reaching the roundabout in the middle of the village I saw a name I recognised. It hadn't been listed in any of the tourist guides so I was delighted to see the Hotel Adler still alive and kicking nearly eighty years after Giles Playfair had rued narrowly missing the man with two stomachs. The outside still looked much as it would have done in the twenties, save for the addition of a Mediterranean-style terrace stuck to the side, part of the building now having been converted into an Italian-style bar called Vanini.

To the right of the Adler was a pedestrianised thoroughfare

that I guessed was the main focus of Vaduz. Expensive jewellery and watches glinted from shop windows. There were a couple of restaurants and a marquee going up on a terraced area next to the town hall. Outside a souvenir shop stood a table covered in t-shirts and sweatshirts. I went over to have a look. 'Switzerland' they all read.

Inside I found the usual range of tat. Key rings, bookmarks, beer glasses, metallic stickers, those huge pencils with tassles on the end: I was in souvenir hell. Unlike the rest of Vaduz, however, the shop was packed with people. American people. Men called Irving in terylene trousers stood around while their well-upholstered wives shouted to each other across the shop. 'Irma, look at this! It's a piece of wood with a cow drawn on it. Isn't that the cutest thing?'

This, it turned out, was the heart of Liechtenstein tourism. Coaches would pull up behind the town hall and disgorge their occupants on to the tarmac. They would move as one into the souvenir shop to stock up on tea towels and snowstorms before having a quick photo opportunity with the castle in the background, piling back on to the coach and heading for Austria. They spend barely an hour in Liechtenstein, it's just another name to cross off their list of countries. They can have their passport stamped at the tourist office for a small fee, but otherwise most of the cash goes over the counter at the tourist shop. Hence the only money that the Liechtenstein Tourist Board sees from these flying visits is the odd couple of francs for a passport stamp. Indeed, nobody knows how many tourists visit Liechtenstein each year, such is the transient nature of the industry. The owner of the shop, however, enjoys a cash bonanza. And, like all good souvenir shops, the owner is an elderly Russian émigré nobleman with a penchant for winter sports, the arts and a fast buck.

Baron Edward von Falz-Fein invented tourism in Liechtenstein. He had the foresight to open his 'Quick' tourist shop in Vaduz in the fifties, and his name is still over the door. If you're inclined, you can even buy his autobiography, a pile of which sits between teetering towers of Liechtenstein first-day covers. Only trouble is, it's in Russian.

The Baron was, I learned, still alive and now well into his nineties. His family had been elevated to the Russian nobility by Tsar Nicholas II at the turn of the twentieth century. As revolution swept across the country the Baron and his mother had fled, eventually finding sanctuary in Liechtenstein. He was largely responsible for establishing the principality's reputation in winter sports (he has carried the Liechtenstein flag at the opening ceremony of several Olympic Games) and tried to establish tourism there despite local opposition. That the shop is still doing a roaring trade in nick-nacks is testament to the Baron's foresight.

He also had a marketing strategy that had all the subtlety of Bernard Bresslaw dancing the Nutcracker Suite. The Baron penned and published the first English language history of and guide to the principality in the late fifties, a copy of which I had managed to acquire via the Internet. It's a slim volume with some attractive colour plates of the countryside, which gives an outline of the history and attractions of Liechtenstein. He manages to restrain himself until page sixteen, where he starts to discuss the merits of tax-free shopping in the principality, listing chocolate and cigarettes as being particularly cheap.

'All of these articles may be obtained at the Quick Tourist Shop in Vaduz,' he finally blurts out, 'where an English-speaking staff will help you select gifts and souvenirs to give pleasure for years to come.' It's funny he should say that because I have often mused upon how I will never achieve real fulfilment in life until I own a letter opener with 'Liechtenstein' stamped upon its hilt.

At the rear of the booklet are three testaments to the principality by foreign writers. American novelist Paul Gallico eulogises his Liechtenstein-made cuckoo clock and advises readers to 'see my friend Baron von Falz-Fein in the Quick Tourist Shop and let him measure you for yours'.

Temple Fielding of the Fielding Travel Guides adds that tourists should 'go to the wonderful little Quick Tourist Office . . . because you're almost sure to find what you want at this fountainhead for foreign visitors. The proprietor Baron Edward von Falz-Fein is supercharged with enthusiasm for his work and hospitality for his guests'.

Finally this from British writer Gordon Cooper: 'I always regard the Baron as one of the sights of Liechtenstein, even of Europe, for his energy and initiative are amazing. You'll find him most kind and helpful and, of course, English is spoken.' Of course.

Awed by my presence in the Baron's famous shop I bought a rather snazzy t-shirt with the initials FL (Fürstentum Liechtenstein) on the breast in a spoof of the Calvin Klein CK logo (copyright permission obtained, no doubt).

On leaving with my purchase I passed a couple more restaurants, another souvenir shop, the Postage-Stamp Museum and a grey, box-like building which was the new art gallery, due to open a month hence. And then I was back where I started. I had 'done' the centre of Vaduz in about ten minutes. I was here for another four days. The ninety minutes of the Austria game aside, how would I fill my time? I dined upon a cold chicken burger from Vaduz's premier kebab establishment and headed back to the Grünesholz. There was clearly nothing to do here. However, being naturally paranoid I presumed that somewhere in this village there were lots of groovy people having a great time with other groovy people. Sullenly, I trudged back to the guesthouse.

As I walked along, bored, my thoughts turned to the woman at the Grünesholz. Lacking any other form of entertainment, I'd been reading too many gothic novels, and in my mind she transformed into Griselda, a sturdily built, bloodthirsty princess from one of the tales. I snuck back into the hotel via the back door, certain I was about to be attacked by a murderous ghoul with a reluctance to speak English.

Although I had told myself not to, given that I was here to explore the culture and surroundings of a new land, I switched on the television. As a veteran of hotel television I knew what to expect: CNN, German Oprah-style talk shows, *The Simpsons* dubbed into Spanish, and weather forecasts for areas several hundred miles away.

The screen flickered into life at a German music channel for another familiar dose of cathode-ray culture. I know I'll sound like my dad here, but rap music all sounds the same to me. And German rap music sounds even more the same than its American counterpart. A bunch of angry-looking white kids who seem in need of a good bath shout unsyncopated lyrics whilst either travelling on a metro train or standing on a metro platform. The formula is always identical. Pasty-faced kid harangues camera as trains arrive and depart in the background. Another must is to have on the train a respectable looking middle-aged man in a suit reading a broadsheet newspaper and looking very frightened of these scary kids shouting about how they want to do stuff they want to do, not what other people want them to do.

I flicked through a few more channels and arrived at some kind of talk show. My attention was caught by a stunningly attractive girl with long blond hair, sparkling blue eyes and an innocent countenance. She spoke quietly and frequently laughed in a delightfully nervous way. A caption flashed up: 'Gina Wild – Schauspielerin' – (actress). I was smitten instantly; she possessed that childish charm that makes you want to give her a good cuddle and take her home to your mum.

Suddenly the scene cut to a quick flash of what was evidently hardcore pornography carefully chosen so as not to show too much to the early evening audience. My jaw dropped. There looking over the shoulder of a man with an appalling mullet was Gina's face, flushed and panting.

The scene cut back to the faintly virginal-looking Gina in the studio. A caption flashed up again: 'Gina Wild – Erotik-Star'. I nearly fell off the bed in surprise. Not only was this picture of innocence a hardcore-porn star, she was being interviewed on what was evidently the German version of *The Gloria Hunniford Show*.

As my ear began to tune in to the German I deduced that Gina was being asked her views on some of the day's news stories. A short film about the plight of struggling German fishermen was shown. Weather-beaten men clad in oilskins spoke urgently and desperately through enormous moustaches. There was fear in their eyes and their livelihood was clearly at stake. The film finished and the picture cut back to the studio. The interviewer asked Gina her opinion. She thought for a moment and replied, 'I like fish.'

As the interview concluded, the host handed over to her colleague. He was standing next to a man dressed as a chimney sweep covered from head to toe in soot. The sweep answered a couple of questions and the host said, '*Danke schön*. Okay, Gina . . .' The camera panned back and hardcore-porn star Gina Wild rode up to the sweep on a scooter, kissed him on both cheeks and rode away again with a black smudge on both sides of her face. The credits rolled. I have no idea at all what that was all about.

It had been a long day. I flicked through the channels a few more times in the waning hope of finding footage of people shagging each other, gave up and went to sleep, dreaming of horrendous crones on broomsticks flying out of a dark, threatening castle and swooping towards me screeching, 'Schpeeeeeek Engleeeeeeesch!' A sign above the portcullis said 'Welcome to Liechtenstein' in thick gothic script.

Four

At breakfast, where I dined alone, Griselda seemed to regard me with deep, deep loathing. As I devoured the basketful of rolls and croissants that were thumped down in front of me with such force that they scattered to all four corners of the table, she stood in the doorway with her arms folded, tutting every time a crumb dropped. Which was quite often. Fortunately a leisurely breakfast was out of the question anyway, as I had an early appointment to see the saintly Martina and her boss at the tourist board. I stood up quickly and whipped my napkin from my lap with a magician's flourish to ensure that I deposited crumbs over the widest possible area and made to leave the dining room.

The front benches of the House of Commons are placed just far enough apart that their occupants can't reach each other with swords. I employed a similar tactic when bypassing Griselda, judging just the right distance to spot a fangs-first lunge for my throat and take necessary evasive action.

As I walked to the headquarters of the Liechtenstein Tourist Board I wondered why Griselda should have developed such a fearsome misanthropic countenance. Surely it wasn't just me? She was too young to be so bitter, although the way the bags under her eyes were inflating by the day it was clear she was working long hours. This morning they were the size of the croissants.

A difficult upbringing, perhaps, that involved being locked in cupboards for long periods. Maybe she was stuck in a loveless marriage. Maybe there'd been a broken engagement that had left her heart rent irreparably asunder. Unfortunately I then had to stop coming up with further theories because I was chuckling aloud.

I would grow used to looks of incredulity in Liechtenstein when I told people why I was there. Why on earth, they were thinking, would anyone want to write a book about Liechtenstein? In English? Roland Büchel, the head honcho at the tourist board, was one such person. Prematurely grey with small round glasses and a meticulously trimmed beard, he didn't really know what to make of me. Uncharitably sending Martina off to make the coffee after she'd sat down enthusiastically at the table with her pad and pen, he chatted amiably and pushed a number of brochures across the table towards me. I could tell straightaway that he thought I was nuts.

Martina returned with the coffee. She was just as I had imagined – friendly, blond, attractive and wearing horn-rimmed glasses. And she made top coffee, too. I outlined my plans in more detail: as well as following the football team, I said, I wanted to get to the heart of Liechtenstein. The people, the culture, the history. Roland by now clearly thought I was nuttier than a bag of cashews, but tolerated me nonetheless. Martina sat there looking saintly, smiling at me encouragingly every time I said something. A portrait of Prince Hans Adam II hung on the wall behind her. Even his benevolent smile paled behind Martina's.

The Prince remains popular despite the controversial changes to the constitution he wants to introduce. Although the bumph produced by the government's press and information office tells you how the Prince and the people rule together in perfect harmony, the truth isn't quite so Grimm's Fairy Tales.

Every bill of parliament has to be signed by the Prince before it becomes law. Just like in Britain, I hear you cry, where every parliamentary bill has to be autographed by the Queen. Yes, but the Queen never turns to the Prime Minister and says, 'Hey, one has just read the small print, and you know what?

One is not blimming well signing,' before replacing the cap on her Pentel and flouncing out with her nose in the air.

Okay, Hans Adam II probably doesn't do that exactly, but he has been known to refuse to pass bills and use his power to dissolve parliament if he's not happy with the way they are doing things.

It strikes me as strange that a nation that has made itself rich as a result of the free market ethos is governed by the closest thing Europe has to an absolutist regime. It's not quite like the French Revolution hasn't happened, but it's quite a contrast that an economy that is the epitome of laissez-faire falls short of the mark in terms of democracy. I mean, for heaven's sake, women only got the vote in Liechtenstein in 1984. Yes, 1984 – while striking miners' wives in Britain were voicing such a strong opinion for change, their Liechtensteiner sisters didn't even have the franchise. And even then the referendum (blokes only, remember) was so close it almost went to a recount.

The Prince, believe it or not, wants more power. A hard-nosed businessman as well as Europe's richest royal, he's not happy with just being able to veto laws and dissolve parliament when he feels like it, and has proposed a series of measures to take power away from parliament and place it within the castle walls. Indeed, he's even threatened to move the royal seat back to Vienna if he doesn't get his way.

Despite this, his popularity remains undimmed and his portrait is yet to be replaced by images of Che Guevara. Hence Hans Adam peered benevolently at me as Roland and Martina regarded the nutcase in their midst.

Mindful of the previous night's non-activities I asked Roland what people do in the evenings in Liechtenstein.

A flicker of confusion furrowed his brow for an instant. 'Well . . .' he began uncertainly, 'maybe they would go to a restaurant, maybe the theatre . . . or maybe they just stay at home.' The conviction with which he added the last phrase suggested he was on safe territory there. It was confirmed then – you don't come to Liechtenstein for the nightlife. Ayia Napa it ain't.

Martina said she'd sent a bus pass to the Grünesholz for

me and asked if the place was okay. 'Yes, the people are very friendly,' I lied.

Thrusting leaflets and brochures into my bag I headed for the offices of the *Liechtensteiner Fussball-Verband*, situated in a small street behind the Adler.

Liechtenstein is a relative newcomer to international competition. Although the *Liechtensteiner Fussball-Verband* dates back as far as 1933 and they joined UEFA and FIFA in 1974, it wasn't until the qualifying rounds for Euro 96 that the principality stepped on to the field for a competitive match. They had played a smattering of friendlies, most notably chalking up a 2–0 win in 1982 over the People's Republic of China (who had roughly 1,261,800,000 more people to choose from), but their first competitive game was not until April 20th 1994 against Northern Ireland in Belfast. As England looked forward to staging Euro 96, Liechtenstein were just pleased to be in the hat for the first time.

Jimmy Quinn opened the scoring in the fourth minute for the home side, and three minutes into the second half the Liechtensteiners found themselves 4–0 behind. However, a combination of dogged determination and the Irish taking their foot off the pedal allowed the visitors a little more space and, six minutes from time, midfielder Daniel Hasler scored his country's first ever goal. Little did they know at the time, but Liechtenstein wouldn't score another competitive goal for two-and-a-half years.

Defeats followed at home to neighbouring Austria, away to the Republic of Ireland, in Latvia, Portugal and to Austria again. So when the Republic of Ireland came to the national team's former home at the Eschen-Mauren Sportpark, the visitors would have expected a comfortable stroll and the opportunity to take in some alpine scenery during the frequent lulls to allow Liechtenstein to transfer the ball from their goal to the centre spot. After all, Liechtenstein had played six games and lost the lot, conceding twenty-eight goals in the process. The Irish, meanwhile, most of whose players graced the English Premiership every week, had just beaten Portugal's Figo and co. at Lansdowne Road.

Around 3,000 Irish fans descended on the principality for the game, but despite their team having forty efforts (count 'em) on goal and twenty corners, they watched in horror as their heroes failed to break down the Liechtenstein rearguard. Martin Heeb in the home goal was unbeatable. Deep into injury time, Steve Staunton lined up a free kick from twenty-five yards. It passed within inches of the top corner, and missed Tony Cascarino's forehead by a fraction when the slightest contact would have diverted the ball into the back of the net. It was the last kick of the game, and the principality had picked up its first ever international point. The home players did lap after lap of honour as the Irish skulked from the field. The Irish fans applauded the home side just as hard as the home fans. It was a rare great moment for football in Liechtenstein. That evening, when the Liechtenstein team entered a bar packed with Irish fans, they were each carried shoulder high by the visiting supporters.

The rest of the campaign was a relative disappointment. Portugal stuck seven past Heeb without reply in the next game, there was a 0–1 defeat in Riga, with Latvia's goal coming just seven minutes from the end, and finally a 0–4 defeat at home to Northern Ireland.

Liechtenstein were left bottom of the group with one goal, one point and forty goals conceded to show for their ten game campaign. They had hit the bar and had a goal disallowed against Portugal, but for a team made up completely of amateurs representing a country which doesn't even have its own league, the solitary point could be regarded with some satisfaction.

The France 98 qualifying campaign in 1996 brought Ireland to Liechtenstein again after the principality had opened their campaign with a 0–3 defeat in Macedonia. This time there was no mucking about and the Irish were three up inside the first eleven minutes, adding two more before the close. In the next match, away to Lithuania in Vilnius, midfielder Harry Zech scored Liechtenstein's second ever goal to equalise the home team's opener just after half-time. However, straight from the kick-off Lithuania scored what proved to be the winner.

If this performance had been encouraging, the next game against Macedonia was the low point of Liechtenstein's footballing history: 9 November 1996 is a date that will ring hollow down the ages for Liechtenstein. At half-time in Eschen-Mauren, Liechtenstein were 0–6 down, going on to lose by an extraordinary 1–11 margin. But coach Dietrich Weise had a good excuse. The grass on the pitch was too long, you see. The training pitches on which the team had prepared were carefully manicured, thus the players were all crippled with cramp after half an hour, unused as they were to striding through such vegetation. The Macedonians, however, managed to hack their way through the undergrowth without too many problems.

Weise's contract was up anyway and he had already announced that he was off, sparing him the ignominy of the sack or a humiliating resignation. Austrian Alfred Riedl took over, his first match in charge ending in a 0–8 defeat in Romania. There was an improved performance against Lithuania, only a 0–2 defeat this time, but a ten minute David Connolly hat-trick in Dublin helped Ireland to another five goal victory in the next match. Two 0–4 defeats to Iceland and another eight goal mauling by Romania brought the Liechtenstein campaign to a humiliating close. Ten games, ten defeats, fifty-two goals conceded. The Romania game had one consolation, however: Mario Frick scored his first ever international goal twenty minutes from the end of his seventeenth game.

Frick is the closest thing Liechtenstein has to a football legend. Having begun his career in the junior teams of his home village club FC Balzers, the gangly, jug-eared attacking midfielder soon attracted the interest of Swiss professional clubs. Spells at St Gallen and FC Basel saw Frick become Liechtenstein's first ever professional before FC Zurich of the Swiss top flight came a-calling. There Frick played up front alongside South African World Cup striker Shaun Bartlett and tasted top level European competition. His goal against Romania helped to seal Frick's place in the hearts of Liechtenstein's football public.

Riedl went after the World Cup campaign, and Erich Bürzle

took over briefly for a 0–6 friendly defeat in Austria, in which defender Patrik Hefti had been sent off for two bookable offences as early as the seventh minute. For the Euro 2000 campaign, however, the team would be coached by a young German called Ralf Loose. Fortunately for those who see fit to lampoon the efforts of the smaller nations, his surname is pronounced 'loser'.

Loose, who had been in charge of Liechtenstein's junior teams since 1996, became, at thirty-five, Europe's youngest national team coach. The tall defender had begun his career at SC Dortsfeld 09, before being snapped up by Borussia Dortmund. In 1981 Loose captained the West Germany youth side to victory at both the European and World Youth Championships, a team coached by Dietrich Weise. In the World Youth Final in Sydney, Loose scored twice in the final, a 4–0 win over Qatar. He still holds the record for the most appearances for Germany's youth team. The same year he also made his Bundesliga debut for Dortmund at the age of eighteen. Later he moved on to nearby Fortuna Dusseldorf, before injury curtailed his career at the age of thirty in 1993.

Having completed his coaching qualifications, he spent a short while at FSV Mainz 05 where Weise persuaded his former protégé to join him in the principality in 1996.

1998 was an exciting year for Liechtenstein football. Not only had the highly rated Loose stepped up to take control of the national team, but the new national stadium had opened in Vaduz. The sports ground at Eschen-Mauren hadn't met UEFA standards and so the old FC Vaduz ground by the banks of the Rhine was redeveloped into a compact, all-seater venue capable of holding just over 3,500 spectators – more than 10 per cent of the population. In an echo of the great Wembley debate, there was disquiet amongst the Liechtenstein sporting fraternity when the stadium was built purely as a football venue. The Eschen-Mauren Sportpark housed several sports and featured an athletics track. Despite the disagreements, FC Vaduz's rickety old grandstand bit the dust and the swanky new arena went up on the bank of the Rhine. Given that the Rhine doubles as Liechtenstein's border with Switzerland, and there is just a road between the stadium and the river, it's possible for a hefty clearance to leave the country. Fortunately, the absence of customs controls between Liechtenstein and Switzerland means that matches are not held up while LFV officials rifle their pockets to pay export duty on the match-ball.

Liechtenstein's Euro 2000 campaign got off to a bad start in Loose's first game with a 0–7 defeat in Romania, who had now crashed twenty-three goals past the principality in three games. The first international at the Rheinpark Stadion ended with a 0–4 reverse to Slovakia, and four days later, on 14 October 1998, Azerbaijan arrived.

Of all their previous opponents Azerbaijan presented Liechtenstein with their best opportunity so far to earn a point. The former Soviet republic had won only once since entering international competition in 1994, a shock 1–0 success over Switzerland during the France 98 qualifiers. Loose had taken the drastic decision of drafting in four players from the junior teams. These included promising sixteen-year-old goalkeeper Peter Jehle, who was already attracting the interest of a number of major European clubs (and Crystal Palace).

When the match approached half-time goalless there was a sense of expectation amongst the Rheinpark faithful. A goalless draw would do very nicely. Azerbaijan had had most of the play but created little to threaten Jehle in goal.

On the stroke of half-time Mario Frick went tumbling in the penalty area a good three yards beyond the goalkeeper's challenge. As the aggrieved custodian leapt to his feet and waved an imaginary yellow card at the ref for the dive, he was astonished to see a yellow being waved at him and the referee pointing to the spot. Liechtenstein had a penalty, albeit a highly dubious one. It was their first spot kick in international football, and presented them with their best opportunity to take the lead in a competitive match. Unfortunately, Harry Zech succeeded only in placing the ball wide of the goalkeeper's right-hand post. Had Liechtenstein missed their chance?

Two minutes into the second half Frick went over again and, remarkably, Liechtenstein had earned their second penalty of the game. This time Frick picked up the ball himself, placed it on the spot and, as fans covered their eyes, made no mistake. For the first time ever Liechtenstein led a competitive international match. Mario Frick was now their leading international goalscorer, with two.

Barely three minutes later another youngster, Thomas Beck, broke down the left and crossed towards the penalty spot. Martin Telser arrived from midfield and one touch later the ball was in the back of the net. Now things were getting seriously out of hand: not only were Liechtenstein ahead for the first time, they were now two goals up. The stadium erupted.

Azerbaijan roared back and reduced the arrears with a goal on the hour. Liechtenstein defended doggedly and held on grimly despite seeing the Azeris hit the post with ten minutes to go and, frighteningly, the crossbar in the last minute. The 1,450-strong crowd rose as one at the whistle to acclaim the achievement of the young team and their new coach. Ralf Loose's record now read three matches, three points, easily the best of any Liechtenstein national coach to date.

The next four matches saw more customary defeats, 0–5 to Hungary and Portugal and 0–4 in the return with Azerbaijan in Baku. Despite a 0–8 reverse to Portugal, goalkeeper Peter Jehle stood out with a string of excellent saves.

When Hungary came to Vaduz there was no real reason to expect anything other than another defeat. Whilst certainly not the force they once were, Hungary should have been too good for Liechtenstein. However, the home side took the game to the Hungarians and created enough chances to have been two or three up at the interval. Hungary hit the bar just after the break but Liechtenstein held out for a goalless draw and earned their fourth European Championship point.

When you look back at the history of Liechtenstein international football, this match clearly was a turning point for Ralf Loose's side, more so even than the Azerbaijan win. The Ireland 0–0 had been a fluke; just one of those days where it wouldn't go in for the visitors. Victory over Azerbaijan had been a fine achievement, but in football terms the opposition were just as much minnows as Liechtenstein. The Hungary result, however, was something different: a deserved, tangible reward for Loose's ambitious team selection and shrewd tactical nous. It was a ringing vindication of his controversial policy of blooding young players in the full national side.

Liechtenstein then travelled to Slovakia and came back defeated by only 2–0, half the margin the Slovaks had inflicted in Vaduz. Romania came to the principality for the final qualifying game, attended by FIFA supremo Sepp Blatter, and despite having Thomas Beck sent off on fifty-two minutes, more dogged defending restricted Gheorghe Hagi and his cohorts to a 3–0 win. Not a bad result at all in the circumstances, especially when you consider how many goals the Romanians had put past the Liechtensteiners in their previous encounters.

A friendly with the Faroe Islands, who had earned creditable draws with Scotland and Bosnia-Herzegovina in their group, ended with defeat by a solitary goal before the team travelled to Freiburg to face Germany in a match designed to provide target practice for the European champions prior to the Euro 2000 finals.

A sell-out crowd of 24,000 assembled at SC Freiburg's Dreisamstadion, including around 250 travelling Liechtensteiners. When Oliver Bierhoff scored in the first minute, things looked like going to plan. Within a quarter of an hour, however, Martin Stocklasa had capitalised on an error by Lothar Matthäus to equalise. Mehmet Scholl made it 2–1 just after half an hour thanks to a fortunate deflection off Daniel Hasler, but Liechtenstein's resistance was fierce. Half-time arrived with no further goals, and then, ten minutes into the second half Peter Jehle launched a long clearance downfield that was flicked on by Martin Stocklasa. Mario Frick hared on to the loose ball and buried a sensational equaliser.

For the next ten minutes the tiny principality with its mixture of bank workers, students and store clerks held the reigning European champions at 2–2. Indeed, Erich Ribbeck had changed virtually his entire team at half-time, so in effect Liechtenstein were holding twenty-two Germans to a draw. Marco Bode made it 3–2 on sixty-five minutes, and in the last ten, as the visitors flagged against the fresh legs of their illustrious opponents, Ulf Kirsten and Carsten Jancker rattled in five goals between them to earn a flattering 8–2 victory.

The four-point haul and encouraging performance against Germany showed that Ralf Loose's influence was reaping slow but sure dividends. The defence was tightening and erstwhile midfield general Harry Zech was developing into a highly effective libero. Mario Frick was clearly an exceptional talent and now an established professional in the Swiss top flight attracting the attention of some big clubs. Peter Jehle's performances between the posts had earned him a move to the famous Grasshoppers of Zurich. Midfielder Matthias Beck also turned professional in Switzerland with St Gallen, lanky wing back Freddie Gigon of Stade Lausanne had acquired a Liechtenstein passport and was eligible for the national side, and young midfielder Martin Stocklasa joined Frick at FC Zurich. Liechtenstein football was getting serious.

The Euro 2000 campaign had seen Liechtenstein football advance like never before. Qualification for the 2002 World Cup finals clearly wasn't going to happen, but Liechtenstein would certainly be no pushovers and a repeat of the Macedonia farce was unlikely. Drawn with Austria, Bosnia-Herzegovina, Israel and mighty Spain it was hard to see where any points might come from, but Liechtenstein were confident of not being disgraced.

Loose had instilled a professional attitude into the squad, and the team set off for their first World Cup qualifier against Israel in September 2000 in good spirits. 'Although we are more professional in our outlook, this doesn't make the games any easier,' said midfielder Martin Telser. Israel had reached the qualification play-offs for Euro 2000 but had been comprehensively routed by Denmark, 0–5 in Tel Aviv and 0–3 in Copenhagen. Thus ended coach Schlomo Scharf's eight-year tenure as national coach, with Denmark's Richard Moller Nielsen replacing him.

As the team trained before the game in 30-degree heat in Tel Aviv, Loose found himself able to pick from a virtually full-strength squad. Thus it was a strong Liechtenstein team that took the field at the Ramat Gan Stadium in front of 11,000 spectators. The defence had shown in previous matches that it was not as porous as it once was, and Peter Jehle had made a sensational debut for Grasshoppers a month earlier. First choice keeper Stephane Hüber had given away a ninety-fifth-minute penalty in Grasshoppers' match with Basel and been sent off. Jehle trotted on to the field, took his place between the posts and promptly saved the spot kick.

This was clearly the most confident, able Liechtenstein team ever to leave the principality.

They will have been disappointed then to find themselves a goal down after sixteen seconds. From the kick-off Israel pressed forward, Avi Nimny broke away on the left, his cross was missed by Martin Stocklasa, and Alon Mizrahi lashed the ball into the roof of the net from eight yards. It was precisely the start Liechtenstein had wanted to avoid, a goal down inside the first minute.

Many teams might not have recovered from such a devastating early blow, but Liechtenstein are made of stronger stuff these days. Banin and Blackburn's Eyal Berkovic were causing problems but by the time the game had reached the quarter-hour mark the visitors had settled into their rhythm. Indeed, on eighteen minutes they had their first shot on goal when Mario Frick's effort from distance was smothered by Davidovich in the Israeli goal. The spiky-haired, vastly experienced Daniel Hasler was excelling in his deep-lying central midfield role and subduing Berkovic, the main supplier of Israel's creativity.

Early in the second half there were chances for Thomas Beck and Mario Frick, but as the heat began to take its toll Israel began to turn the screw. Jehle pulled off a string of superb saves to prevent the home side increasing their lead, keeping the ball out until ten minutes from time when Pini Balili converted another Nimny cross for the second goal.

The Israel fans were not happy with their side at the final whistle and let them know it. Wherever Liechtenstein play, opposing fans expect a hatful of goals, but Ralf Loose's team were proving the veracity of the old adage that there are no easy games in international football any more. It had been a fine performance from the Liechtensteiners, particularly after such a disastrous start.

A month later, Austria were to make the short trip across the border. As I left the tourist office in search of the LFV, the Austrians' sleek team coach was parked smugly outside the Hotel Schatzmann on the other side of the road. There were forty-eight hours to go before the game. My moment of revelation in a London hostelry on a rainy afternoon had led me from taking initially minor notice of the Israel–Liechtenstein result in the newspaper to strolling through the centre of the Vaduz to meet the man in charge of football in the principality prior to their next match.

I reached the door of the LFV offices, which are situated above a grocer's shop on a quiet street corner a stone's throw from the Adler. A simple brass plate beside a sturdy unmarked slab of heavy mahogany was the only clue that this was the nerve centre of Liechtenstein football. I pressed the bell. A few seconds later the door buzzed but I couldn't open it. I pressed the bell again and the same thing happened. This occurred twice more until someone eventually came down and let me in. I know how to make an impression.

Markus Schaper came out of his office to greet me. A short, bespectacled man with a goatee beard, the General Secretary of the Liechtenstein Football Association bears more than a passing resemblance to Jeremy Spake from *Airport*. He's a cheerful soul dressed casually in jeans, denim shirt and LFV tie. He ushers me into his office, a tidy, almost unnaturally ordered affair with identical ringbinders on shelves along one wall and a desk completely clear save for the LFV pennant suspended from a stand next to his computer.

I asked him about the background to Liechtenstein's improvement.

'It all began back in about 1988,' he explained in perfect English. 'The LFV noticed that football in Liechtenstein was at a particularly low ebb, both in terms of quality and quantity. We were down to about nine hundred players in all categories, from under ten to senior level. That's when the concept of

"Liechtenstein Football 2000" was launched in order to improve football here. We wanted to enter international competition, and we wanted to do this for two reasons: mainly because playing at that level would improve our football, but also it would produce extra income in terms of television rights and advertising. This we hoped would enable us to employ a professional coach to improve our youth teams.

'So we entered a team into Euro 96 under a German coach named Dietrich Weise who had been in Liechtenstein since 1993. The income from television rights enabled us to improve our administrative infrastructure and rent offices for the Association. We also negotiated with the Swiss FA to pool resources at youth level, such as training and medical facilities. So our junior teams also include Swiss regional players but are still called Team Liechtenstein. Although our population is thirty-two thousand, only around twenty-one thousand are Liechtenstein nationals so we have to cast our net a bit wider to improve the teams at junior level. That way the step up to the full national squad isn't so great.

'We're continuing to improve the youth set-up, giving the young players a complete education, not just football training. We have arrangements with schools and businesses, which mean that youngsters can have the best football coaching without detracting from their general education. At the moment things look very good in the long term. A year or two ago we had only one professional, now we have six or seven. Who knows, maybe by the time the next World Cup comes around, the whole team will be professional.

'It's a very young team now. Peter Jehle our goalkeeper is a very promising player who was until recently the goalkeeper for both the national team and the national under-nineteen team. He's now the number two goalkeeper at Grasshoppers, whose main goalkeeper plays for the Swiss national team.'

I suggest to him that the Euro 2000 campaign was the pinnacle of Liechtenstein international footballing achievement.

'Yes, without a doubt. It was our best ever qualifying performance. I know you should never say never, but we know that we will never be world champions. Our aim is to help reduce the gap between the smaller nations and the rest. If we can achieve that then we will have been successful, and the Euro 2000 campaign went a long way towards this ambition.

'The main problem for us in Liechtenstein is that football isn't that important to people. We don't have the support that other countries have. The game isn't important in people's minds, probably because we are not a poor country. Hence the social aspect of football is not the same and we don't really have the concept of the "fan" here. I hope that this will change; maybe it will as the national team becomes more successful. The new stadium helps, and it's something of which I am very proud. It was completed in 1998 to all UEFA and FIFA specifications and seats 3,548 people. To me it is the greatest stadium in the world, and in per capita terms it's probably the biggest. When it's full, that means there is around twelve per cent of the entire population there.'

I ask whether the stadium will be full for the visit of neighbours Austria.

'The match is very nearly sold out. There are many Austrians living and working in Liechtenstein so we have decided not to segregate the supporters. I don't see there being any dangers from the supporters being mixed.

'On the pitch I think we have to be realistic. There are at least two classes between Austria and Liechtenstein, but nothing is certain in football and anything can be possible. We played very well in Israel, apart from the disastrous start. It was very hot and our part-time players were very tired in the last twenty minutes of the game. We have prepared hard for this match. The professional players trained this morning and those players who work during the day will train this evening. We have secured agreements with their employers when they need time off but it's usually not a problem because we pay the players for the time they lose. We usually get goodwill from their bosses as it's kudos for their companies, having an international footballer working there.

'Was I happy with the draw for this group? Yes, very happy. Austria is our neighbour, Spain is obviously a fantastic team.

Israel is a very good side and beat Austria 5–0 in the Euro 2000 qualifiers. Bosnia has a young national side with some famous players. So yes, we were very happy from both a sporting and financial point of view.'

What, then, are Schaper's hopes for the rest of the campaign?

'Martin Luther King said "I have a dream" and I have dreams too, dreams that we will win another game. It would be a wonderful moment for me to wake up in a year to find that we had done as well as we did in the Euro 2000 qualifiers and earned four points. But we have to be realistic and just try to do the best job to get the best result for Liechtenstein.'

Schaper almost bounces on his chair with enthusiasm. As the only full-time administrator of Liechtenstein football he's a busy man, and our meeting is cut short by the arrival of the tall figure of Otto Biedermann, the president of the LFV, on some urgent business. I managed to leave the building in a less spastic manner than I'd entered, bought a copy of the *Liechtensteiner Vaterland* and ensconced myself in the Old Castle Inn, a pub and restaurant which I had walked past several times and only just registered that its name was in English.

Not certain of the protocol (do I sit and wait to be served or do I go to the bar and order?) I compromised by sliding on to a stool at the bar and ordering '*ein gross Bier*'. It was mid-afternoon and there were only a few figures slumped along the bar like a collection of Barneys from Moe's Tavern in *The Simpsons*. My request caused the place to fall silent, and I was conscious of everyone turning to look at me. '*Gross?*' asked the girl behind the bar, incredulously. I nodded assertively. She reached beneath the bar and heaved out an enormous glass stein. She slid it beneath the tap and started pouring. And pouring. And pouring. It took for ever. Grunting with the effort, she eventually heaved the froth-topped behemoth on to the bar and slid it towards me. It took both hands and necessitated placing her foot against the wall behind her for extra purchase. The stein was absolutely enormous. I swallowed nervously, and glanced from side to side. The Barneys, I noted, had far more modest drinks in stalked glasses in front of them. They were all looking at me.

I took a couple of deep breaths and placed both hands around the glass. My fingertips didn't meet on the far side. Realising that the slightest tilt would send a torrent of beer into my lap that might feasibly wash me clean out of the door, I placed my mouth over the glass and attempted to hoover up some of the froth. Some went up my nose and I sneezed, sending a blizzard of foam around a four-foot radius. Finally I gripped the glass again and after some effort managed to lift it clear of the counter. I took a gulp and allowed it to drop again with a thud that made the picture frames on the wall rattle. The effort had left me panting, the only noise breaking the awe-struck silence. I glanced from side to side again and the hubbub of conversation recommenced. When I spread out the newspaper and pulled out my German dictionary, the Barneys all nodded knowingly to each other. Ah, they seemed to be saying, he's English. No wonder he's a pisshead.

I ploughed through the previews and learned that sweeper Harry Zech, one of Liechtenstein's best, most experienced players and a winemaker by trade, would be missing from the team against Austria. 'It's a hard loss,' said Ralf Loose, although I looked at the wrong word in the dictionary at first and thought he was calling Zech a tosser. There was specula-tion as to what Loose would do in Zech's absence. The sweeper system had been very effective for Liechtenstein, and to lose Zech would be a major blow. Daniel Hasler would be an alter-native as he'd played there before, but his performance in the centre of midfield was excellent in Tel Aviv, leading Loose to lament that he didn't have two Daniel Haslers, one to play in midfield and another in defence.

Loose promised to attack the Austrians, a part of Liechtenstein's game he said had been neglected. Austria had had a poor Euro 2000 campaign, losing 0–5 to Israel and astonishingly 0–9 to Spain. I'd seen them a couple of months earlier playing out a tedious 1–1 draw with Hungary on a sweltering night in Budapest in a 95 per cent empty stadium and they hadn't been all that. And this game was almost exactly ten years after the Austrians famously lost to the Faroe Islands in the North Atlantic country's first ever competitive match.

With half a gallon of beer still to be consumed, I turned to the front page to see what was concerning the people of Liechtenstein in October 2000. Electronic Signatures Should Be Legally Valid, ran the front page headline on the day after the parliament building in Belgrade had been stormed by the people. Intelligence Is Not Innate screamed page three's leader.

I meandered back to the Grünesholz with the enormous beer I'd somehow managed to finish swilling around inside me. When I got back to my room I discovered that the builders next door had dug through the cable television connection. I didn't deduce this at first, of course. Oh no, first I had to spend twenty minutes fiddling with the aerial and pressing all sorts of buttons before I became aware of a commotion outside the window. Anita, the woman who owned the place, was haranguing three workmen whilst brandishing a rolling pin. They were clearly working frantically to repair it, presumably because they knew that Griselda was lurking inside with access to a kitchen full of sharp implements. Ten minutes later, the picture came back. I was reading quietly on the bed at the time, when suddenly the room was filled with shouty German rap music and some pimply youths appeared pressing their faces against the inside of the screen. Given that I was reading another spooky gothic novel and the sun had just gone down, it's no surprise that I fell off the bed.

I picked myself up and reduced the volume (why I'd thought turning the volume up full would help get the picture back, I don't know), pulled my coat on and ventured back into town. It was deserted, of course, and the dark streets echoed to my footsteps. There was a ten-foot-high smiling plastic cow outside the Chinese restaurant, advertising chocolate. Some Americans had been having their photograph taken in front of it earlier in the day (rather than the magnificent fourteenth-century castle on the hillside behind) saying, 'Gee, we gotta get a picture in front of the big plastic cow!' Now, as it loomed at me out of the gloom, the cow had taken on a sinister countenance. I looked through the windows of a couple of bars and found them almost totally deserted. I was filled once again with the feeling that there were lots of groovy young Liechtensteiners somewhere all having a really great time. Without me. I couldn't face the Old Castle Inn, fearing that my experience with the giant beer earlier had created something of a rod for my back. If I went in again everyone would be nudging each other and pointing and I'd be forced to consume another bucketload to preserve my reputation.

I noticed a glow from the direction of the stadium and remembered that Markus Schaper had told me the team would be training tonight at eight o'clock. It was a quarter to eight, so with nothing better to do I wandered towards the Rhine in the direction of the floodlights. The Swiss Alps loomed large and menacing out of the gloom beyond the stadium. Behind me Vaduz Castle was bathed in orange floodlights, looking from a distance like it was suspended in mid air. It had been Baron von Falz-Fein's idea to light the castle at night. The current prince's father had apparently been reluctant for the understandable reason that it would keep him awake at night ('Is it dark yet, dear?' 'Haven't the foggiest, love.'). Having been in the north Norwegian town of Tromsø during its three months of continuous sunlight a few weeks earlier, I'd seen just how doolally continuous daylight sends people. The Prince would have been doing all sorts of weird things (running naked through the streets, if Tromsø was anything to go by), so I presume the soft orange light was a compromise. All the same, it looked wonderful.

I entered the stadium just as the squad came out of the tunnel in their blue-and-black training suits. With characteristic Swiss timing it was exactly eight o'clock. The stadium has a small, modern stand along both touchlines with the seats picked out in the national colours of red and blue. There was no spectator accommodation behind the goals, just tall fencing to keep the ball from disappearing into the car park. I sat high up in the seats and watched for a while as the players jogged backwards and forwards across the pitch in their 'Liechtenstein' emblazoned warm-up suits. I recognised Ralf Loose, his tall countenance oozing natural authority even though he's still only in his mid-thirties. His eyes are deep set and he has a square jaw not dissimilar to Glenn Hoddle's. His hair sprouts from just above his forehead and is brushed back in a way that only Germans seem to achieve. I also managed to pick out Peter Jehle, the young goalkeeper, and the team's star player Mario Frick.

After fifteen minutes of watching the squad jogging backwards and forwards I realised that I wasn't going to glean any great insight into the Liechtenstein set-up. Plus, a couple of players seemed to have spotted the lone bloke in the stand and identified me as a weirdo. 'Hey,' they might have said to each other under their breath, 'I bet that's the guy that went into the Old Castle Inn today and asked for '*ein gross Bier*'.

Suddenly the two cans of Belgian lager that were warming gently in my room seemed appealing, and I set off home. I got into bed, drank the beer and watched an American straight-to-video film dubbed badly into Italian before nodding off.

Five

Griselda's hatred of humanity appeared to have mellowed overnight. She actually bade me 'good morning' when I appeared for breakfast, and just set down the coffee instead of throwing it over me (I'd taken the precaution of diving under the table anyway).

Whilst concentrating again on scattering crumbs widely and this time making sure the little foil butter wrappers were placed face down on the table after use too, it occurred to me that the bus pass Martina had sent down hadn't appeared. Liechtenstein's bus service is extraordinarily efficient and economical. In an effort to wean people away from their cars and on to public transport to ease some of the daily gridlock, a weekly pass costs less than three pounds, offering unlimited travel on a service that guarantees a bus every ten minutes on the main routes. This also includes travel into Switzerland and Austria. I tracked down Anita and asked her if an envelope had arrived for me. She threw her hands up to her face and said with genuine horror, '*Ich habe vergessen!*' She bustled off behind the bar and came back with a tourist-board-branded envelope. As she handed it to me she asked which room I was in, as if not knowing that was the reason she hadn't passed it on to me. Given that I was evidently the only guest, I wasn't convinced.

I went back to my room and discovered that the workmen

had drilled through the television cable again. Deciding to leave before Griselda learned this and came out shooting, I crossed the road outside the Grünesholz just as the heavens opened. The mountains were invisible behind the misty rain and I was instantly soaked. The endless stream of traffic hissed by, splashing water over my shoes as I trudged up the road. The rain fell harder as I reached the parliament building and I decided to take shelter inside, only then realising that I could, of course, have used my snazzy new bus pass to avoid a soaking. Two women at the reception desk looked at me quizzically as I skidded through the door shaking droplets of rain from my head like a small terrier after a bath. I stood dripping and chatting with them in broken English. When I explained why I was in Liechtenstein, once they'd got over the now customary incredulity, they insisted I visit the government's office of press and information where I would find all sorts of useful leaflets and assorted gubbins.

Still sodden, I was led along the immaculately polished marble corridor that runs the length of the ground floor. An immense sweeping staircase in the centre takes you upstairs to where the business of parliament is done. It was rather like diving headlong into the House of Commons to avoid a cloud-burst and being shown into the cabinet offices instead of riddled with bullets.

The echo of my squeaking wet trainers bounced around the walls, amplifying the sound to the proportions of a badminton doubles tournament in St Paul's Cathedral. The two women knocked on a thick wooden door and retreated whence they had come. A genial man called Peter emerged, shaking my hand and laughing heartily. He took me into an adjacent office, handed me all sorts of booklets and invited me to help myself to the stacks of publicity photographs in the filing cabinets nearby before returning to his office still chuckling away.

There were some panoramic shots of the castle in snow and sunshine, the sights of Vaduz (both of them) and, finally, the members of the Liechtenstein government. I helped myself to half a dozen signed colour portraits of the head of government whose name happened to be Mario Frick. I had discovered this before I left and become very excited at the possibility of a country's head of government playing up front for the national football team. Alas, they were different people. Eight years previously this Mario Frick had, at the age of twenty-seven, become Europe's youngest leader. The pressure had clearly told as he was now as bald as a coot. He had a kindly face, however, and you never know when a signed picture of the Liechtenstein head of government might come in handy (central Asian border crossings, job interviews, pick-up joints: the list is endless). I also snaffled a picture of a member of his cabinet, on the puerile grounds that her name was Andrea Willi.

The rain had eased a little by now and I ventured back into the centre of Vaduz. Surprisingly, there weren't many people around. A large group of American schoolchildren tumbled out of their vehicle, pushing each other and shouting. Their brightly coloured cagoules and rucksacks stood out on this grey, miserable day against the grey, miserable buildings and the braces on their teeth glinted in the little available light. 'Gahd, this place is, like, so dull,' said a sulky blond girl. 'Are we not in Switzerland any more?' asked a boy with greasy hair. 'No man,' a friend replied before delving into his ruck-sack and pulling out a sheaf of paper stapled in one corner, 'this is . . . Ly-chen-steen.'

I followed them into the Baron's souvenir shop where, as I thought they would, they had a good look around, poked and prodded things, held them up for each other's noisy inspection to the accompaniment of their scraping nylon rainwear, and then didn't buy anything.

I wandered back in the direction of the Grünesholz, which took me past the art museum. It was across the road from the almost-completed grey cube that would shortly house the impressive Liechtenstein art collection, but was in complete contrast to its successor. The gallery occupied the two floors of an anonymous building above the tourist office and the Postage-Stamp Museum. The woman on reception felt guilty in charging me admission, explaining that there was not much to see. Everything was being packed up ready for the move.

There was, however, an exhibition of photographs and slides detailing the conversion of various European buildings into artistic spaces. Not what those spaces actually contained, you understand, just the buildings themselves.

The curator was clearly bored as most of her exhibits were packed away in boxes and decided to accompany me around what I thought to be the most stupefyingly dull exhibition I have ever seen. There are only so many photographs of empty warehouses in which you can feign interest. 'This one's in Berlin,' she'd say, before moving on to the next identical shot and saying wearily, 'This one's in Prague,' in a tone of voice that said, 'Look, we both know this is ridiculous but let's just go with it and get it over.' She wore jeans and a stripy blouse whose collars were turned up. Her brown hair was streaked with grey and, with her half-moon glasses, she bore an uncanny resemblance to Germaine Greer. When I asked her about the new building, to my surprise she rolled her eyes to the ceiling. The museum had taken a couple of decades to plan, three years to build and was to be the focal point for attracting visitors to the principality, but its curator wasn't impressed. 'It's horrible,' she said, looking at me over the top of her glasses. 'It's too cramped in there, there's no space to do anything. And look at it, it just sits there like . . .' She paused, waving her hand contemptuously in the direction of the new building, trying to find the right word. 'It just sits there!'

I mentioned that I had recently visited the remarkable titanium-plated Guggenheim in Bilbao and she sighed wistfully. It was clearly more what she'd had in mind for Vaduz than the squat grey cube that she'd got. And killing time in a draughty building presiding over a collection of pictures that would have even architects rushing to the window and hurling themselves into the street below clearly didn't help her mood.

I left her to her warehouses and visited the Postage-Stamp Museum, thinking that at least I couldn't find this as dull as what I'd just seen. And you know what? I was wrong. At the risk of becoming the target of some philatelic fatwa, once you've seen one stamp, you really have seen them all. The museum is housed in just one room, with the displays contained in pull-out racks. After looking at the first few of these, I became aware that I was pulling them halfway out and shoving them back in with a metallic crack at a tempo that called to mind a desktop Newton's cradle. The floor had clearly been polished by the same expert cleaner who polished the parliament building, and every step I took sounded like I was attempting to skate around the room on a pair of Marigolds.

I made the best of it and hung around for a full three minutes, killing time by reading some of the information on display. Liechtenstein's first postage stamps had been produced in 1912, and judging by the popularity of the principality's stamps among collectors these would now be worth an absolute fortune. Curiously the stamps are not actually produced in Liechtenstein, but in Austria and Switzerland. In 1980, one of my newly acquired booklets told me, postage stamp sales accounted for more than 10 per cent of the nation's revenue, but since then high finance has taken over and philately is not as important to the economy as it once was. Which presumably put paid to the boom years of the stamp museum.

Having had my fill of gummy-backed perforated squares for one lifetime, I headed for the exit giving a cheery smile and nod to the attendant as she sat behind a desk reading a newspaper. She smiled back, looking at me sideways in that faintly pitying way that an enthusiast does when it's clear you don't share their passion in the slightest. If it wasn't for me and those that came before me, she seemed to be saying, those postcards you've just bought would be going nowhere, chummy.

Stuck for something to do I meandered back to the Grünesholz, pausing at the supermarket on the way. I'd walked up past the Prince's vineyards on one of my longer excursions and thought I really ought to try Liechtenstein wine. The supermarket had shelves and shelves of red and white, none of which was from Liechtenstein. Tucked away in a corner, on a shelf by itself, was a single bottle of Liechtenstein rosé with a screw top. I took it back to my room and drank it whilst watching a German confessional programme hosted by a sturdy blond woman with short hair and chiselled features. The wine was better than the programme, but there wasn't much in it. CNN was showing footage of the Belgrade parliament being overrun by the populace. No one knew where Slobodan Milosevic was, but I was fairly sure he wasn't in Liechtenstein.

From the outside the Belgrade parliament did not look dissimilar to its Vaduz counterpart. It was hard to imagine the contented people of Liechtenstein becoming that fed up with Mario Frick and his cohorts that they'd start lobbing petrol bombs through the windows. There had been no visible security as I blundered through the door, and I'm pretty sure the two elderly ladies at reception wouldn't have put up much resistance if I'd been waving a Molotov cocktail in one hand and a hammer and sickle flag in the other. It's a safe bet that revolutionary socialism has never had much of a following in the principality (although I like to think that the only reason Lenin didn't set off for St Petersburg in his sealed train from Liechtenstein was the regrettable absence of a train), where an overdue library book probably provokes letters to the papers predicting anarchy and the imminent collapse of society.

Yes, I thought to myself as I raised the bottle of pleasant pink liquid to my pursed lips again to the televised soundtrack of breaking glass and Serbian political chants, my chosen assignment was probably the safest I could have undertaken. It crossed my mind fleetingly to shove a load of toilet paper into the top of the bottle, light it and career into the middle of the street shouting incomprehensible slogans, but decided against it. They'd probably just have set Griselda on me.

As evening fell, emboldened by the 75cl of sweet sticky liquid swilling around inside me, I ambled back into the centre of Vaduz in search of action. It was Friday night: if Vaduz was going to come alive at any time, it was tonight. My cheeks flushed red with the wine and my breathing had become slightly laboured. Ahead of me I thought I saw some flashing bright lights and, remarkably, what appeared to be the silhouettes of people. On the streets? After dark? Enjoying themselves? In Liechtenstein? Surely not.

When I heard the familiar 'dumph, dumph, dumph' of distant loud music above the solemn sound of the church clock chiming the hour, I realised that I wasn't seeing things. There was a fairground in full swing not far from the Old Castle Inn. There was even a policeman directing people across the road. Stunned, I wandered in and bought a beer in a flimsy plastic glass. It was the sort that sends its contents squirting into the air whenever you exert any kind of grip, like when Popeye pops a can of spinach.

Having thus drenched my shoes, I watched a group of teenage boys gathered around one of those see-how-hard-you-can-punch machines. Every time one of them made the bell ring, they would quickly glance around to see if any girls had noticed. One boy succeeded in ringing the bell three times in a row. For some reason, and I blame the Liechtenstein rosé for this, I wondered whether he could do the same thing with his head. I tapped him on the shoulder and pointed first to the punchball and then to my head, smiling idiotically. He didn't seem to understand, so I repeated the mime only this time more imploringly and assertively. He started glancing sideways at his mates who were all looking at me agape. I then realised that he probably thought I was inviting him to punch me in the face, and so retreated waving and grinning pathetically.

In doing so I bumped into a huge man with a beard so full and hair so long that at first I thought his head was on backwards. He was wearing a sleeveless denim jacket over a black t-shirt and his huge forearms were smeared with ancient gothic-script tattoos. I'd spilled his pint, so it looked like I was going to get my punch in the face after all, and I quickly resigned myself to walking around with the imprint of his skull ring on the bridge of my nose for the rest of my life. I waved and grinned pathetically again, only for a giant hand to reach out and clap me on the shoulder so hard I felt the nerves in my teeth rattle. Piercing eyes stared out from somewhere within the hair, looking so deeply into me I feared he could actually see right down to my rapidly constricting sphincter.

As I braced myself for the pain, and glanced around for a safe spot to spit out my broken teeth, his face creased into a vast grin. He said something in German, laughed, clapped me on the shoulder so hard I feared he'd dislocated it, and turned away. I noticed then that the back of his jacket bore the legend 'Hell's Angels Liechtenstein'. I'd spilled the drink of a Hell's Angel and lived. I felt pretty cocky as a result and so had a go at the punchball thing. My first effort missed completely, and my second was so wild it hit the spring from which the ball was suspended (which hurt quite a bit, actually). The third made a glancing contact that moved the ball slightly. I might as well have asked for a paper bag to punch my way out of. That seemed to be more my level.

After my lucky escape I ventured into a heaving Old Castle Inn. The place was full up and sweaty. Ruddy-cheeked Liechtensteiners sat at the tables drinking, chatting and laughing. Skinny waiters dodged between them carrying huge plates of steaming food. I perched on a stool and ordered a beer of more modest size than the one I'd had before. I was curious to know why Vaduz had suddenly sprung to life and asked the girl behind the bar as she plonked down a beermat and placed my drink on it.

'It's *Jahrmarkt* tomorrow,' she replied. 'It's a traditional autumn festival when the farmers bring the cows down from the mountains before winter. Tomorrow there'll be a big parade through the town and more drinking.'

I sat there for a while watching my fellow patrons. Everyone seemed to know each other and everyone looked happy. When all's said and done Liechtensteiners don't have it bad really. Their nation is stinking rich, there's very little crime and, most impressively, they get to look at great big mountains when-ever they like. Their nation has been transformed in around half a century from a backward, poor, rural economy to one of the richest in the world. Consequently, everybody seems happy. Nobody seems poor. And, despite the millions of pounds' worth of business that takes place in the principality every day, a few farmers leading their cows up the street is cause for drinking, funfairs and debauchery. Well, drinking and funfairs anyway.

From the inside pocket of my jacket I pulled out a slim booklet I'd picked up in parliament earlier in the day called

Liechtenstein in Figures 2000 and began to leaf through it. Did you know that in the whole of 1998 there were only four deaths in Liechtenstein as a result of accidents or violence? Considering the sheer volume of traffic that snakes through the principality, I found this quite remarkable. I read on in search of more jaw-dropping stats.

In 1941 only ten people commuted into Liechtenstein to work. In 1999 that number had risen to just under ten thousand out of a total workforce of twenty-five thousand. There is no better illustration of the remarkable transformation of the Liechtenstein economy in the last half century. Where once the tiny principality fuelled its hand-to-mouth existence by taking bulls to market, today it makes a fortune trading on the bull markets and now does so much business that over a third of the workforce travels in from outside its borders.

The unemployment figures also made interesting reading. No, honestly. In 1980 for example, unemployment stood at three. Not 3 per cent, three people. Working for the Liechtenstein DSS must have been a cushy number in those days. In 1999 that figure had risen to 299, still barely 1 per cent of the workforce. I had not seen a single person sleeping rough, and Vaduz is surely the only European capital that can make that boast. A Liechtensteiner's idea of sleeping rough is probably dozing off in a chair in front of the telly.

So no wonder the eyes of the Old Castle Inn's patrons were sparkling, the grins widening and the laughter becoming more hearty by the hour. Liechtenstein is, in economic terms, a roaring success. Whether that success has been at the expense of its architectural charm and its natural resources (with almost one motor vehicle for every man, woman and child of the population, and with new banks and offices springing up at every turn, Liechtenstein could find itself with severe pollution problems in the future) remains to be seen.

As I nursed my beer among the happy locals I wondered how this would reflect on the football team. Was theirs a different type of success? Would, say, a narrow defeat or a draw against Austria tomorrow be viewed by these people as an achievement or a failure? In finance, success and failure are easily measured, but the distinctions are blurred when it comes to international football.

As Liechtenstein proves, economic potential is not restricted by the constraints of your boundaries. When it comes to international football, however, the situation is quite different.

Six

Matchday dawned damp, drizzly and dingy. I squelched into the centre of Vaduz again for the main festivities of *Jahrmarkt*. The funfair was yet to open for business and where the previous evening there had been bright lights, music and happy faces, the rides were stationary and the kiosks boarded up. The collected rainwater made sagging paunches of the kiosk awnings, and it could have been Weymouth on a wet Wednesday. There was a small market on the car park behind the town hall, but where I'd expected cattle pens and exotic cheeses there were just the ubiquitous cheap children's toys, rows of dark brown and tan leather goods and tables piled high with rectangular boxes marked Reebok and Nike.

A few tourists poked around the goods as the rain dripped from the plastic sheeting over the stalls and landed on the backs of their necks. The hiss of braziers and the smell of roasting chestnuts filled the air, but it was all rather miserable. The Alps had vanished behind the misty drizzle and everywhere you looked shoulders drooped beneath anoraks. Disappointed, I bought the *Vaterland* and the *Volksblatt* and returned to the Grünesholz.

Keine Angst Vor Den Österreichen claimed the front page of the *Volksblatt* sports section, reporting the comments of Austria's coach Otto Baric. The squat, tubby Croat, topped permanently and liberally with hair-oil, had taken over the reins of the Austrian side after the calamitous 0–9 defeat to

Spain during the Euro 2000 qualifiers ('Remember folks, this is football, not skittles,' said an Austrian radio announcer before giving out the score). That result saw the end of previous boss Herbert Prohaska, but Baric didn't fare much better. Despite a 7–0 win over San Marino in his first match in charge, Austria then went down 0–5 in Israel, a performance regarded by many as being as awful as the Spain debacle.

Since then things had improved slightly, but it was clear that Baric presided over the weakest Austrian team to take the field for a number of years. However, whilst Liechtenstein had been playing their first game of the qualifying campaign in Tel Aviv, Austria had been returning to form of sorts with a 5–1 friendly victory over Iran.

What loomed largest for the Austrians, however, was that the game at the Rheinpark Stadion fell almost exactly on the tenth anniversary of their 0–1 defeat to the Faroe Islands in the qualifying tournament for the 1992 European Championships. It had been the Faroes' first ever competitive match and had been played in Landskrona, Sweden owing to the absence of a grass football pitch in the rocky North Atlantic outcrop. Austrian striker Toni Polster had predicted double figures for the Austrians, and coach Sepp Herberger happily admitted that he knew nothing about the Faroes.

Incredibly, a goal just after the hour from a timber salesman called Torkil Nielsen was enough to win the game for the Faroese, a result that still haunts the Austrians ten years on.

We must not have a repeat of the Faroes game [said Baric, who was taking this so seriously he had assembled his squad six days before the game rather than the customary four]. I have instructed my team to win. Anything other than a victory will be a disaster for us. We must treat this match as if it were a cup tie. We had Liechtenstein watched in Israel, and it's clear that their defence is very good. The longer the match stays goalless, the more confident Liechtenstein will become, so it's important for us to have wrapped up the game before half-time.

Ralf Loose had opted for Thomas Hanselmann of FC Balzers at sweeper to replace the injured Harry Zech. He would play behind the highly rated Daniel Hasler and the experienced Patrik Hefti, who had played professionally in the USA in the mid-nineties.

The midfield would consist of young professional Jürgen Ospelt, Martin Telser (the scorer of Liechtenstein's last competitive goal), Martin Stocklasa, who played with Mario Frick at Swiss top flight side FC Zurich, his brother Michael, and Stade Lausanne's semi-professional schoolteacher Frédéric Gigon. Up front, Frick and Thomas Beck would be attempting to register Liechtenstein's first competitive goal since the Azerbaijan game more than two years earlier. Beck told the *Volksblatt*:

> I'm going into this game highly motivated. I'll be giving everything for the team and my country. We'll be trying to open up the game early – if we can reach half-time goalless or even just one goal behind, it will make the Austrians nervous. If we can keep the Austrians at bay then maybe the crowd will get behind us.

Loose was asked if he attached any significance to the fact that Liechtenstein had lost only 0–2 in Israel, where the Austrians had shipped five goals a few months previously.

> Obviously I haven't added up the two results and concluded that we'll win 3–0. You can't really compare the two games. Against Austria, Israel were motivated by a full house of 30,000 and had a great day. Against us last month there were only 11,000 people there and the pressure was not so great. Don't forget that Liechtenstein's last two matches with Austria have ended 0–6 and 0–7 – from these defeats it's clear that you can't predict even a 1–0 victory for us.

That afternoon England took on Germany in the last match at Wembley Stadium, so I returned to my room to watch it on television. On a soggy day Dietmar Hamann's free kick was enough to inflict defeat on Kevin Keegan's boys. The German pundits could barely contain their gleeful surprise at the result. As the stands emptied behind him, the German anchorman turned to camera and closed the programme with the words, 'Bye-bye Vem-blee!'

At that moment a huge tinkling of cowbells drowned out the television, as just about every cow in Liechtenstein was led up the street. *Jahrmarkt* was about to reach its climax. I hung out of the window watching the bovine convoy as it made its way towards the centre of Vaduz. Some cows had small bells around their neck that produced a tinkle similar to those that ring in the servants' kitchen in period dramas. Others had huge great sonorous things that caused their neck to stoop as they walked. I learned later that the bigger the bell, the more milk the cow has produced over the previous months.

As the rain continued to fall I managed to drag myself away from live coverage of Switzerland against the Faroe Islands. I left the Grünesholz and set off into the dark, rainy Vaduz night behind swaying bovine backsides that deposited hillocks of dung on to the road with impressive regularity.

Reaching the main roundabout by the Adler, having danced up the street avoiding the cowpats, I turned left down the road to the stadium. It was still an hour to kick-off and there was a trickle of hooded figures making their way to the ground. The further from the town centre and nearer to the riverside stadium, the quieter it became. I passed a small house where a trio of goats galloped around inside a small pen, their bells tinkling daintily. A woman on a horse trotted past me on the other side of the road to a backdrop of five-feet-high maize stalks. Wembley Way this wasn't, something emphasised for me by a text message that arrived at that moment to tell me Kevin Keegan had just resigned live on national television.

I reached the stadium, where a table had been set up by the entrance to sell Liechtenstein scarves and badges. The inclement weather saw everyone scurrying straight inside, which meant a slow night for Liechtenstein's merchandising entrepeneurs. I bought a pin badge and a red-and-blue scarf bearing the legend

'Hopp Liechtenstein' in yellow letters, sold to me by a girl who could have been no more than twelve years old. At least her pink anorak provided a bit of colour to the dreary evening.

On entering the press room I discovered that due to the huge demand for press tickets, I had been placed in the *Gegentribune*, the stand opposite the main one, where some pasting tables had been set up behind the spectators for the overspill from the press box.

As the teams came out to warm up, three Austrian supporters in the front row rose to their feet emitting what can only be described as a primeval bellow. One was a bearded man with glasses, who wore an expression that suggested a permanent unpleasant odour in his nostrils. He wore a motor-cycle jacket beneath a frayed sleeveless denim number covered in sew-on patches displaying the logo of just about every football club in Austria. His hands were thrust into the pockets of his saggy, faded black jeans and his shoulders were hunched like a pedestrian turning to avoid being splashed by a truck going through a puddle. He had a grubby, lank scarf tied around each wrist, and jammed in his right armpit was an Austrian flag on a stick. Next to him was a youngster, probably in his late teens and apparently still dressed by his mother. He wore stone-washed jeans, white trainers and a blue-and-yellow cagoule beneath a face with more spots than a cheetah. The one who appeared to be the leader of this pulchritudinous triumvirate was a skinhead in his early twenties. His cranium was shaved smooth to its deep pink skin which, combined with his dark eyes and protuberant nostrils, gave him a porcine appearance. His jeans were tucked into the top of his black eighteen-hole Dr Martens, with a shiny green bomber jacket completing the ensemble. I guessed, rather uncharitably but such was my mood, that none of them had ever known the physical love of a woman. Most alarmingly for their neighbours, Man-pig was also wielding a megaphone.

Their roar of greeting not having elicited a response from the Austrian players warming up below them, Man-pig decided that his amplification aid should be put to use. He put his finger on the trigger and let off an ear-splitting siren. This was followed by a distorted, tone-deaf rendition in German of 'Stand Up for the Austrians'. At most stadia staging an international match, you wouldn't really have noticed this. But in the genteel surroundings of the Rheinpark Stadion, where everybody else was waiting quietly and patiently for the match to begin, their presence was as incongruous as Napalm Death supporting the London Symphony Orchestra at the Albert Hall.

At least, I thought, they're not next to me. A couple of Liechtenstein policemen, startled no doubt at actually having something to do for the first time this millennium, went over and told the Austrians to sit down. Not an unreasonable request given that they were at the front of the stand, which meant that they were blocking the view of the pitch for the half dozen rows behind them. In response to this, however, Beardy threw the most extraordinary paddy. He hurled his flag to the ground and proceeded to harangue the policeman at high volume, waggling a grubby forefinger in his face.

Whether he was given confidence by the fact that there were clearly no opposition fans here who would give him the pasting he deserved I don't know, but Beardy was treading a very fine line. Not only could the policeman and his colleague justifiably take him outside the ground, give him a thorough twatting and dump him in the Rhine, they were also carrying guns.

The gist of Beardy's tirade seemed to be that the three amigos travel to every game involving Austria and, boy, do they stand up. And he was buggered if he was going to have that unblemished run of steadfast uprightness interrupted by some two-bob, jumped-up boy scout who doesn't even live in a proper country. At least I think that's what he said. As I put down my pen in order to enjoy fully the imminent spillage of Austrian blood, the policeman, startled, decided upon a compromise. Speaking quietly, he appeared to be telling them they could stand up as long as they moved to the back of the stand. Behind the journalists, he was clearly indicating. And guess who he was pointing them towards. Beardy nodded, grunted, picked up his flag, returned his hands to his trouser pockets and slouched up the gangway. He was followed by Man-pig and Mummy's Boy, who judging by the look of sheer adoration he was aiming in Beardy's direction was clearly not all that fussed about knowing the physical love of a woman for the foreseeable future.

The three of them came and stood right behind me. The megaphone siren went off again, and 'Stand Up for the Austrians' crackled out, into my right ear, out of my left and then on around the rest of the stadium. Ho hum, only another two hours to go.

There was clearly not a seat to be had, save for the three vacated recently at the front. That meant a 3,548 sell-out, gathered in the two stands on either side of the pitch. From my position at the back, I could look across the stadium towards Vaduz, behind which the last traces of enormous alpine silhouette were being submerged by the night. Beyond and above the white luminescence of the floodlights, and bathed in its own artificial orange light, the castle looked eerily as though it was suspended just above the roof of the stand opposite. Behind me, barely twenty yards away, the Rhine swept by invisibly in the darkness.

Below me the players warmed up in their 'Liechtenstein'-emblazoned sweatshirts. Despite the gulf in class, not to mention earnings, between them, as the two teams went through their stretches, as the goalkeepers caught crosses and as the coaches strolled among them with their hands behind their backs, these two neighbouring but wholly disparate nations had been levelled. Whatever the difference in size, population, resources and gross national product, these could have been two evenly matched sides. Would the illusion continue past the kick-off?

The players trooped from the field to the accompaniment of the ubiquitous 'Go West' by the Pet Shop Boys. The pitch was empty, save for the small brass band marching towards the centre circle. The 'Official FIFA Anthem' thundered from the speakers, a PA system clearly borrowed from Pink Floyd for the occasion. There were probably more woofers and tweeters in the ground than there were people. The FIFA anthem will be familiar to anyone who has attended an international football match in recent years. Sounding like the theme music to a 1980s US soap-opera pilot that never made it to a full series, the bombastic combination of brass and drums has only the weediest of melodies into which to sink its teeth. It's a lot of noise and bluster over very little substance, and it's the 'Official FIFA Anthem'. Go figure.

As the final cadence died away and the spectators dabbed at the blood seeping from their eardrums, the referee led the teams on to the field. Andreas Herzog led out the visitors, Mario Frick the home side. There was polite applause from 3,545 people in the stadium. No prizes for guessing who the other three were, as from behind me the siren wailed and Man-pig, Beardy and Mummy's Boy whooped, hollered and bellowed like the audience at a US sitcom when the main character walks on to the set for the first time. Beardy ran down the steps, hung over the front of the stand, did a curious double punching motion like a drunken uncle trying to do the Locomotion at a wedding and ran back up again. 'Stand up for the Austrians,' rasped into my right ear again but this time paused on its way through, halted just behind my forehead to kick my head in from the inside whilst simultaneously pummelling my eardrums, and proceeded on its way. No one, it hardly needs to be said, stood up for the Austrians.

The teams lined up on the field in single file and the band played the Austrian national anthem, a turgid affair. The crowd remained standing for the Liechtenstein anthem but, to my surprise, the gentle chords of the opening bars of 'God Save The Queen' oozed from the horns of assorted trumpets, trombones and euphoniums of the Harmoniemusik band of Triesen. Crikey, I thought, that's awfully decent of them.

But this was, indeed, the national anthem of Liechtenstein. Back in the 1850s, Liechtenstein realised that if it was to be regarded as a nation in its own right it needed the basic trappings of a nation state at the very least. So, the Liechtensteiners listened to a few anthems of other countries, decided they rather liked the lack of bombast in 'God Save The Queen', and asked a German clergyman called Jausch, who lived in Balzers, to come up with some words. Jausch obliged, and Liechtenstein had its anthem.

So, what will happen when Liechtenstein meets England? Will they just play the anthem once? And if they do play it twice, how will the England fans know which one to boo?

The teams broke and commenced their final warm-ups. Austria wore their traditional white shirts, black shorts and white socks. Liechtenstein wore navy blue shirts with white flashes from hip to shoulder, red shorts and red socks. The princely crown was worn over the heart.

The match began in near silence and but for my three new friends, you could hear the shouts of the players. The trio was given a chance to up the volume inside the first few seconds, when Patrik Hefti slid in to block a through ball from Stranzl only to present it to Christian Mayrleb. The blond Austria Vienna striker took the ball into the area and hit a right foot shot that Jehle turned around the post at full stretch. It was a fine save, and one that prevented a start as disastrous as the Israel game.

Unsurprisingly the opening minutes were spent in the Liechtenstein half of the field, with Markus Schopp making inroads down the right supported by skipper Herzog. Frick was looking lively, tackling back and chasing hard, but the match had opened at a leisurely pace with the home side content to sit back and let the Austrians come to them.

In the eighth minute, however, the Liechtensteiners made their first foray into the Austrian half. A long clearance from Jehle found Frick wide on the left deep inside the Austrian half. The rangy forward put his head down and charged into the area, where he came up against two defenders. Stranzl got a foot in as the Liechtenstein forward twisted and turned, but succeeded only in rolling the ball out to Martin Stocklasa, who curled a first-time left-foot shot fractionally wide of Wohlfahrt's right post from twenty-five yards. It was a tremendous effort, and had it bent a foot further, the Austrian keeper would have been powerless to prevent Liechtenstein from taking a shock lead.

Even this promising move failed to rouse the home crowd and the atmosphere remained muted. Admittedly the match was not being played at breakneck pace, but it was enlivened slightly in the fourteenth minute when Martin Telser allowed the ball to run away from him in the centre circle. As Austria's Martin Hiden moved in to clear, the young Liechtensteiner sent the highly rated defender spinning into the air with an ill-advised, over-exuberant challenge that earned him a yellow card.

Liechtenstein were coping well. Frick continued to be a handful on the left, whilst in the centre Martin Stocklasa seemed most likely to create something for the home side. Jürgen Ospelt was keeping tabs on Herzog on the right. Austria were being allowed few clear chances – a speculative shot from distance by Herzog on the quarter-hour was their first effort since Mayrleb's in the first minute.

In the twentieth minute, however, the visitors took the lead. Telser gave away a free kick forty yards from the Liechtenstein goal in an inside-left position. As Herzog struck the kick, the Liechtenstein defence hurtled upfield as one. As arms went in the air for offside, the ball reached Markus Schopp on the right, who had sprung the trap and was now all alone inside the area with the ball at his feet. As the defence span round and attempted to recover, Schopp curled the ball towards the six-yard line where Thomas Flögel arrived to poke the ball home, despite Ospelt's desperate challenge and Hanselmann's valiant effort to clear.

Schopp had been threatening to make an incisive contribution all evening, and the Liechtenstein offside trap had failed miserably. There was an initial suspicion of offside about the goal, as the Austrian front men ran back with the Liechtenstein defence, but Schopp's run had been timed to perfection. The goal stung Liechtenstein into positive action. Beck and Frick were running hard up front and Martin Stocklasa was showing great vision with some ranging passes. Unfortunately, on the greasy turf, they were proving too strong for Frick and Ospelt on the flanks.

Meanwhile, Man-pig was dominating the megaphone like a drunk nursing a microphone at a karaoke night. A tuneless, lengthy rendition of the closing cadenza to 'Hey Jude' is what finally triggered the headache that would remain with me for the rest of the night. He cranked up the rendition on half an hour when Daniel Hasler lost possession to Kühbauer, who threaded the ball through to Mayrleb with his back to goal. Mayrleb was allowed to turn in a circle wide enough for a small yacht, and his stinging right-foot shot from the edge of the area thudded into Jehle's chest.

Two minutes later, Hefti joined Telser in the book. A Liechtenstein move broke down and the ball was played out of the Austrian defence. Mayrleb turned the big defender, who is probably the most appropriately named footballer since Luxembourg's Patrick Posing, on the halfway line and made to escape. Hefti was having none of it, however, and yanked the Austrian forward back by the collar of his shirt. He accepted the booking with a wave of culpability.

It wasn't a pretty game, and the muted atmosphere was punctured frequently by the Scottish referee's whistle as he blew for foul after foul. There was one moment of quality in the thirty-fourth minute, when Austria had the ball in the net again. It was a free kick from an identical position to that which produced the first goal, and this time the Liechtenstein defence stayed deep. Schopp again stole around the back to ping a volley across Jehle and low inside the far post. Just before the ball hit the net, however, the referee's whistle pierced the alpine night to penalise some Austrian pushing in the melee that wrestled for position as the ball came over.

Although the goal was ruled out, it again demonstrated the danger posed by Schopp. Liechtenstein were dealing comfortably enough with the rest of the Austrian attack, but it was the midfielder with the lank blond hair who was threatening to unlock the defence with increasing regularity.

Ten minutes before the break, Liechtenstein produced their second foray into the Austrian box. Ospelt headed a Schopp cross out to Martin Stocklasa midway inside the Liechtenstein half. The cultured, chiselled-featured midfielder threaded an immaculate pass to Frick on the left, who in turn played the ball first time into the inside-left channel where Telser had made an impressive run. The midfielder made it to the edge of the area and crossed low, but as Beck closed in Wohlfahrt pounced on the ball for his first serious touch of the game. Liechtenstein had transferred the ball from the edge of their penalty area to the other end of the field with impressive speed, and once again the elder of the Stocklasa brothers and Frick were at the centre of the principality's attacking creativity.

Six minutes later, they were at it again. Stocklasa found Frick on the left, and the gangly forward set off. Cutting inside and beating two players, he threaded the ball to Telser, a perfectly weighted ball that left the youngster with only Wohlfahrt to beat. The crowd sucked its breath in sharply and there was a crescendo of expectation. Seemingly in slow motion, Telser drew the goalkeeper expertly, but then, from all of eight yards, somehow managed to spoon the ball high over the bar.

It was the sort of chance that coined the cliché 'gilt edged'. It really would have been easier to score, and what a goal it would have been. The Stocklasa/Frick/Telser combination had carved open the Austrian right once again, and in Telser's defence, the ball did bobble slightly before he shot. But I was left with the feeling that Liechtenstein might not be allowed a better opportunity to score.

As the ball was moved swiftly to the other end, Christian Mayrleb contrived to miss an even easier opportunity. The ball came over from the left, evaded everybody, and found the striker all alone to the right of the penalty spot. It needed one touch and a shot and Austria would have been two up. Instead, Mayrleb dithered long enough to allow the formidable figure of Hefti to move across and intimidate him into a pathetic toe poke that rolled gently into Jehle's arms.

Mayrleb had been barracked by the Austrian fans around me for most of the game, but this miss amplified the volume from my three chums to thunderous levels. He had the previous weekend scored a controversial goal for Austria Vienna when he should have given the ball back after an opposition player had been injured. This latest misdemeanour, now in the shirt of his national team, was enough to have Man-pig ranting into his megaphone like never before.

It was the last incident of the first half, and as the players trooped off Liechtenstein could enjoy their half-time brew with

greater satisfaction than their opponents. Had their offside trap
been just a fraction of a second quicker, they might have gone
in at the break with the match still goalless. Indeed, but for
an unfortunate bobble, they might even have scored their first
competitive goal for two years.

As it was, their plan of frustrating the Austrians and
restricting them to one goal before the interval had worked,
and Baric's pep talk must have been given in a more urgent
voice than Loose's. Austria attempted to ooze confidence, but
the number of misplaced passes and sliced clearances would
have rung alarm bells for Baric.

In the *Gegentribune*, a young man in front of me started
up a conversation. It turned out that he and his two friends
from Stuttgart travel Europe watching football matches. The
week before they had been in Azerbaijan watching Neftchi
Baku, and the week before that in Edinburgh watching Heart
of Midlothian ('Jambo! Jambo!' he bellowed suddenly, to my
alarm). With my Man-pig induced headache increasing by the
minute, I wasn't feeling particularly sociable, so he soon turned
his attention to the three amigos where bonding began to take
place. Banter went backwards and forwards, with the
Stuttgarters going through a repertoire of their club's terrace
routine, much of which was in English ('Vee are Stuttgart,
super Stuttgart, no one likes us, vee don't care, vee hate
Freiburg, zey are fucking bastards . . .' etc). With these guys
in front, and the Austrians behind me, how I was relishing the
second half.

The half began at a leisurely pace with the shouts of the
players again the noisiest in the ground. Even the three amigos
had gone relatively quiet, and Man-pig had pulled up a chair
next to me at the table and laid his megaphone down. I
considered pointing behind him, shouting, 'Oh my God, look
at that!' and, while his back was turned, hurling the megaphone out of the back of the stand and into the Rhine, but
then considered the size of his Dr Martens and thought better
of it.

In the meantime, Liechtenstein had created the first opportunity of the half, a twenty-five-yard effort from Thomas Beck

that flew way over the crossbar and into the children's playground behind the goal. Shortly afterwards, Jehle athletically punched clear a Herzog cross from the right with an impressive swallow dive that drew applause from the stands.

Austria were trying to commit more players forward, but Liechtenstein's solid defence was restricting their opponents to nothing more than speculative efforts from distance. Gigon and Ospelt were snuffing out the threat from the wide men, with Schopp noticeably quieter, and crosses into the danger area were rare. Those that did arrive were dealt with confidently by Jehle. Hefti and Hasler were preventing Mayrleb and substitute Kitzbichler from making significant inroads into the home penalty area with Mayrleb in particular dropping deeper and deeper as the match progressed. The Austrian fans became increasingly critical as the avalanche of goals they had expected failed to materialise. Their whistles grew louder once Telser had seen a shot from distance gathered by Wohlfahrt.

Suddenly Flögel sent a perfect through ball down the middle for Mayrleb who turned Hefti and was left with just Jehle to beat. He produced the shot of a striker lacking in confidence. Hit high and unconvincingly to Jehle's right, the Liechtenstein keeper leapt into the air and clung on to the ball. It was another great chance spurned by the Austrians.

With twenty-five minutes remaining, Hiden missed his header as Hefti launched a long ball towards Frick. The Liechtenstein striker, seeing the ball for almost the first time in the second half, ran on to the pass and cut inside from close to the goalline on the left. Beating two players, he might have done better than shooting over from an acute angle as Michael Stocklasa and Thomas Beck arrived in the six-yard box. It was obvious, however, that Frick posed the most serious and potent attacking threat to the Austrians. But with Liechtenstein penned into their own half for most of the match, and with two Austrians marking the FC Zurich striker, his opportunities to threaten Wohlfahrt's goal were rare.

Shortly afterwards, Liechtenstein will not have been disappointed to see Schopp leave the field as Baric chose to withdraw him in favour of Alfred Hörtnagl, a defensive midfielder for an attacking one. Baric had clearly given up hope of racking up a substantial score to boost Austrian goal difference in favour of ensuring the three points in the face of an impressive Liechtenstein performance. The substitution was a victory of sorts for Loose; an admission by Baric that Austria were not controlling the game in the way he would have wished.

It was when Jürgen Ospelt went down injured after a clash of heads with Kitzbichler that Man-pig charged up his megaphone again, with a song to the tune of 'Land of Hope and Glory'. He was really, really getting on my nerves, and my headache was now one of epic proportions. It was after an amplified harangue of Mayrleb that he decided increased altitude might improve his acoustics, so imagine my delight when he climbed on to my table and began to jump up and down. Finally I snapped, and yelled up at him in language that may not have had his decibel level, but was infinitely more colourful than anything he'd produced all night. He climbed down from the table, but showed no sign of giving up his megaphone. How I wished that I'd grabbed it when I had the chance.

With twenty minutes remaining, Kitzbichler went into the book for diving under pressure from Hefti. Given the immense size of the Liechtenstein defender booked in the first half, attempting to get him sent off was probably not such a good idea. Mind you, so huge was the Liechtenstein stopper I'd have probably fallen over if he'd come anywhere near me too, unbalanced by the sheer perspective of the banker from Vaduz. Soon afterwards, Loose withdrew Michael Stocklasa in favour of the FC Triesen midfielder Thomas Nigg, a player who couldn't have contrasted more with Hefti. Just seventeen, little Nigg was earning his first cap and with his voluminous shorts and a shirt hanging limply from his shoulders, might easily have been mistaken for the team mascot.

Meanwhile, Mayrleb's nightmare continued. Again put clean through, his nerve failed him when faced with the not exactly towering figure of Peter Jehle. Instead of slipping the ball past the Liechtenstein keeper, he chose to square it for Kühbauer. Given that his teammate's arrival was closely accompanied by

Ospelt, this wasn't such a good idea. The Liechtenstein defender produced a fantastic saving tackle, the chance was wasted and the whistling reached new levels. Surely Baric would bring him off and put him out of his misery?

Austria's performance was degenerating rapidly. Mayrleb was being jeered and whistled with every touch, and when Flögel sent an intended cross into the trees behind the goal, you could sense their frustration increasing by the minute. Liechtenstein were keeping their shape well, and in their own half managed to have two players marking each Austrian. Even the Austrian crowd was starting to lose interest, and as the final minutes ticked by the three amigos slumped into a sullen silence as their heroes failed to produce the slick performance they felt their support warranted.

They perked up a little six minutes from time when Herzog found space opening up in front of him twenty-five yards from goal. His rasping shot flicked off Hefti on the way through, and Jehle did well to grab the ball at the second attempt. The best they could manage, however, was a truly horrendous 'You'll Never Walk Alone' which thankfully petered out within seconds.

After two minutes of injury time the referee ended the match to a chorus of whistles from the Austrian fans. The three amigos were exchanging telephone numbers with their new friends, and as I made to leave I hoped upon hope that I would never, ever be in the same football ground as any of them ever again. My head was thumping, it was cold, it was raining and I was feeling thoroughly miserable. It had been an excellent perform-ance from Liechtenstein and a poor one from Austria, but I was feeling more sorry for myself than pleased for my adopted team.

I made my way out of the ground, passing a grim-faced Otto Baric being interviewed on the pitch for television. Wrapped in a beige, belted raincoat with the collar turned up, his face set in a grimace and his eyes cold and emotionless, the Austrian coach looked like a throwback to the Cold War. I walked away from the stadium as the rain continued to fall. It was a twenty-five-minute walk back to the Grünesholz, during which the grating non-witticisms from Man-pig and his megaphone still bounced around my aching head.

It was a miserable evening. I was cold, wet and had a headache so bad it felt like someone had unscrewed the top of my skull, dropped in an anvil, and screwed the top back on. I reached the Grünesholz with a heavy heart. As I got to the gate, my right foot suddenly slid from under me and I toppled sideways into the hedge. As I picked myself out of the soggy undergrowth, I looked down to see that I had slid through an enormous cowpat left by one of Liechtenstein's finest bovines earlier in the day. It just about summed up my night.

I went straight to bed, the thumping in my head accompanied by the patter of raindrops on the window as I drifted into a restless sleep.

Seven

I awoke from my gloomy slumber to find the sun streaming through a slim crack in the curtains and falling across the bedspread in a dust-flecked golden shaft. It had been so long since I'd seen sunshine, I wondered at first what it was. After breakfast I went for a stroll around Vaduz and felt my self-pity evaporating with the morning mist. The sun shone out of a deep-blue sky dotted with cloud. A couple of puddles and a skiddy footprint through a cowpat were the only evidence of my miserable end to the previous evening. It was a crisp autumn morning, and as I walked up the street into the centre of Vaduz I noticed that something else was different – there was barely a vehicle on the road. Without the clank and rumble of construction work as well, Liechtenstein was genuinely peaceful for the first time since I had arrived.

I walked down to the stadium. Where twelve hours earlier I had squelched along dark and sodden tarmac, my head thumping and melancholic, I walked along the same pavement in the other direction feeling my affection for this speck of a nation growing with every step. The maize field lining the road up to the stadium was a vibrant riot of green and yellow against the blue sky. Given the miserable greys and dark greens of the previous few days, it was as if someone had snuck into my room during the night and given my eyeballs a good scrub. The goats came out to greet me from their pen, bells tinkling.

I breathed deeply the clear mountain air, the sharp chill knifing into my lungs. I reached the Rhine, the sun glinting from its ripples as it babbled along the border, and above the sound of the river, churchbells began to peal all along the valley, echoing around the mountains from high-pitched treble to booming resonant tenor. Suddenly I loved Liechtenstein. It's amazing what a fresh autumn morning can do.

I peered into the stadium. The red, blue and yellow seats shone bright in the sunshine, and the pitch glistened a deep green, betraying just a few scars from the night before. I walked back into Vaduz, calling at a tobacconist's on the way. I picked up a newspaper, the national Sunday tabloid *Liewo* (short for *Liechtenstein Wochenende*, or Liechtenstein Weekend) and when I went to pay for it the shopkeeper waved her hand, smiled and said, '*Ist frei*' – it's free. I sat on a bench in the sunshine and leafed through to the sports coverage. *Liechtenstein Super!* said the headline. *Superresultat für Liechtenstein* began the report.

Hearing music, I made my way to the marquee next to the town hall, where a brass band was just getting into its stride. The lighting inside glinted back from meticulously polished instruments and gold buttons fronting double-breasted military uniforms. Families sat at long tables, swaying gently to the music. And although it was only just past eleven o'clock on a Sunday, people were getting thoroughly stuck into the beer and hot wine.

It struck me that in the unlikely event Liechtenstein was to be invaded that morning, the band would be pressed into service in defence of their motherland on the grounds that they were the ones with the uniforms. A mixture of pensioners and teenage music students, Liechtenstein's only hope would rest with the slim chance that the band could polka the enemy into submission.

After a bratwurst, a glass of hot wine and a bit of a sway, I made my way back to the Grünesholz feeling as happy as I had since leaving London. The saintly Martina had arranged for an English woman now resident in Liechtenstein to show me around the whole country. 'It should only take a couple of hours,' she had told me. Sure enough, I found Sheila waiting for me at the bar in the Grünesholz, and we walked outside to her car. A middle-aged woman with greying hair, she told me in an upper-class English accent with the tiniest Germanic tint that she had come to Liechtenstein in search of adventure more than forty years previously and remained here ever since.

'The first time I came to Liechtenstein was in 1956,' she said when I asked what she was doing here. 'I was trying to find a job in Switzerland, but it was hard to work as a secretary then because it was difficult to get a permit. So in the end I came to Vaduz and worked in the souvenir shop for Baron von Falz-Fein. I came for a couple of summers and then found I was missing Liechtenstein when I wasn't here, and then when I returned I met my husband and stayed for good.

'Liechtenstein was very underdeveloped at that time,' she said, as I asked how much the place had changed. 'The main street through Vaduz had been tarmacked, but the pavements were just gravel. There was a horse and cart that would come through Vaduz once a week to collect household rubbish, and the same horse and cart was used as a hearse for funerals. The coffin would go on the cart and the whole village would walk behind.'

We drove into Vaduz, stopping at the government building. A beautiful piece of architecture, the white, three-storey building is fronted by a balcony beneath a tiled fascia of the Liechtenstein coat of arms. Its steeply sloping roof is zig-zagged with red and black tiles. Until as recently as twenty-five years ago, the building also served as Liechtenstein's police station and prison. The prison was a laid-back affair, with the inmates allowed out for walks in the woods while their meals were being delivered from the kitchen of the principality's finest hotel.

'Vaduz has certainly changed since I arrived,' said Sheila. 'There were only about twelve thousand people living in the whole country; now that number has nearly trebled. Coming from London, it was like a fairy story living in this little country. I was fascinated by it all. At that time it was very friendly here, and because we were so few, everybody knew everybody else. If you were away from Vaduz for, say, two or three weeks, everyone would descend on you to ask where you'd been when you came back. It's different now.

'I was lucky then that the Liechtenstein people were so open towards foreigners. Maybe they still are today, but life has become so busy that one doesn't have the time to really get to know people like one used to.'

We drove through Vaduz and up towards the castle.

'Liechtenstein has grown up terrifically since I first arrived,' Sheila continued. 'Vaduz has lost its village character, and with it some of its identity. The big problem in Liechtenstein is that there is so little ground. Two-thirds of the country is mountains, and only one-third can be built on. That means there's not much room to live, so land has become incredibly expensive.'

As we pull up outside the castle, I comment on how much building work I've seen in Vaduz.

'Yes, Liechtenstein is a permanent building site now. It's a problem at the moment but we're hoping that in one or two years Vaduz will be looking a little more respectable. It has definitely resulted in a loss of character. When I first came here, Vaduz was all lovely old buildings, but it's all gone commercial now, and the feeling is that what land there is can't be wasted on rickety old buildings. So they've all been pulled down and modern buildings have gone up. You can probably tell that a lot of Vaduz was built in the sixties, when architectural style was very poor. Some things are being corrected now but Vaduz has a characterless feel.'

We climb out of the car and walk to the castle gate.

'It's not open to the public, unfortunately,' says Sheila. 'It was restored by the current prince's father, who was the first of the princely family to live in Liechtenstein. It was little more than a ruin when he first arrived. The current prince renovated the interior, where the art collection is kept. It's an extraordinary collection, stored in the bowels of the castle. The paintings are kept in rows on vertical pull-out racks. There are apparently six kilometres of these racks in the castle cellars, which gives you an idea of the scale. No one can really accurately put a figure on its worth.

'It was believed to have been started by Prince Karl at the turn of the seventeenth century. The collection became so vast that a building had to be constructed in Vienna to house it, before it was moved here in 1940.'

Sheila described how Franz Josef II set about relaunching the principality when he arrived at the castle in 1938.

'When the Prince and his wife Gina arrived in Liechtenstein they were shocked at what a poor country it was. They were genuinely concerned for the well-being of the people here, and Princess Gina even worked for the Red Cross. Meanwhile Franz Josef set about moving the country away from its poor rural status and towards industrialisation.

'The present prince, Hans Adam II, is a real businessman, and he's continued his father's work. Although he didn't succeed his father until his death in 1989, Hans Adam was heavily involved with the administration of the family wealth from the early seventies, and Franz Josef handed over most of the business duties of the principality to his son in 1984. Hans Adam is certainly no fool when it comes to business – he's acquired ninety per cent of the shares in Liechtenstein's main bank, the LGT.

'The people here are worried that if he doesn't get his way over the constitutional changes he wants to make, the Prince will move the family back to Vienna. I understand that he eventually wants to hand over most of his power to his son Alois, but is reluctant to do so until this constitutional mess is sorted out. It's difficult for the people here, because the Prince is very popular, yet his proposals are interpreted as moving Liechtenstein further away from democracy and towards autocracy.

'I do think there is a danger of the rapid growth here spinning out of control. We're being overrun by foreign banks, and there are hardly any private homes in the centre of Vaduz now. The place is dead in the evenings as a result.'

Tell me about it, I thought.

Curiously the castle is less impressive viewed from close

range than it is when seen from a distance. Its most formidable battlements are on the mountainside: from the road behind it just looks like your common or garden stately pile. The triangular roof of the tower is its most identifiable feature: a relatively recent addition. Later, I found a book of pictures of Vaduz. In most of the engravings, paintings and early photographs, the castle is a ruin, its tower roofless, with battlements like a row of broken teeth.

We climbed back into the car and headed along to the hillside village of Triesenberg, which overlooks Vaduz and neighbouring Triesen on the valley floor below.

As we swept along the winding mountain roads, I asked Sheila something about which I had been curious ever since my arrival in the principality. What makes a Liechtensteiner a Liechtensteiner? What differentiates the population of this tiny riverside community from the people of Austria and Switzerland?

'I think Liechtenstein is a unique place, at least it has been until now,' she said. 'Of course we don't know what the future will bring, but there is something rather special about the country. The Prince plays a large role in giving the people an identity, as there is no royal family in Switzerland, Austria or Germany. I think we are privileged to live here because it's possible for everyone to live well; the people are well looked after by the state. Basically we're happy. That's one thing the Prince's mother used to say: it's a happy country.

'Life's fairly easy here. And maybe Liechtensteiners are bigheads in a way. I think they feel they're untouchable, which can make them a bit narrow-minded. A lot of them won't travel, and if they do they still think that they're the king of the castle. But I think they have a lot to learn about the world, because don't forget it's only fifty years since this was a purely agricultural nation. They've made a lot of headway, but they're not quite experienced enough yet.

'On the other hand, Liechtenstein is very influenced by the Föhn, the warm wind that sweeps through the valley. I think this affects people psychologically and is why so many people here drive like maniacs, for example. Many people become depressed, and Liechtenstein does have a high suicide rate. We also have our share of problems with drugs and alcohol, the same as any other country.

'The people here are very nice, but the friendliness has its boundaries. In England if someone you know came to the door, you'd invite them in for a cup of tea, but that's very rare in Liechtenstein, and in Switzerland too, I think. I lived in Zurich for three years working for American Express. I met a lot of people at the company but in all that time, not one of them invited me to their home. Liechtensteiners are better than that, but I'd say they're fairly reticent sometimes too.

'There isn't a lot for young people in Liechtenstein. They're trying to change that, putting on concerts and film screenings at the stadium and so on, but some young people find it very limited, especially at weekends.'

Triesenberg is more what I had expected from Liechtenstein. It's a jumble of chalet-style houses on a steep hillside, with a charming church at its centre topped by an onion-shaped steeple.

The village was established by the Walsers, the farming community from the Wallis canton of Switzerland who were escaping starvation at the end of the thirteenth century. They settled at the valley floor initially, but the regular flooding of the Rhine persuaded the Walsers to move further up the hillside. The community has managed to retain its character, customs and even its language, a dialect spoken by only a few families, all of whom live in and around Triesenberg. Even other Liechtensteiners regard the Walsers as being almost of a different nationality.

For hundreds of years, Triesenberg's lofty position allowed the community to maintain a high level of seclusion. The Walsers were never a rich community, and the back-breaking work farming the steeply sloping pastures prompted many to leave the region. Walsers travelled as far as Russia and the United States in an attempt to be something other than dairy farmers or herdsmen. Indeed, Triesenberg wasn't opened up until the construction of the first road from Vaduz in the 1860s.

It's only in recent years that the Walser way of life has come under threat. Liechtenstein's rapid development and improved infrastructure has seen many Triesenbergers working down in the valley in Vaduz, whilst other Liechtensteiners have moved to the village, attracted by its peaceful remote location and breathtaking views across the Rhine to the Swiss Alps. Agriculture, on which the community was founded, now employs only a handful of Triesenbergers.

We stood for a while and looked across the valley. It's an impressive view to the snow-streaked peaks in the distance, a panorama that encompasses most of this tiny country. Away to the left, following the river, is Balzers, with Gutenberg Castle a speck on its conical mound. To the right is the hotch-potch of Vaduz, its higgledy-piggledy arrangement of banks and buildings staggering out from the central roundabout towards the Rhine. The Rheinpark Stadion sits in the distance by the river, trees growing up around it as if the people were attempting to hide the ground from view. The sky is still deep blue and the previous day's rain has rinsed the air to provide a sharp, defined vista miles into the distance.

'I've lived away from England for so long now that I really feel this is my home,' Sheila said suddenly and with feeling, as the breeze teased her hair away from her forehead. 'I still love going back to visit friends and relatives, but this is my home. I think I'd have to have a very important reason to go and live in England again. I think I'd find a lot of things very difficult and would always want to come back here.'

After an appropriate silence I asked whether it would be difficult for her to come to Liechtenstein now as a foreign national.

'The rules have relaxed a little bit since we joined the European Economic Area,' she replied. 'Because of that we've had to adapt to their rules. It used to be difficult for foreigners working here because you had to renew your permit each year and it was very hard for a foreigner to change jobs, but that's a lot easier now. If you're a woman and you marry a Liechtenstein man, as I did, then you have no problems. When I married I took out Liechtenstein citizenship and got my passport straightaway. Today though, the woman has to wait twelve years before she can obtain a Liechtenstein passport, to stop marriages of convenience.'

What is the status of women now, I asked, mindful of the relatively recent enfranchisement?

'The mother of the Prince campaigned energetically on this issue for many years,' Sheila said. 'She thought it was a huge priority, but it took until 1984 to have the law changed by referendum. Things have changed slowly. Some men still think that women should be seen and not heard, but it's gradually becoming better. Women are becoming more visible in government, and most women work now, which certainly wasn't the case when I first came here. A woman's role was as a wife and mother, nothing more.

'Now I work part time for the tourist office, part time at a law practice and give private English lessons, so that's quite a contrast. It's a good life. There's a terrific demand here for people who can speak English, so I'm keeping busy.'

As Sheila drove us higher through the mountains towards the skiing resort of Malbun, she told me of the time she dined with ex-King Farouk of Egypt, an invitation wangled for her by Baron von Falz-Fein due to the deposed monarch's predilection for young blond girls. Faroukh had a full entourage and a personal bodyguard who followed his master everywhere. Even, in the days before plumbing, when he went outside for a wee.

The ex-King was naturally a talking point for the locals during his visit, not least when he was caught in the middle of the night climbing out of the hotel window, entourage in tow, in order to avoid paying his presumably substantial bill.

We passed through Steg, a hamlet noted for its cross-country skiing trails and ancient, tiny, whitewashed chapel. As we emerged from a lengthy mountain tunnel, we were overtaken by a BMW, which roared past irritably and was out of sight by the time we reached the next bend. 'Oh, I recognise him – he was in our last government,' said Sheila. 'He always drives like that. When even the politicians drive like maniacs, what do you expect from the rest of the people?'

We rounded a bend and were upon Malbun, more than five thousand feet above sea level. The village is set in a natural bowl near the top of the mountains and is the heart of Liechtenstein's winter sports industry, the most lucrative aspect of Liechtenstein tourism. It's so popular that some chalets have to be reserved a year in advance.

A ski resort out of season is a curious place. The skeletal steelwork of the lifts marches up the mountainside and over the crest to the higher slopes, a strange sight when there is no snow. We passed the bottom of the lift, where the seats dangled motionless six feet above the grass. In the control room, chairs were pushed under desks and computer terminals lurked beneath dustsheets.

Malbun is virtually deserted during the summer, coming emphatically to life when the snows arrive. Sheila's is the only car in the large car park, and there is nobody around. Indeed, when Malbun was first settled in the nineteenth century, the area was thought to be haunted by ghosts and evil spirits. These would have the run of the place when the cattle farmers left in winter until the snow melted in the spring and the farmers returned. Now, the ghosts can enjoy the summer instead. We walk up towards the 'Peace Chapel', constructed in the late forties to give thanks for Liechtenstein being spared the horrors of the Second World War, and look across the village to the mountains.

It's a real ghost town – hotels and shops have their shutters closed, and the only things missing are tumbleweed blowing down the street and Lee Van Cleef stepping out from behind one of the buildings, shaping to draw.

There is a sprinkling of houses scattered about the hillside. Each has a triangular wooden construction slightly uphill, designed to deflect, or at least break up, the slips of snow that are a constant threat during the winter. On the upper slopes of the valley are horizontal structures designed to prevent avalanches from descending on the village before they have the opportunity to get up a good head of steam.

'There's a serious avalanche here roughly every fifty years,' said Sheila. 'I think the first was recorded in 1837, and destroyed a house. There was one in 1951 that destroyed four houses – but no one knew about it for two days because there was nobody here at the time. The most serious was in 1971 when two skiers were killed, but two years ago there were two on consecutive nights, which destroyed quite a few houses. Fortunately, everyone knew it was coming and the village had been evacuated.'

We drove back down the mountain and went south to Balzers, passing the castle once again.

'It's not easy for the Prince at the moment,' said Sheila. 'He wants more power, the government wants more democracy. He wants to abdicate and hand over to Alois, but won't until this mess is sorted out. We hope they find a compromise because it would be a complete catastrophe if the Prince were to run off to Vienna. Liechtenstein would certainly lose its image, and to have the castle sitting up on the hillside without the Prince would be disastrous for Liechtenstein tourism.'

Balzers is dominated by the castle on Gutenberg hill, a structure that the author Grete Gulbransson described as the most beautiful place on earth. She wasn't too wide of the mark either. It was once owned, Sheila told me, by a Liechtenstein woman who was married to a successful Mexican film producer.

When the film producer died, his widow could no longer afford to keep up the castle and sold it to the state, keeping a few rooms for herself as an apartment and making a considerable profit into the bargain. In her mid-eighties she married a man who was some forty years her junior, and the couple travelled the world, rarely returning to Liechtenstein.

The castle is sometimes opened for concerts in the winter, but, sadly, is otherwise closed to the public, which meant there was no opportunity to recreate the farmyard repertoire of the Austrian soldiers. Having been practising my animal impressions for several days, this came as a great disappointment to me.

That evening, the *Jahrmarkt* festival came to a conclusion. The beer stalls began to close, the fairground wound down, and by nine o'clock Vaduz was back to its normal empty self.

The next morning I left Liechtenstein. On the bus to Sargans I opened out the sports section of the *Volksblatt*. Sensation In The Air! screamed the headline. Liechtenstein Only Lose 0–1!

Eight

By the end of March nearly five months had elapsed since my visit to Vaduz. The nights had drawn in and were beginning to shuffle out again, the sensible knitwear and soap-on-a-rope industries had enjoyed their customary Yuletide bonanza, and snow had fallen and melted to bracket a bumper Liechtenstein winter tourist season. Yet despite this considerable World Cup hiatus, it was still a last-minute decision to go to Spain. Whilst I would have been first in the queue to see Liechtenstein in the Bernabeu or Nou Camp, the Jose Rico Perez in Alicante somehow didn't quite have the same appeal. Plus, friends and family were starting to question my sanity given my growing obsession with watching one of the world's most unsuccessful football teams.

It was hard trying to explain to people how losing 0–1 at home to Austria is a great result. When your friends follow Premier League clubs and the England national team, my excited tales of narrow defeats and moral victories were being met with raised eyebrows and uncertain glances. No, I thought, going to Spain would be too much. This didn't mean that I was going to miss the game altogether, however. It was an evening kick-off on a Saturday, so there was surely a Spanish bar in London that would be showing the match via satellite. I'd take the train into town and watch my boys battle away over tapas and a few bottles of San Miguel. I might even wear my Liechtenstein scarf, just to show why I was there. So, in the week leading up to the game, I started phoning around London's Spanish establishments. Most didn't know there was a match on, let alone think they'd be showing it. The rest just said an incredulous no, as if I'd phoned up to ask whether they served sprouts and soda in a tall glass.

As the days passed, my sense of urgency grew. Phone calls to friends and acquaintances with satellite television failed to secure an agreement to have me in their front room on a Saturday evening watching a match that could have been arranged to define the term 'foregone conclusion'. I started to have visions of following the game on an Internet score-ticker. And that's when I realised I had to be there. Sitting in front of a computer screen hitting 'refresh' every couple of minutes would be no good at all. How then would I appreciate Jürgen Ospelt's saving tackles, and Patrik Hefti's juddering challenges on Raul? How could I not be there to see the left-sided tussle between Gaizka Mendieta and Freddie Gigon, who would have had to plead for time away from his school to play against the best in the world? Surely I couldn't afford to miss the sight of little Thomas Beck running at Real Madrid's Fernando Hierro?

Thus, two days before the game I logged on all right, but this was to find last-minute flights to Alicante. After an hour or so of looking at prices from the expensive to the extortionate, I booked my passage and a hotel room. I would fly out on the Saturday morning, coming back the next day before setting off for Vaduz twenty-four hours later ready for the match against Bosnia-Herzegovina on the Wednesday. It was a ridiculous schedule, granted, but as long as I was there for that ninety minutes on Saturday night, no matter.

And so I was there, sitting high in the stand at Alicante's 30,000 capacity Jose Rico Perez stadium on a humid evening on the east coast of Spain, as the pride of Liechtenstein marched on to the field alongside one of the world's greatest teams.

The stadium was sold out. It's an uncovered arena, the seats arranged in banks of blue and white stripes in tribute to the colours of Hercules, Alicante's leading club currently languishing in the second division. The upper tiers of the stands along each touchline are steeply banked, frighteningly so. Fortunately I was close to the front.

As the players entered the field I wondered how the eleven men and boys from the principality must have been feeling. The ground is compact and claustrophobic, with spectators pressed right up against the touchlines. The Alicante public, given a rare opportunity to see their national side in the flesh, were out in force. They were also making enough noise to intimidate even the most experienced sides, let alone the mixture of small-time professionals and amateurs from a country who could almost fit their entire population into the stadium.

Liechtenstein were, thankfully, at full strength. Harry Zech was back at sweeper, Hefti and Hasler were in the centre of defence with Gigon, the Stocklasa brothers and Jürgen Ospelt strung out in front of them across the deep-lying midfield. Martin Telser and Thomas Beck were there to back up Mario Frick, who would operate as a lone striker. Frick's performance against Austria five months earlier had persuaded former Italian international Antonio Cabrini to sign him for Arezzo, where he was now banging in goals with joyous abandon in Serie C. However, the ambitious Liechtensteiner was already hoping to progress further. Rayo Vallecano would be watching Frick in Alicante, along with a number of clubs from Serie A and Serie B.

Spain, meanwhile, fielded an awesome-looking team, with names familiar to anyone with even the most cursory knowledge of international football. The front pairing of Raul and Javi Moreno alone was enough to give Jehle nightmares, let alone Mendieta, Munitis, Guardiola and Helguera following in behind.

The Spanish newspaper *Marca* had run a poll in the week running up to the match, canvassing opinions on what the score might be. Eighty-five per cent thought that Spain would score at least eleven goals, whilst a straw poll among the Spanish players produced 6–0 as the most pessimistic prediction. The crowd wanted blood, and there were probably a few dry Liechtenstein mouths walking out into this cauldron.

On a humid evening the visitors, playing in their change strip of yellow shirts, red shorts and yellow socks, produced the first chance of the match. Mario Frick robbed Hierro in the third minute and released Telser, whose shot from distance had Casillas scrambling across his goal. It was an early sign that Liechtenstein were not intending to provide Spain with a bit of shooting practice. Predictably, however, play soon switched to the Liechtenstein half and stayed there.

The early indications were that Munitis would give Ospelt a busy evening on the Liechtenstein right. The tricky little winger from Real Madrid sent over two telling crosses in the opening minutes, the second of which Raul headed into the arms of Jehle. Hierro, the Spanish captain, was also having a fierce tussle with Patrik Hefti when he moved forward for corners. Hierro was just one goal behind Emilio Butragueno in the all-time Spanish scorers' list, and clearly thought he could overtake the legendary striker before the night was out. Encouragingly though, Gigon, watched by his pupils on live TV back in Switzerland, was having the better of his early skirmishes with Mendieta.

The Valencia forward was drifting further infield to escape Gigon's attentions and, just after the quarter-hour, this allowed him to set up a chance for Guardiola, whose shot from twenty yards flew comfortably over Jehle's crossbar.

Two minutes later, Ospelt was in the referee's notebook. As Munitis looked to cut in from the left, the Liechtenstein player stood his ground just outside the corner of the area and let Munitis run into him. As the winger hit the deck the crowd bayed, and the yellow card was waved in the warm night air. After Munitis had climbed gingerly to his feet, Guardiola curled in an exquisite free kick. Just when it seemed that the ball would creep in under the crossbar, Jehle arched his back and touched the ball wide. It was a fantastic save, causing the Spanish fans to arrest a roar of triumph in their throats. Jehle is not the biggest goalkeeper in European football, but here he demonstrated once again the extraordinary agility that had attracted the attention of some of the continent's top clubs.

Parity lasted barely a minute, however. Mendieta received the ball wide on the right and showed in a simple feint the quality that makes him worth several million pounds more than Gigon. The Liechtensteiner was left rooted to the spot as Mendieta ghosted past him and sent over a cross towards the six-yard line. Raul couldn't get there, Daniel Hasler couldn't get there, but Ivan Helguera arrived two yards ahead of Ospelt to turn the ball home from close range, stooping so low his nose must have left a furrow in the turf. There was a suspicion that the plunging midfielder might have scored using his upper arm, but the stadium exploded with colour and noise. Liechtenstein had weathered the first twenty minutes without too much discomfort, but one flash of brilliance from Mendieta showed just how many gears the Spanish possessed to step up into as and when they needed.

After the goal, the Spanish pressure resumed. Munitis continued to probe down the left but Ospelt, arguably to blame for Helguera's unchallenged arrival for the goal, was combining well with Beck and Daniel Hasler to prevent the ball from entering the Liechtenstein box. On the left Hefti and Gigon worked well together to prevent Mendieta taking a firm grip on the Spanish right. Liechtenstein were managing to prevent the home side creating clear chances, with Jehle coming out to catch a couple of crosses and Martin Stocklasa heading clear a Hierro header that looped over the visitors' keeper.

The lack of goals was starting to unsettle the crowd, and when Raul was caught offside for the second time, whistles began to fill the night air. But still Liechtenstein couldn't get the ball out of their own half. Frick cut a lonely figure in the centre circle as he stood, hands on hips, watching his teammates battling away on their own eighteen-yard line. On half an hour, Mendieta wriggled into the penalty area, only for Michael Stocklasa to wrest the ball from between the Valencia star's feet. Still the Spanish were not creating clear chances. When Raul chased the referee for thirty yards after he tumbled under Daniel Hasler's challenge whilst trying to reach a high ball from Hierro in the penalty area, you sensed that Liechtenstein were getting under the Spanish skin. However, where many teams might have become frustrated and started fraying at the edges, the Spanish continued to build patiently, sensing that their quality would pay off in the long run. They might not reach double figures, as the readers of *Marca* desired, but Spain knew that if they kept calm the goals would come.

And that's exactly what happened. In the thirty-fourth minute Fernando Hierro had thundered a twenty-five-yard free kick straight at Jehle after Martin Stocklasa had been booked for tripping Raul. In fact, Raul was already falling after being caught around the throat by Hefti.

Two minutes later, Munitis floated a ball to the edge of the Liechtenstein box. Javi Moreno got up above Daniel Hasler and nodded it back towards Mendieta, standing some twenty-five yards from goal. Mendieta allowed the ball to bounce, set himself, and cracked a thunderous left-foot shot that swerved away from the diving Jehle and into the top corner of the net. It was a shot of immense power, hit from a standing position with minimal backlift: a strike of the highest quality. The crowd rose as one to acclaim a moment of inspired brilliance.

If Liechtenstein were relieved to see the departure of Munitis shortly afterwards, still feeling the effects of the challenge by Ospelt that had earned the Liechtensteiner a booking, they had an even bigger let off in the fortieth minute. Full back Manuel Pablo overlapped down the right and sent over a tantalising cross towards the six-yard box. Raul arrived, escaped Daniel Hasler but mistimed his header, which flashed across the goal and safely out for a goal kick. It was a cross almost identical to the one that had produced the opening goal, an outswinger moving away from Jehle, and again Liechtenstein couldn't deal with it. It was clear that the visitors were susceptible to crosses whipped in towards the six-yard box, so Ospelt and Gigon strove to snuff out the wide men.

In first-half injury time Liechtenstein won a corner, following some excellent work down the right from Ospelt, Telser and Thomas Beck. It was the first time since the third minute that they had been anywhere near the Spanish goal, and the team might have been forgiven for trotting off on a lap of honour. Beck sent over the corner, which Daniel Hasler met with his head ten yards from goal. It bounced comfortably into the arms of Iker Casillas, but at least Liechtenstein had created their second clear chance of the game. However, Casillas's long throw eventually found Raul on the left of the area, and the Real Madrid star forced a diving stop from Jehle at his near post to concede another corner.

The second half began with the Spanish again laying siege to the Liechtenstein goal. Two minutes into the half, Ospelt gave away a free kick wide on the right. Guardiola sent an inswinging cross towards Raul, whose perfectly timed run allowed a clear glancing header angled towards the far post. Jehle flashed across the goal, however, and produced a marvellous reaction save at full stretch to fingertip the ball beyond the post for a corner.

The Spanish were gradually increasing the pressure – how long could Liechtenstein hold out? Although this was one of the most one-sided matches I'd ever seen, Liechtenstein's solid rearguard was making it an engaging spectacle. I was on the edge of my seat as if the game were delicately poised at 0–0 with chances at both ends, willing the ball away from Jehle's goal.

In the fifty-third minute, however, disaster struck. From deep inside his own half, the influential Guardiola arrowed a wonderful through ball towards Moreno. Hasler and Zech were beaten, and with one touch Moreno was bearing down on goal. Jehle came racing out but his angle was wrong. Somehow, he was the wrong side of Moreno, with nothing between the striker and the goal. Jehle lunged to his left as Moreno touched the ball forward, but succeeded only in bringing the Alaves striker down and conceding a penalty.

My first thought was that the young goalkeeper would be sent off. But fortunately Zech had got between Moreno and the goal, meaning that Jehle was not the last man and hence escaped with a booking. He still had to face the penalty, however. My mind went back to his sensational debut for Grasshoppers, when Jehle came on to replace the sent-off Stephane Hüber in injury time to save a penalty. The pressure was on again – could he respond?

Hierro stepped up and sent Jehle the wrong way, clipping the ball to the goalkeeper's left as he went right. You could sense the relief in the crowd as the teenage goalkeeper hooked the ball from the back of the net and kicked it upfield. The Spanish players descended on their captain, who had now equalled Butragueno's record.

Still the home side didn't let up. Mendieta appeared on the left to curl a tantalising ball towards the far post. It drifted over Gigon and on to the chest of Raul, who found Jehle out quickly to smother the chance. Almost immediately, Guardiola again pinged an incisive ball into the inside left channel. Javi Moreno controlled it on his instep, and despite the close attentions of Harry Zech and Daniel Hasler, swivelled and shot into Jehle's midriff from an acute angle.

In the warmth of the evening, you began to sense that, with twenty minutes remaining, the Liechtensteiners were beginning to tire. Little gaps were beginning to appear in the reardguard, and the clearances were becoming more desperate. In the penalty area, Mendieta and Javi Moreno were starting to find space where previously there had been none.

In the seventieth minute, Guardiola sent over a corner from the right, Hierro clipped the ball towards goal and Raul escaped from Martin Stocklasa to cut across Jehle and flick the ball home with his heel for Spain's fourth goal. Two minutes later, Raul slipped the ball between Hefti and Hasler as Zech challenged. Moreno took the ball in his stride and finished low beyond Jehle and just inside the far post. As the crowd erupted again, the whistle had already gone to penalise Zech's late lunge on the Real Madrid striker: the goal wouldn't stand. Mendieta lined up behind the ball, took two steps and curled an immaculate free kick that cannoned back from the crossbar with Jehle beaten. Fortunately, Gigon was on hand to head the ball clear as Raul threatened to turn in the rebound. Liechtenstein were rocking for the first time in the whole game.

More and more crosses were coming over as Ospelt and Gigon began to tire from their perpetual patrolling of the flanks, but you felt that Liechtenstein might just hold out for a highly respectable 0–4. Jehle reacted sharply when Nadal hit a shot from a tight angle towards his left-hand post, scrambling the ball behind for a corner as Raul looked set to pounce, and you felt that the young keeper would not be beaten again.

With eight minutes remaining, however, Jehle fluffed an attempted clearance under pressure from Raul. Javi Moreno nipped in and carried the ball towards the corner flag. Mendieta called for the ball on the corner of the box, turned inside and hit a right-foot shot into the far corner of the net. It had precisely the same precision, pace and control as his first half strike, hit with his other foot. Jehle retrieved the ball from the net, kicked it upfield, put his hands on his hips and hung his head, mouthing quiet recriminations to himself.

It was hard on the tiring Liechtensteiners, but it could have been worse three minutes later. Javi Moreno was twisting and turning in the area, attempting to get away from Zech, when Hefti arrived and appeared to trip the Spanish striker with a weary challenge. Hefti raised both palms, usually an admission of guilt designed to be otherwise, but the referee waved away the imploring gestures of the Spanish. It was quite a let off.

Nevertheless, the heavy-legged Liechtensteiners saw out the final minutes without further mishap. At the whistle, the crowd rose. Impressive as the Spanish had been, I hoped that some of the crowd's applause was directed at the plucky team from the principality. As the Liechtenstein players shook hands with their illustrious opponents, you could see them blowing hard, their socks around their ankles as they dragged heavy feet across the turf.

Memorable as the occasion had been, and well though they had played, the team still had to motivate themselves to face Bosnia-Herzegovina in Vaduz four days hence. Would it be a case of the dustcart following the Lord Mayor's Show?

Nine

Two days after the match in Alicante, I left London for Vaduz in order to watch Liechtenstein play Bosnia-Herzegovina on the Wednesday. Britain was in the middle of the foot-and-mouth crisis. Signs at Heathrow forbade departing Brits from taking anything remotely related to agriculture abroad in an attempt to confine the disease. Even books by James Herriot were banned, and anyone confessing a fondness for *The Archers* was liable to be turfed off the plane.

Scary images of mountainous carcass bonfires dominated the press, orange skies over a horizon punctured by a jumble of hoof-topped legs. Liechtenstein is full of cloven-hoofed creatures and I was leaving my disease-ridden nation to wander amongst them. Hence I took quite a risk in going back to Vaduz as I could have been quite happily taking with me a virulent disease that would sweep devastatingly through the Rhine Valley fractionally faster than the rampaging mob of Swiss, Austrians and Liechtensteiners in hot pursuit of my hide.

Having squelched across the disinfectant mats at Zurich Airport and boarded my train, I headed out of the Swiss capital once again and for the border. Zurich, I had decided, is a fine example of Europeanness. On the brief train ride between the airport and the main station, the ticket inspector had been a young woman with a mop of brown curly hair. She slipped as easily between German and English as she did between the items of luggage that littered her passage through the carriage. Opposite me a man with a Swiss passport peeping over the top of his shirt pocket conversed with his wife in Italian. An elderly woman moved to sit next to me, asking in German if the seat was free. She sat down and pulled out a French magazine. When we left the train I stopped to allow a young woman to step out in front of me. '*Merci*,' she said with a smile.

Zurich is also a great city to travel from by train. Before you know it you have glided seamlessly from the bustling city centre to cruise along the banks of the gargantuan lake that spreads south-east from the city. From the cracked plasterwork of the Zurich suburbs, suddenly you're looking at sailing boats bobbing on clear blue water. The vast cat's cradle of cabling as you leave the station soon gives way to the rigging of dozens of yachts. It's like travelling from King's Cross to Frinton-on-Sea and the journey taking five minutes.

The saintly Martina from the tourist office had arranged for me to stay at the Grünesholz once again, and this time on reaching Vaduz, I managed to alight at the correct stop. Martina had also warned me that the place would be closed on the day I arrived. 'You may enter at backside of the hotel,' she had told me in an e-mail. 'If there should not be anybody, please find the key beside the phone. Sorry, it is a very small hotel and they have their own rules.'

Finding the door locked at the front, I made my way to the rear of the building to enter as advised at backside of the hotel. The grubby building site of five months earlier, where the workmen had merrily sliced through the Grünesholz's television cable twice daily, had been replaced by a glass-fronted Toyota showroom. Where previously workmen in Tyrolean hats had set about the Grünesholz's only contact with the outside world, there sat gleaming new cars amongst strategically placed pot plants on a vigorously polished floor.

I approached the door with caution, expecting Griselda to be waiting behind it ready to garrotte intruders with a violin string. I pushed it open and threw myself to the floor. There being no assaults on my life from the darkness I fumbled for the lightswitch. At the end of the hall I could make out a key and a big piece of card, just as Martina had predicted. 'Nr 8 – Cornelli', read the card.

It was a fair Chinese-whispers approximation of my name, I thought as I mounted the stairs. The place was entirely deserted. I had a different room this time and, to my alarm, there was no television. I would therefore be unable to brush up on the piscine tastes of German porn stars and my knowledge of German white rap would remain underdeveloped.

It was late afternoon and the sinking sun was casting long shadows over the valley as I took a stroll into the centre of Vaduz. Nothing much had changed other than even more building work appeared to be going on than six months earlier. The pedestrianised street in the centre was being resurfaced: drills drilled and steamhammers pounded the bricks into place. I bought the *Vaterland* and the *Volksblatt* and retired to a bench to read in the evening sun. I opened out the *Vaterland* to discover an extraordinary lead story. *Status Quo Komt Nach Vaduz!* screamed the front page. It was true, Liechtenstein's biggest news story of the day was the impending arrival of the British dinosaur rockers to headline Liechtenstein's premier rock event of the year: the Little Big One open-air festival in July. I lunged for my bag to take out my diary and make a note to be elsewhere.

I glanced at the match reports from Alicante. Big-Spirited Struggle Defeated By Elegance said the *Volksblatt,* while the *Vaterland* led with A Valuable Lesson At The Highest Level. Both papers were filled with admiration for the ability of the Spaniards and praise for the dogged determination of the Liechtensteiners to keep the score at a respectable level. LFV president Otto Bierdermann said in the *Vaterland*:

I am content with the result and also with the performance of our team. The result went according to the status of the two teams. With France and Portugal, Spain is currently one of the best teams in the world, and clearly there is a considerable gulf in class between them and a country such as Liechtenstein. Nevertheless, everyone could see the improvement in our team, particularly in defence.

Peter Jehle was a little dejected, however:

> The fourth and fifth goals disappointed me, and took the shine off the performance. Basic errors that wouldn't normally happen, happened to me. These will torment me and keep me awake at night. I told the Spanish reporters before the game that I'd be fairly happy to concede up to five goals. With hindsight, however, that's not the case.

> We were glad just to get out of our own half [said Mario Frick]. I think I had one chance, otherwise it felt like the time I played up front in an under-sixteen match against Spain and never saw the ball once. Even without service though, I didn't have my best game. I was running out of patience in a way, because playing for the national team is completely different to playing with Arezzo. In Italy, every second pass goes up to the strikers, so in Alicante I felt a little starved.

'The 0–5 defeat is still another good result for us,' Martin Telser told the *Vaterland*'s Ernst Hasler, 'particularly when you consider that the crowd was like an extra player to Spain.'

On the Spanish side, Fernando Hierro was 'very content. We achieved our target, which was the three points. I scored my twenty-sixth goal for the national side, which puts me level with Emilio Butragueno in the all-time scorers list, and that's a great way to celebrate my thirty-third birthday.'

Gaizka Mendieta, one of the greatest players in the world, had been impressed by Jehle. 'The Liechtenstein goalkeeper played very well, and Liechtenstein are not disgraced in defeat.'

The following morning, I renewed my acquaintance with the Grünesholz's breakfast room. The owner appeared surprised to see me there and asked for my room number. Her name, I had discovered, is Anita Hug – a friendly appeal belied by her powerful appearance (say it out loud and you'll see what I mean). But there was no sign of Griselda, I was obviously devastated to see. After breakfast, I went out and bought a hiking map of the country because in a brief fit of energy I had decided to walk up the mountain to Triesenberg, the home of the Walsers. I'd read that there was a museum devoted to this extraordinary community and decided to pay it a visit. According to the map, the route would take me out of Vaduz up past the castle and on up the mountain to the village inside a leisurely two hours.

Possession of the map made me feel like the rugged outdoor type that I plainly am not. It was a large map with lots of tightly spaced relief lines depicting the peaks of the principality. A tourist map it certainly wasn't. Advice on the back suggested that stout, well-worn hiking boots and waterproofs were advisable. I had on a pair of flimsy Adidas trainers and an anorak that Katie had bought me for a tenner in C&A's children's department. No matter. I went to the supermarket and bought a plastic bottle of water (one of those where the top turns into a nozzle to make you feel really sporty) and a bar of chocolate for energy. A big bottle of peach yoghurt drink was despatched down my throat followed by two squares of chocolate. Unsatiated by this combination I decided that my trek needed better sustenance in its preparation stage, so I went and had a kebab. It was foul, but I valiantly forced it down.

The hiking trail begins via a small street to the side of the Chinese restaurant in the main street. I walked up the lane and found myself at the bottom of an enormous flight of wooden stairs that disappeared into the trees above the village. I zipped up my anorak, stashed the chocolate and water and began to climb. The stairs seemed to go on for ever. Within a couple of minutes I was breathing hard and a sheen of sweat had already begun to appear on my forehead. Before long my thighs were screaming for mercy and I slumped gasping on to a bench before the next flight. I yanked the water out of my pocket and gulped about half of it down. I was sure the air was getting thinner.

It was when a middle-aged man in a suit skipped lightly past me up the stairs with a newspaper under his arm that I realised that I hadn't actually reached the outskirts of Vaduz yet. I'd already reached the outer limits of my endurance yet local people do this when they nip out for a paper and don't even get out of breath. I climbed some more stairs and found thankfully that they gave way to a bark-strewn footpath of a less achilles-stretching gradient. The path zig-zagged up the mountainside in the same way that yachts tack through difficult stretches of water.

The path was lined with dense trees, but an occasional break in the foliage allowed a glimpse of Vaduz retreating into the distance below. After a few minutes I saw a sign ahead. Great, I thought, it might tell me how high I'd climbed so far. Instead the sign read as follows:

> THE STATE. The Principality of Liechtenstein is a constitutional hereditary monarchy upon a democratic and parliamentary basis. The power of State is invested in the Prince and the People. The Prince is Head of State. The Diet is elected by the People. Laws come into force only on receiving the consent of the monarch. State administration is carried out by the government. There is a complete system of Courts of Justice.

An incongruous location for a mini lecture on Liechtensteiner democracy, I thought. The austere way in which the information was disseminated reminded me of the Progress Publishing books of Soviet politics I'd picked up on a school trip to Moscow in the mid-eighties. Dogma has to be written this way. Short sentences are essential. There is then no room for compromise. Neither must there be any room for dissent.

The sign had been defaced by a badly drawn swastika. I presumed that this had been put there by the same Lithuanian graffiti artists who had written the name of their country, helpfully in four different languages, in the same pen on a nearby tree, declaring in English that they had 'made it at last'. I was surprised that the conquest of Liechtenstein had been such a longed-for event amongst Lithuanian Nazis.

After twenty minutes or so of leisurely climbing I emerged from the undergrowth at the princely seat. I hadn't been this close to the castle since Sheila had shown me around. I was '*grüss Gotted*' by a party of middle-aged walkers who, despite my flimsy footwear and child's anorak, obviously recognised a kindred back-to-nature spirit. I fixed each with a firm gaze, walker to walker, bonding with these fellow slaves to health and fitness. However, I might have stared a little too hard as the women started to look a bit frightened.

Following the road that leads past the castle I came across a deserted car park. This may have once been a popular beauty spot, as the spaces were designed so that you parked your car facing out into the valley. However, since the tarmac had been laid, the roadside shrubbery had grown to such an extent that you couldn't see a thing. The physical exertion of my climb coupled with the horrendous kebab I'd consumed before departure had produced some alarming rumblings from my digestive system. I had visions of diving into the undergrowth and scrabbling around for dry leaves, until I saw a toilet block at the end of the car park.

I was instantly wary. Such establishments in Britain are without exception worse than the latrines of Valhalla and only the most clinically desperate of people would even consider entering their brown-streaked portals and attempting to breathe the mixture of effluent and chemicals that masquerades as air within. But this was Liechtenstein, I thought, a nation far more civilised than my own. My grumbling bowels urged me towards the block. I opened the door and peered inside. Bliss. The place was as clean as my bathroom back at the Grünesholz. The floor was completely dry and the toilet paper holder was present, in one piece, and fulsomely stocked with soft two-ply. The light worked. A pristine porcelain toilet drew me forward as if it had blinked a large pair of coquettish blue eyes at me from within the bowl.

There were even instructions in English on how to wash your hands. Whether they chose English because it was the most commonly understood language by users of public conveniences, or just assumed that only English speakers would be filthy enough to wonder what the big white thing with two metal attachments was, I couldn't say. But, in accordance with the sticker I 'wet the hands completely!' I then proceeded to 'take the soap and lather thoroughly!' If it hadn't been for the exclamation marks I would doubtlessly have performed my ablutions in such a haphazard cavalier fashion as to render any hygiene defunct. The instructions finished there, however, and it was left to my own initiative to work out what to do next.

I was reluctant to leave this temple to toilet technology. I could happily have stayed for longer, had a coffee and read the papers, but the call of the Walser Museum was strong so I strode on into the trees. The route continued to be a succession of steep double backs. I was gasping for breath again and a dull ache was commencing at the base of my spine. My thighs were aching in a way they hadn't since our sadistic primary school PE teacher used to have us doing circuit training so rigorous the SAS would have wilted.

As our class of exhausted ten-year-olds crawled back to the changing rooms begging for mercy, he would give us just two minutes to shower and dress. The moment those minutes were up he would throw any unworn clothes out of the door and on to the playing field, followed by me and my classmates, whatever our state of undress, whatever the weather. As a sickly, uncoordinated child with skinny legs and thick glasses, there were two things that terrified me most about this teacher. One was the human pyramid he insisted on building at every school sports day. Being a short, skinny drink of water I was always earmarked for the upper layers. Horrified parents, who had expected to watch nothing more adventurous than a couple of egg-and-spoon races, would look on as their offspring were either staggering at the bottom of the pile with the weight of several classmates on their shoulders or scrambling skyward to teeter alarmingly at the top of the pyramid. Invariably the pyramid would plummet to the tarmac in a jumble of tangled limbs, as the disgruntled pedagogue went puce and exploded.

Gymnastics was the other thing I feared most. The image of the vaulting horse in the middle of the gym is one that still makes my mouth go dry and my stomach turn over even now, more than twenty years on. As a succession of small boys would rise from the springboard, execute a forward roll over the horse and land on their feet with arms outstretched, I used to wait my turn in absolute terror. The final straw came one day when I gave it everything and charged headlong towards the springboard. My trajectory was a little flat and my head arrived at the near end of the horse with my body in a straight line behind it like a human torpedo. My teacher tried to remedy the situation by grabbing the back of my shorts and pulling me over in a forward roll. He took a fistful of waistband and heaved. There was a terrific tearing sound and the next thing I knew I was falling sideways from the horse.

The rest of the class burst into high-pitched hysterics. I looked up to see him holding up what remained of my shorts in his right hand. For some reason he always insisted that we wear just shorts for PE, no underpants. So, there I was, legs spread wide, in just a white vest and displaying my undescended privates to my peers. Even the teacher was laughing, the bastard.

Still today the sight of lithe young eastern European Olympians twisting and turning through the air brings those traumatic memories flooding back. Muscular complaints stemming from physical exertion have the same effect, and that's why, high on an alpine mountainside, when my legs declared war upon the rest of me, I found myself thinking of my teacher.

My gasps grew more desperate and my backache throbbed as the endless trail of double backs continued skyward. The sound of running water preceded a rest stop at the edge of a babbling torrent of pure mountain water gurgling over the rocks. Around the next bend I realised I would have to cross the raging torrent in order to continue on my way to Triesenberg.

It's at times like this that I remember why I choose the safer parts of the world to do this sort of thing. A frown of puzzlement darkens my forehead whenever I read of people who hack through Amazonian rainforests or cross African plains without the safe surrounds of, at the very least, an armoured people carrier with a fully-stocked bar and a pizza oven. If I'd been doing this walk in the forests of Peru or somewhere, there was every chance that an enormous, hairy, multicoloured spider would come spinning out of the trees and plant itself on my face. Or I'd suddenly feel a tightening around my calves, look down and see a huge boa constrictor tying itself around me in a prelude to calling me elevenses.

I can't understand this sort of adventure travel in the slightest. Great feats of daring were surely all taken care of by our Victorian forefathers, for whom the height of bravery was shooting harmless indigenous people and animals from a safe distance with a hearty 'tally ho'.

In the forests of Liechtenstein, however, the most dangerous thing that can happen to you is a bird shitting on your head. I stepped up to the rushing torrent of icy mountain water and pondered how to get to the other side. Your average adventurer would not think twice before planting their backpack on their head and wading across as the water laps against their chin, hoping at the same time that all the crocodiles are looking the other way.

Here, however, the water was no more than an inch deep and the only danger appeared to come from slipping on wet leaves. I took a couple of deep breaths, identified the most likely footholds and skipped across. The water didn't even reach over the top of my trainers. Despite my most dangerous mission to date not even having dampened my socks, I still felt liberated. I'd walked through a puddle and suddenly I was Grizzly Adams.

Eventually I reached the top of the tree line and emerged on to a grassy meadow. A small cluster of houses lay ahead and I fully expected a kindly Alpine couple to be waiting at their gate for me, the weary traveller, with home-baked bread and coffee. The place was deserted, however, save for the flabby sound of a diesel engine somewhere nearby. One of the buildings appeared to be incredibly old; it was in typical chalet-style but the wood was dark and ancient, and several window panes were missing. I peered inside. There was no evidence of habitation other than some straw on the floor. It looked as though animals had been billeted there at one point but now the place was deserted and had been for some years.

But as I passed by, I noticed that a pair of antlers had been affixed to the outer wall. Not only that but they had been recently adorned at the crown of the skull with a small bouquet of fresh wild flowers. Similar bunches had been placed at each side. It was a bit spooky, to say the least. Here I was, alone, halfway up a mountain in a strange country as a mist descended, having stumbled on what appeared to be a deserted forest house with some kind of satanic shrine attached. I started to wish I'd never seen *The Blair Witch Project*. From a barn nearby came the mournful sound of cowbells. In the distance, a chainsaw roared into life, and *The Texas Chainsaw Massacre* was added to the list of films I wished I'd never seen. I walked on quickly, much to the disgust of my put-upon thighs.

A brief clearing in the mist showed that I was now high above the valley floor. The air was much colder, and the water in my bottle was now chilled so deeply that I could feel its coldness all the way down to my stomach as I took a couple of large gulps.

Although I couldn't see Vaduz, I could certainly hear it. The relentless rhythmic clanking of heavy machinery betrayed the capital from its misty camouflage. It appeared that if you wanted to make your fortune in Liechtenstein, the best thing to do would be to start a construction company. When the mist parted briefly, I could see Vaduz spread beneath me and began to count the huge T-shaped cranes that dominated the town's skyline. There were seventeen. In a community of only five thousand people. That's roughly a crane for every three hundred inhabitants. Some were so closely spaced they could have jousted with each other. This didn't seem right somehow. A place that prides itself on being the Valley of Peace was now making more noise than a small tank battle.

Part of the charm of Liechtenstein is its beautiful rural setting and its relative lack of industrial development. It's already one of the richest countries in Europe – the frenzy of office and factory construction below me suggested a zealousness for the accumulation of cash that could eventually see the tiny nation overstretch itself and come crashing down. From my lofty vantage point I felt like Lemuel Gulliver. I wanted to squat down on my haunches, pick up the government in the palm of my hand and tell them, enough!

I sat for a while listening to the cacophony until the mist

closed in again. Within minutes I was on the outskirts of Triesenberg. The climb had taken me two and a half hours and I was knackered. I stumbled into the centre of the village and located the museum. But first, I didn't half fancy a pint. However, it was mid-afternoon on a Tuesday and everywhere was closed. I walked up to the museum and checked the opening times – unusually for me, I had arrived within them. I pushed open the door and went inside.

A kindly looking elderly woman sat behind a counter strewn with tourist leaflets. She seemed slightly startled to see me. '*Grüss Gott*,' she said, raising an eyebrow. I replied in kind, expecting her to stand up and sell me a ticket. She didn't move, instead continuing to regard me with a mixture of wonderment and suspicion. 'Er . . . museum?' I ventured. She drew her breath in sharply and pushed her hands against her cheeks. 'Museum *geschlossen*,' she said with genuine sorrow.

It turned out that the Walser Museum was closed for two weeks for renovation work. Arse, I thought. Instead I bought a hardback book about Triesenberg which had some stuff about the Walsers in it. The old woman looked even more amazed. When I unwrapped the plastic around the book I realised why – it had been produced in 1978. For twenty-three years the book had lain beneath the desk waiting for a purchaser.

I went for a look at the church with its onion-shaped belfry and sat for a while on a bench in the adjoining cemetery. Most of the headstones featured photographs of the graves' occupants. An elderly couple called Beck smiled out from their headstone, having died within just three days of each other in 1996. In the corner was the headstone of a child who had died aged just one month in 1961 – the grave was still immaculate, with fresh flowers and a lit candle in front of the stone. Some headstones were simple wooden crosses draped with strips of black netting. I spent a sobering half hour in the cemetery wondering about the people who had been born, lived and died in this tiny mountain hamlet. Mist in the valley obscured the rest of Liechtenstein and it was easy to forget that the rest of the world was out there somewhere. Generations of the same families were here. A plump blond woman pottered between the wall mounted tap and the grave she was tending, keeping up a one-sided conversation with its occupant in a soothing voice as she positioned fresh flowers in a vase.

The walk back to Vaduz was much quicker than my ascent. It was downhill, for a start. When I reached the capital, following the thumping and clanking from the misty valley below, I looked up but couldn't see Triesenberg in the low cloud.

I felt healthily exhausted. I popped into the supermarket and bought six bottles of beer, determined to undo all the good work my Triesenberg odyssey had instilled in my put-upon physique. I could have imagined it, but I'm sure I received a number of disapproving looks as I strolled back to the Grünesholz, sixpack in hand (the only type of sixpack I'm ever likely to possess). I lay back on the bed and drank three bottles in quick succession. I was tired, but it was still only early evening and I was hungry. Earlier I'd passed a restaurant that had advertised its special of the day as *Szegedische Gulasch mit Spätzle*.

I'd had this dish in the town of Szeged itself a few months earlier. Deep in the south of Hungary I'd sat alone on a restaurant terrace in the near-deserted town as a hot wind blew and thunder rumbled menacingly in the distance. The mournful sounds of a cimbalom and violin duo accompanied the scene. I thought that this would make an impressive conversational gambit in Liechtenstein and before long the whole restaurant, from customers to kitchen coolies, would surround my table listening with rapt attention to my tales of the Great Plain.

The restaurant was empty. I wolfed down the passable goulash without a single anecdotal opportunity and blundered out into the evening with another couple of beers inside me to add to the three I'd consumed in my room. As usual, the centre of Vaduz was deserted but I was diverted by the huge flashing neon sign over the Crash Bar. Its doors and windows were heavily smoked so I couldn't do my usual trick of passing the place three or four times risking head/lamp-post interfaces as I peered inside whilst at the same time attempting to look nonchalant.

Taking a deep breath, in I went. Three people sat at the bar whilst a thirtysomething woman with dark hair polished glasses. Some tired-looking musical instruments hung from the nicotine-beige walls. German pop music came from the speakers, and there was the thud and clack of a pool game from an adjoining room. I ordered a beer in flawless German. Or so I'd thought. 'Where are you from?' asked a man at the end in heavily accented English. 'London,' I replied. None of the people assembled at the bar could quite believe that I'd travelled from England in order to watch Liechtenstein play Bosnia at football. Günther, the man who'd rumbled my nationality in the face of my immaculate German pronunciation, was just as surprised that I'd pronounced his name correctly (more 'Gewnter' than 'Goonter') as he'd always thought that the English were physically incapable of mastering the umlaut sound. Günther had had a few by this point and he swayed on his stool as he informed me that he had played for the Liechtenstein national team at under-sixteen level. But he didn't like football, he said. It turned out that the woman next to me was studying English, and should have been poring over her Cambridge Advanced English books rather than propping up the Crash Bar. We fell easily into conversation.

Eventually Günther and his girlfriend staggered away into the night with a flurry of kisses, handshakes and shoulder clasps. So it was just me and Stefanie, and Vaduz was our oyster. She'd make a lovely wife, said Günther, pointing at Stefanie as he departed.

Stefanie was from the south-west German province of Baden-Würtemberg and had come to Liechtenstein to work for the environment department. She'd been in the country nearly a year and was still trying to work out the people. 'They are friendly up to a point,' she said running her finger around the rim of her beer glass, 'but they don't seem to like strangers getting too close. Günther's different. I work with his girlfriend Jacqui and they are very friendly. He's not normally like that; I think he's so drunk because he's bought Jacqui a CHF4,000 (about £1,600) piece of jewellery. And he doesn't have a job.'

I had warmed to Günther instantly, as I was now warming

to Stefanie. When I asked her what she thought of Liechtenstein she said 'small'.

'On my first day in the job I had to go to a meeting and the head of government was there. I was shocked – it was like going to a meeting in Germany and Gerhard Schröder walking in. But later that evening I saw him in the supermarket pushing his trolley. He gave me a cheery wave and carried on getting his groceries.'

At that point we were joined by another woman whom Stefanie introduced as Claudia. She looked miserable, and all the while Stefanie spoke, her friend smoked and drank in a manner which suggested she was trying to look moody and mysterious.

I told Stefanie about my mountain trek earlier in the day, and how I'd counted seventeen cranes.

'Yes, it's madness,' she agreed. 'The development in Vaduz in particular is getting out of control. The long term effects on the environment could be disastrous but no one will do anything about it. Small Rhine tributaries are being dammed for building work, which is just madness.'

We talked for an hour but by this time the beer was taking hold. I know we covered the Berlin Wall, an old German girl-friend of mine and how Stefanie polishes up her English by listening to Leonard Cohen records in her bedsit in Balzers. She suggested moving to another bar further down. Gallantly I offered to settle the drinks bill but didn't have enough money. My beer-fuelled drinks-all-round generosity had got the better of my wallet. Sheepishly I had to leave Stefanie and Claudia as collateral while I staggered off to the cashpoint.

We moved on to an upstairs bar called Schwefel on the road to Triesen. Soon afterwards Stefanie headed for home, and I began gamely trying to get something out of Claudia. I commented that I'd never noticed the place before. 'Well, everything in Liechtenstein is hidden,' she said mysteriously. Then as we sat at a small table drinking beer and eating deep-fried jalapeno peppers it all suddenly came rushing out.

Claudia was seeing a married man called Manfred. He worked in the same building, he was forty-four, she was twenty-nine. He had three children. 'I don't normally go for older men,' she confided, 'but the first time I saw him I thought, hmmm, you're dangerous.' A month previously they'd managed to escape to Vienna together for a few days where they'd smoked a lot of grass and had inordinate amounts of rumbustuous sex. Two days before we met, Claudia, tired of the secrecy, had told him it was all over. He was still sending her erotic e-mails.

'Do you love him?' I asked. 'Yes, I love him,' she replied. She talked non-stop for nearly an hour. I think my transience in the country had made me an ideal shoulder to cry on. Liechtenstein was so small that everybody knew everybody else's business. It was remarkable, in fact, that the affair had stayed secret for so long (she even said that no doubt we had been seen together and the word would be around that Claudia was out drinking until the early hours with that scruffy-looking foreigner). So when I turned up, just passing through, no vested interests anywhere, the burden of Claudia's troubles was lifted from her shoulders and into my booze-shrivelled brain, which churned out ill-conceived advice about blokes, 'You can't trust 'em', 'He'll never leave her, you know', and so on.

'I know there's no future,' she sighed. 'I mean, how can I go home to my parents and say, this is my new boyfriend, he's fifteen years older, married with three children and grows the best cannabis in the whole of the Rhine Valley?'

We parted outside the bar. Claudia kissed me on the cheek, climbed into a taxi and was gone. I headed back to the Grünesholz for a drunken, restless and sweaty sleep.

Ten

The construction workers of Vaduz had started particularly early. When I was woken on the morning of the Bosnia game by a loud thumping, I cursed anew the relentless development of this part of the Rhine Valley and buried my head beneath the pillow. The volume didn't diminish, and it took me a minute to realise that the pummelling was not coming from the building sites that surrounded the Grünesholz but from inside my own head. I also had a thirst so raging I could have happily drained Lake Zurich with a straw.

Having thrust my suffering head under the shower I staggered down to breakfast. There were just two places set, one opposite the other. I sat down gingerly, ready to leap upon the coffee pot when it arrived, place the spout against my pursed lips and gulp down its volcanic contents in one. Frau Hug appeared in the doorway, looking from side to side and then eyed me suspiciously. '*Sind Sie allein?*' she asked. Was I alone? '*Ja*,' I mumbled. My eyebrows jerked instinctively towards the ceiling in surprise, rousing the timpanists in my cranium from *forte* to *fortissimo*. With a confused shrug she removed the place setting opposite me. Had Claudia been right? Did everyone know everyone else's business? Had somebody noticed the two of us apparently getting on famously the previous night and forewarned Frau Hug that I might have company the next morning?

Surely not, I thought, as my dry mouth tried in vain to soften up a bread roll. Surely being seen talking to a young woman one night didn't automatically lead to an extra place setting at breakfast? I looked down, still rolling the spongy dough around my mouth, and considered the place mat, which advertised a competition to win a trip to the Sydney Olympics. A great prize, had the Sydney Olympics not finished some seven months earlier. I wondered how Claudia was getting on at the bank. She'd been punctuating the conversation with the phrase 'I'm so bloody drunk' all evening and now she'd be at her desk, with a hangover as raging as mine, waiting to download the latest saucy e-mails from her erstwhile lover.

I had an appointment of my own, however. The previous evening, thankfully just as I was starting on my first bottle, my mobile had rung and it was Martin Frommelt, the Press Officer of the Liechtensteiner Fussball Verband. 'Would you like to come to a press conference at ten a.m. tomorrow?' he had asked. I agreed readily, thankful for something to do that involved other human beings. It was to be held at the box-like new art museum in the centre of Vaduz, which had opened since my last visit. Normally when I get such last-minute invitations to press conferences it's because the organisation is expecting the turnout to be low, and hence the ringaround of the freelancers commences in the hope of making up the numbers. I presumed that this was the case here too. Luckily, I'm not proud and will turn up to anything if there's the off-chance of a free sandwich.

So off I staggered. I was delighted to see that I was following Roland Büchel from the tourist board into the building. I said a breezy hello, breathing sharp alcohol fumes over him. I recognised also Peter, the jovial man from the government information office who had furnished me with signed photographs of the cabinet on my last visit. Mario Frick had been surprisingly voted out of office a couple of weeks previously, and by a considerable majority too. Considering the two main parties, the Reds and the Blacks, were virtually indistinguishable to the outsider, this was quite a turn up. I'd heard that you have to have lived in Liechtenstein all your life to discern the ideological differences between them.

Once I had entered the room, suddenly everyone began to speak English. A smiling man in a grey suit even started talking about cricket. Martin Frommelt introduced me to a skinny young man encased in a huge anorak, with sticky-out ears and a shiny outdoor complexion. He was Marcus Hasler, a Liechtensteiner cross-country skier ranked sixth in the world. He looked nervous and out of place in a windowless, neon-lit room full of men in suits and this scruffy foreigner smelling of drink.

It turned out the press conference was to publicise a cross-country ski race to be held in Balzers later in the year. It was given in machine-gun-fast Swiss-German of which I could understand not a word. My hangover really and truly kicked in and as soon as the conference finished, while the Liechtensteiners adjourned for coffee and cake, I blundered through the corridors and out into the street. Within minutes I was back in my bed in the Grünesholz.

Fortunately I awoke in plenty of time for the match. I showered, changed and headed into Vaduz for an early evening pre-match perambulation. There was no evidence that an international football match was taking place in the town. In fact there were no indications of anything really as I took a leisurely stroll through the empty centre. I sat down on a bench outside the Rathaus and sorted out a few notes. Around the corner came a small group of men. Three of them were middle-aged, slightly overweight and wearing shabby, ill-fitting blazers. The two men escorting them were immaculately dressed in tailored three-piece suits. As the group drew nearer I recognised the badge on the larger group's blazers – they were dignitaries of the Bosnian FA.

I had seen Bosnia in action twice before. Once in the Faroe Islands two years previously where they held on for a 2–2 draw, thanks mainly to the Faroes missing a second-half penalty, and once in Sarajevo for a 'Football For Peace' match with a FIFA World XI.

I remember going to the Faroese FA offices in Torshavn on the day before the game to sort out my press pass. 'That's assuming the Bosnians turn up,' said Heidi, the jolly FA secretary. 'We've had no word from them to say they're coming. It was the same when we played one of their teams in the UEFA Cup – the first we knew they were actually coming was when the plane appeared in the sky requesting permission to land.'

Fortunately the Bosnians did arrive. They had no supporters with them, and when they scored the only cheers came from the players and the knot of Bosnian FA dignitaries waving a flag in the main stand. Bosnia to the Faroes is one of the longest distances to cover in European football, and with the Faroes being one of Europe's most expensive countries, it was no surprise that the Bosnian fans gave the game a miss.

The match in Sarajevo was a different affair, and I arrived early at the Olympic Stadium for the game. I soon discovered that the press entrance is also the entrance to the best seats. The tickets for the match with the FIFA World Stars were neither numbered nor segregated so the whole 25,000-strong crowd was trying to squeeze through that gate for the best view. When I saw two journalists walking across people's heads and diving headlong through the two-foot gap between the crowd and the top of the gate I decided to try a different route and found another less densely populated entrance.

Somehow I ended up on the pitch. A combination of waving my press card and shouting 'BBC!' seemed to do the trick, even to the extent of crossing the moat around the playing area at a gate guarded by armed police with dogs. Looking up at the press box I saw it was full of flag-waving, chanting Bosnian fans. In front of me on the running track was a man in a suit whom I took initially to be a Bosnian FA official. I tapped him on the shoulder and he turned round.

It was Sepp Blatter, FIFA President and the most powerful man in football. The man he'd been talking to leaned over to see who I was. 'Er, *bonjour Monsieur Platini*,' I mumbled before scuttling away.

Armed with a press card though I was, I still had no accreditation for the game. A polite lady from the Bosnian FA sympathised but was on the point of throwing me out. My pleading expression led to her going to find the Bosnian press officer.

Back he came, saying he hadn't received my faxed and e-mailed applications. Generously, however, he gave me his own pass for pitchside access. Somehow though, I didn't really look like Fuad Krvavac. I scuttled off to hide with the photographers behind the goal where I was to take a stray Bosnian first half shot full in the midriff.

One of the men now strolling towards me was the very same Fuad Krvavac. I hoped that given the year that had passed since our last encounter he wouldn't recognise me. Fortunately the group was distracted by the Rolex watches in a nearby shop window. They rushed over and pressed their noses against the glass, cooing admiration for the thousands of pounds' worth of timepieces ticking away in a substantial display of Liechtensteiner opulence.

Finally they moved off in the direction of the stadium. Eventually I set off too. I was about to pass the Adler when a teenage girl standing alone on the corner said something to me in German that I didn't recognise. 'Sorry, I'm English,' I replied with a shrug. 'Oh,' she said, pausing to think. 'Do you want a ticket for the football game?' She held out a shiny piece of card with 'Liechtenstein v Bosnien-Herzegowienen' written upon it. I'd encountered my first Liechtensteiner ticket tout.

'Oh,' I replied, 'I already have my ticket, thanks.' She didn't understand. 'It costs forty francs,' she said, pointing to the price on the ticket. Not only was she the unlikeliest tout I'd ever encountered, she was also selling the ticket at face value. 'It's okay, sorry,' I said. A brief cloud of confusion skittered across her brow. I didn't want to be rude and just walk away. Her kindly demeanour instilled in me an urge to explain why I couldn't take up her offer of a ticket. I reached into my back pocket for my press card. Her eyes lit up – she thought I was going for my wallet. I felt terrible as I showed her the card with an apologetic shrug. 'Ohhhh . . . *Scheisse*!' she said with genuine anguish. Half an hour before kick-off in the deserted streets of Vaduz, evidently I was her last hope.

As I walked up towards the stadium, I doubted whether the ground would be full to its 3,500 capacity. Were the Bosnians, talented team though they were, a big enough draw for the less than committed fans of Liechtenstein? It was unlikely, I thought, that many Bosnians would have made the trip. They'd drawn at home with Austria the previous weekend, and coach Drago Smajlovic was jeered as he left the field. Having lost their opening match at home to Spain, then suffered a disappointing 1–3 defeat in Israel, the Bosnians' chances of qualifying were rapidly diminishing. Plus Liechtenstein is an expensive country to visit.

As I approached the ground through the fields and past the goats I could hear drumming and singing. Given the almost funereal atmosphere of the Austrian match (apart from my personal trio of amplified cheerleaders), I was puzzled. As I drew nearer I realised that hundreds of Bosnians were chanting and singing outside the stadium entrance. They were draped in flags, and many sported replica shirts. I spotted at least three Zeleznicar Sarajevo and a Velez Mostar amongst the Bosnian national shirts. Many fans wore t-shirts that announced they were 'Hardcore Bosnians on tour', and listed their nation's group games.

I went in and found my seat. This time I was located in the press box proper, next to a middle-aged man with grey hair and a barcode moustache, dark and flecked with grey. This, as it turned out, was Ernst Hasler from the *Liechtensteiner Vaterland*, whose work I had been deciphering with my dictionary since I first arrived in the principality.

The players jogged out on to the pitch to warm up. I noticed that there were a number of Italian journalists at the game and asked Ernst why.

'Ah, they're here to see Mario Frick,' he explained. The Liechtenstein forward had been an instant hit in Serie C at Arezzo, for whom he had signed shortly after the match against Austria in Vaduz. Frick had hinted that he might be on the move after that game: 'I would like to move from FC Zurich and I have had strong interest from another club outside Switzerland. I can't really say much more at the moment.'

Within three weeks, the gangling forward was happily ensconced in his Tuscan villa with his girlfriend and baby, and making an instant impression at his new club. Two hundred

Big Brother is watching you: the Prince's castle overlooking Vaduz (Matt Wright)

Liechtenstein football's field of dreams: the 3,548-capacity Rheinpark Stadion
(Matt Wright)

It's forty minutes to kick-off and the fans flock to the stadium (Matt Wright)

The pride of a principality. Fortunately the other players persuaded
Martin Telser to remove his lucky tall hat before kick-off (Matt Wright)

Eyal Berkovic and Harry Zech congratulate each other on not having a haircut as bad as the linesman's (Matt Wright)

Yes, a 0–3 home defeat to Israel really can feel this good. Jürgen Ospelt, Frédéric Gigon, Patrik Hefti, Hanno Hasler and Harry Zech in the Schwefel bar after the match (Matt Wright)

LFV General Secretary Markus Schaper insisted on answering every question through 'Mister Thumb' (Matt Wright)

Ralf Loose unburdens himself to the greatest sports journalist in the world, Ernst Hasler of the *Liechtensteiner Vaterland* (Matt Wright)

The beating heart of football commerce in Liechtenstein (Matt Wright)

Peter Jehle performs a familiar duty (Matt Wright)

Mixed Zone

Liechtenstein football
supporters: a rare sighting
(Matt Wright)

The happy-go-lucky Liechtenstein bench enjoying the game (Matt Wright)

Ralf Loose attempts to deflect criticism after the defeat in Bosnia by crooning a selection of hits from the shows (Charlie Connelly)

Harry Zech: master winemaker first, World Cup footballer second (Charlie Connelly)

Mario Frick (left) takes on Igor Tudor, Verona v Juventus: November 2001
(Fabio Corba/*Liechtensteiner Vaterland*)

Mario Frick addresses the nation via Ernst Hasler (Fabio Corba/*Liechtensteiner Vaterland*)

fans turned out for his first training session, rather different from the crowds at Liechtenstein sessions which appeared to consist of me. He marked his debut with two goals in a 2–1 win over Lucchese, and scored again in his second game. By the time the Bosnia game came around he had already broken the goalscoring record for a foreign player in Serie C with eighteen. Hence the interest from the big boys.

'Perugia and Torino look the most likely,' said Ernst, 'but whoever signs him will have to pay around six million francs [approx £2million]. I also heard that Verona and Chievo are interested.'

Torino, going for promotion to Serie A, had watched Frick in Spain at the weekend, but their Chief Executive Sandro Mazzola, a former Italian international, hadn't been able to draw any significant conclusions.

'He's a strong, quick player whom I see as a second striker for us,' he said. 'In Spain he played as a lone attacker and didn't have much to do, so it was hard to make any firm judgements.'

The teams emerged to the familiar tinny accompaniment of the FIFA anthem. The Bosnians received a rousing reception from a crowd that almost filled the stadium. Whilst they have hardly set the football world ablaze, Bosnia boast a highly talented team capable on their day of beating just about anyone. They have a quartet of players who would be worth a place in most of Europe's top teams in Elvir Bolic, Sergej Barbarez, Hasan Salihamidzic and Elvir Baljic.

Bolic is probably best remembered in Britain for scoring the goal that ended Manchester United's unbeaten home record in European competition in 1996. Back then Bolic had just begun a highly successful spell at Fenerbahce, where he stayed until a move to Rayo Vallecano of the Spanish top flight in the summer of 2000. Barbarez arrived in Liechtenstein as the leading scorer in the German Bundesliga, having netted sixteen times for SV Hamburg, who had recently announced that they would only listen to offers for the striker beginning at £42million. When somebody told them that this was more than Luis Figo's record move from Barcelona to Real Madrid,

Hamburg pointed out that Barbarez scored more goals than Figo.

Salihamidzic was in his third season at Bayern Munich, whom he had joined from Hamburg. A promising young player with Velez Mostar, Salihamidzic was sent to Hamburg to stay with relatives when war broke out in the region in 1992 and before long he had signed for his local team, making his Bundesliga debut whilst still in his teens. Baljic was the current darling of Bosnian football. Real Madrid paid Fenerbahce £13million for his services in 1999, but a foot injury saw him return to Istanbul to recuperate. Fenerbahce wanted to buy the midfielder back, but Baljic was intent on returning to Spain. A public falling-out with Fenerbahce coach Mustafa Denizli didn't help, particularly when, a month before the game in Vaduz, Baljic was seen out on the town with Denizli's daughter on the night before a match.

Despite this considerable array of talent, Bosnia were still just a point ahead of Liechtenstein after three matches. They had opened the campaign at home to Spain and were unlucky to lose by the odd goal in three. A 1–3 defeat in Israel had followed in October where, despite a stunning thirty-five-yard goal from Energie Cottbus' Bruno Akrapovic to level the scores, two second-half defensive lapses gave Israel the points. While Liechtenstein were putting up their valiant resistance in Alicante, Bosnia were picking up their first point of the campaign thanks to a 1–1 draw with Austria in Sarajevo. Bosnia had taken the lead just before half-time when Franz Wohlfahrt had spilled a Baljic free kick for Barbarez to pounce. Austria equalised on the hour when Michl Baur headed home a corner from Andreas Herzog. Barbarez and Baljic both had chances to win the game, but they arrived in Vaduz still looking for a first victory to keep their already slim qualification hopes alive.

Bosnia lay four points behind the third placed Austrians, who in turn were a point behind Israel. Spain had opened up a four-point lead at the top thanks to their win over Liechtenstein, but had played one more game than the rest of the group. Despite their team's poor run, the Bosnian supporters were in good voice, not least when the tannoy announcer revealed that the FIFA observer at the game was Zdravko Jokic, from Yugoslavia. Jeers and whistles echoed around the ground. Liechtenstein were at full strength and able to field seven players with more than twenty caps in the starting eleven despite having such a young side.

Bosnia started the game positively, being caught offside three times in the first five minutes alone. On seven minutes Baljic threaded a lovely through ball down the left to Vedin Music that caught the Liechtenstein defence flat-footed. The Bosnian midfield raced up in support, Music's cross to the far post was knocked back across the face of goal by Salihamidzic, but neither Barbarez nor Baljic could apply the finish.

A minute later Frick made his first significant contribution to the game – a foul on Akrapovic that resulted in a long lecture from the Latvian referee. The Italian journalists scribbled furiously. From the resultant free kick Baljic raced down the left and arrowed a cross towards the six-yard line that Jehle did well to scramble away as Barbarez thundered in. Liechtenstein were on the rack.

On ten minutes, Bosnia achieved what they had threatened to do on three previous occasions and sprung the offside trap. As Akrapovic slid the ball through the inside right channel Barbarez timed his run to perfection, ran on to the ball and finished low past Jehle into the bottom corner. Playing so far up the field against such a nimble front two was always going to be dangerous. The roar from the Bosnian fans that greeted the goal would have been heard in Switzerland.

Already it was clear that Music was causing major problems for Jürgen Ospelt on the Liechtenstein right, with Akrapovic doing likewise for Frédéric Gigon on the opposite flank. After the goal, however, the home side began to settle and on eighteen minutes made their first significant foray into the Bosnian half. Martin Telser released Thomas Beck down the right, but the diminutive Grasshoppers' midfielder delivered a cross that was too deep for Frick. Michael Stocklasa tried to recover the situation, but Faruk Hujdurovic was quick to close him down and the opportunity was gone.

Midway through the half, Music broke down the left again. As Barbarez and Akrapovic raced into the danger area, Ospelt slid in to turn the cross behind for a corner. Four minutes later, Tomislav Piplica in the Bosnian goal was called into action for the first time when some good work from Mario Frick allowed Ospelt to send in a fizzing effort that thudded into the goal-keeper's chest. Liechtenstein were beginning to come into the game at last after the early Bosnian onslaught. The Liechtenstein crowd responded. Well, somebody clapped.

On half an hour Beck chased down a through ball from Patrik Hefti on the right. Escaping the attentions of Mirza Varesanovic, he did well to send over a cross. Piplica fumbled the ball, but managed to smother it as Frick looked set to pounce. From the resultant clearance the ball was moved swiftly to the other end, where sweeper Harry Zech gave away a free kick in a dangerous position on the edge of the penalty area. Baljic, who'd scored from an almost identical position in Bosnia's opening game against Spain, drove the ball in low, but Jehle had read it well and clutched the ball into his chest. The game was picking up pace.

On thirty-four minutes, the Liechtenstein crowd was stirred into audible action. Salihamidzic chopped down Ospelt in the middle of the field to a chorus of whistles. Shortly afterwards a poor clearance from Jehle landed at the feet of Salihamidzic, but the Bayern midfielder's dipping thirty-yard effort flew over the crossbar. It was all very comfortable for the Bosnians, though. Five minutes before the break, Baljic found himself unmarked in the box with the ball at his feet. Zech, however, was able to close him down quickly enough to force his attempted chip wide of Jehle's left-hand post. When the half-time whistle came, Liechtenstein were happier to hear it than the visitors. Although the home side had had a couple of promising moments and coped reasonably well defensively, the subtle promptings of Akrapovic and Music were still the main threat.

Liechtenstein came out for the second half far tighter than they had been in the first. The defence was beginning to snuff out the threat from the Bosnian wide men and there was not a hint of a chance for the visitors for the first fifteen minutes.

As a result the Bosnians began to grow noticeably more irritable, giving away niggling fouls and hurling themselves to the ground with almost canine yelps of pain at the slightest contact. The Latvian referee finally pulled out his yellow card on fifty-five minutes when Salihamidzic committed one clip too many at Ospelt's ankles.

It made for frustrating viewing. The Bosnians were clearly a talented side, yet the moment frustration set in they started going to pieces, and a game that had hitherto been played in good spirit suddenly was in danger of spilling over. The Liechtensteiners were growing angrier at the Bosnian antics and it appeared to be only a matter of time before pushing and shoving began. Bolic saw a long-range effort fly narrowly over the crossbar on the hour, which seemed to settle the visitors down a little, and the conjuring of a clear chance seemed to shift the visitors' focus back to football rather than cheating. The shot proved to be Bolic's final contribution, however, as he was substituted almost immediately by Marko Topic, a stocky striker from Austria Vienna.

With twenty minutes remaining, Liechtenstein produced their best effort of the match so far. The ball came in from the right, and FC Vaduz's Martin Telser hit a first-time shot from the edge of the area that Piplica only just managed to scramble around the post, drawing warm applause from the Liechtenstein crowd. This seemed only to sting the Bosnians into action once again, however, and within two minutes they had doubled their lead. Baljic sent a low cross into the area where Barbarez stood all alone on the six-yard line to turn the ball into the net. All around the tiny ground the Bosnian supporters leapt from their seats to celebrate what looked to be the decisive goal.

Having come close to equalising so soon before conceding such a sloppy goal, Liechtenstein were clearly disheartened by Barbarez's strike. Loose withdrew Thomas Beck in favour of FC Triesenberg's nippy eighteen-year-old striker Thomas Nigg, earning his second cap, but it failed to lift the game as the Bosnians seemed content to play the ball around their midfield until the referee blew for time.

With ten minutes remaining, a scrap for the ball in the

Liechtenstein area saw Topic go over and the referee point to the spot. There were a few muted protests from the home players which were waved away in imperious fashion by the Latvian official. Barbarez, looking to complete his hat-trick, had marched straight over to pick the ball up and place it on the spot, and he stood, hands on hips, at the end of his run up waiting for the whistle.

After a short run, the Hamburg forward clipped a left-foot shot low to Jehle's left. A burst of yellow flashed across the goalmouth, and the young keeper dived full length to push the ball away for a corner. It was a terrific save and the Liechtenstein crowd stood to applaud.

It looked to be the final highlight of the game as the clock ran down in a subdued atmosphere. A 0–2 scoreline was no disgrace for the home side. With just a minute of normal time remaining, Barbarez opened up the Liechtenstein back line with a measured through ball. Substitute Almedin Hota, who had replaced Baljic barely eight minutes earlier, raced on to the pass and as Jehle came out to narrow the angle, Hota slipped the ball through his legs and into the net.

At the final whistle the Bosnian fans swarmed on to the pitch. For all their talent and fancy tricks, it had taken Barbarez to mark the tangible difference between the two sides. It hadn't been a particularly memorable game, but once again Liechtenstein could be proud of their performance. Their opponents had fielded six players from some of Europe's top leagues with experience at the highest level of European club football, whilst Liechtenstein's team had an average age of twenty-three. They had frustrated the Bosnians for long periods and even created a couple of chances themselves, and the late goal had distorted the scoreline a little. Jehle's penalty save to deny Barbarez his hat-trick was clearly the highlight of the game for the home nation, and the teenage goalkeeper had produced another superb performance between the sticks. Mario Frick had had a quiet game after a promising start, and once again it would have been hard for the watching Italians to have gleaned much about his capabilities.

After the match, in the Rheinpark Stadion's windowless press room, Loose commented on what great support the Bosnians had enjoyed, lamenting that the atmosphere was more like an away game for his side. Barbarez entered the room and took his place at the table next to Loose, who looked at him admiringly and shook his hand in congratulations. As usual, Liechtenstein were gracious in defeat.

Eleven

It's a fourteen-hour return train journey between Vienna and Innsbruck. That's seven hours each way.

I mention this as a convincing argument against forward planning. A matter of months earlier I had, in an uncharacteristic moment of foresight, checked the Group Seven fixture list. This confirmed my assumption that Austria would face Liechtenstein in the Prater Stadium close to the Danube in Vienna at the end of April for Liechtenstein's fifth qualifying match. A quick phonecall to Austrian Airlines, and my passage was booked. This would be an easy trip, I thought, because I know Vienna well. No curious guesthouses with murderous staff there, I thought. For once I could exit the airport, know exactly which bus to get on and be able to find my hotel practically with my eyes closed, I thought. And the stadium, an impressive bowl set in the leafy, riverside Prater Park, would be barely half an hour's stroll away through the spring sunshine. And then, without having the courtesy to tell me personally, the Austrian FA moved the game to Innsbruck. Right on the other side of the flipping country.

Liechtenstein are not the biggest crowd pullers in the international game and their away matches can often be shunted to the provinces. Where most teams visiting Spain will play in Madrid, Liechtenstein took on the home side in Alicante. In Slovakia during the Euro 2000 qualifiers, it was the uninspiring town of Dubnica Nad Vahom that hosted the Liechtensteiners rather than the charming, historic capital Bratislava.

Fortunately I noticed this particular change of venue shortly before departure, and thus avoided turning up at a deserted Prater like a friendless partygoer who's got the wrong night. Innsbruck made sense. FC Tirol's new Tivoli stadium had been open barely three months so was still in its post-natal breath-less flush, it wasn't so far for the Liechtenstein squad to travel, and it gave Austrian football fans in the west of the country the opportunity to see their national side in the flesh. And faced with the choice between banks of empty seats in the Prater or a full house at the state-of-the-art but modest capacity Tivoli, the ÖFB made the right choice. From now on though, I shall wait until the very last moment before making travel arrangements.

Hence, despite a pre-dawn start from south London, it was nearly dark when I reached Innsbruck. Being a traveller who largely confines his expeditions to Europe, I'm used to reaching my destination within four hours of leaving my house. Hence the seven-hour slog across Austria was like a transatlantic flight to me. As we clattered through the countryside I ensured that I walked up and down the carriage every half an hour to coun-ter the onset of deep-vein thrombosis.

Like Liechtenstein, Innsbruck is surrounded by mountains, which hunkered down for the night in the darkness behind the looming Habsburg architecture. The clear, starry sky was criss-crossed by a grid of overhead tramwires. A tram rumbled past in the darkness, which in the sharp chill of the evening made me feel as if I were in Vienna but the post-war Vienna of *The Third Man*. I half expected Orson Welles to step out from behind a telephone box and give me a guilty, knowing half smile.

Innsbruck looked better in the morning. It was a brisk spring day, sunny and chilly, as I strolled through the town, gliding through the wispy clouds of my own breath. The Alps looked fantastic, their snowy peaks reflecting the sunshine. Every few minutes an aircraft would barrel low over the streets in its final descent into Innsbruck's airport. Innsbruck is a pleasant place, unhurried, with a relaxed atmosphere and an old quarter that dates back to the fifteenth century when Maximilian I chose the alpine town as his imperial capital. The city is like Liechtenstein in many ways. It's surrounded by alps for a start, and the fact that virtually every other shop is a jeweller's betrays the opulence of the place and its inhabitants. Its centre is certainly more charming than Vaduz. The narrow streets of the old town provide shady cool in the arcades beneath medieval buildings, where yet more expensive jewellery glints at you in the gloom from shop windows. This, I thought, is what Vaduz needs. A recognisable historic quarter where you can walk on ancient flagstones, smoothed and shaped by a hundred generations of footsteps. Innsbruck is almost an enlarged version of what Vaduz could have been. The old town gives the place focus and a sense of historical perspective. Unfortunately historical perspective is not something you can create. Thus where Vaduz was fifty years ago little more than a collection of old farmhouses tugging their metaphorical fore-locks to the ruined castle on the hill, its lightning development has concreted over much of Vaduz's history and the old farming tracks now thrum to the wheel rhythms of Mercedes Benz. Sigh.

I bought a newspaper and turned to the sports section. Amid the Austrian team news there was a coloured box, listing Austria's record victories. There was an 8–2 hammering of Hungary in 1932, and an 8–1 mauling of Switzerland a few months before that. Luxembourg were dispatched 7–0 in 1956, Cyprus 7–1 in 1968. Pride of place went to the 9–0 tupping of Malta in 1977, when Austrian legend Hans Krankl lashed in a double hat-trick.

The implication was obvious. Hey, Liechtenstein are coming to town. Sit back and watch the goals rattle in. Hey, I thought, yes Liechtenstein are coming to town. The team that almost snatched a draw with your two-bob team about six months ago. And hey, 9–0, that's a familiar sounding scoreline, isn't it? Same scoreline as a Spain v Austria match barely a couple of years ago? A team who only scored half that amount against this Liechtenstein team whom you expect to go belly up like an old whore this evening? Am I getting warm? Hmm?

As my hackles rose, so did the realisation that I was becoming a Liechtenstein fan. Possibly the only Liechtenstein fan in fact. Mario Frick might not have usurped Charlton's play-off-final hat-trick-legend Clive Mendonca in my personal hall of fame, but he was closing in fast. And he hadn't even scored a goal yet. Indeed, Liechtenstein hadn't scored a goal either, not for the last two-and-a-half years in a qualifying game. In fact that's one record that Ralf Loose could be proud of: whenever Liechtenstein score a goal in a qualifying game under his tutelage, they go on to win. Austria beware, I thought, when Super Mario makes the net ripple tonight, you're guaranteed to be on a loser. Then you can read your record scores and weep. The hubris of Polster and co. against the Faroes a decade earlier had clearly not been the object lesson it should have been.

I returned to the hotel, where I had arranged to meet Ernst Hasler from the *Vaterland* for lunch. He arrived with his nephew Romed in tow, whom I recognised as the only person I had ever seen wearing a replica Liechtenstein shirt. He also carried to games a flag so large I suspected that it had been snaffled from the princely castle itself. A short, tubby man with grey hair, Ernst bustled into the restaurant apologising for being late. The strappy sandals he wore over his socks and beneath his grey suit trousers slapped against the tiled floor. I joined him and Romed in ordering a dish evocatively named *Händl-Pfändl*, a mishmash of meat and potato served in a huge skillet.

Ernst had driven to Innsbruck from Liechtenstein the previous day, and it had taken barely two hours. I chose not to mention my curiously roundabout route via the whole of Austria. In the train leg alone, Ernst could have nipped home and come back again three times. He spoke excellent English, all the while dabbing at his red, weepy eyes with a handkerchief.

Ernst has seen every Liechtenstein international bar one, a match in Portugal that he watched on television. Just as he was telling me this, his mobile rang: it was somebody giving him the Austrian line-up. The big news was that Markus

Schopp, who had tormented Liechtenstein in Vaduz, had suffered a muscle strain in training the previous evening and it had just been confirmed he wouldn't play. As he told me this Ernst was jabbing at numbers on his phone. After a brief dialogue in machine-gun German, Ernst switched the phone off, satisfied. 'That was Loose, I was just giving him the Austrian team. It's a good job I phoned because he was basing his defence on stopping Schopp.'

We talked about Liechtenstein politics. Ernst told me there were many differences between the Reds and the Blacks, but they were hard to explain. He said that Mario Frick (the politician) had been usurped basically because the Blacks were better at PR this time around. Liechtenstein politics were as much about personalities as issues. The *Vaterland* and the *Volksblatt* were aligned to the Reds and the Blacks respectively, I discovered, and Ernst was a committed lifelong Red.

He'd been to the Austrian press conference the day before, and said that Otto Baric looked nervous. 'Austria are missing a few players,' said Ernst. 'He's worried that Liechtenstein has a good defence and they might frustrate his team. He's missing Wohlfahrt the goalkeeper and the strikers Didi Kühbauer and Christian Mayrleb. So Austria have no strikers this evening, and everyone's talking about a record score because it's only Liechtenstein, which might work in our favour. Baric said that whatever people expect, he'd be happy with two or three nil. He said the public shouldn't expect the six or seven goal wins that Austria used to inflict on us. I told Loose about the newspapers predicting a record score, and he said that would help to inspire the team.'

Austria's captain Andreas Herzog, who would be facing Liechtenstein for the fourth time in his international career, was also trying to play down the clamour for goals in the Austrian newspaper *Kurier*.

We know that the first game only narrowly went our way. We must win, but we are very aware that it will not be easy. I saw on television the international match less than a year ago when Liechtenstein played Germany. After sixty-five minutes it was 2–2, which would be a terrible situation for us. Liechtenstein have learnt how to defend in recent years, and you can no longer expect to beat them by six or seven goals. Against Israel, Liechtenstein restricted their opponents to very few clear chances. Many players are playing in Switzerland now, and one even plays in Italy. This has improved the players' game as well as instilling them with far more confidence than they used to have.

Ernst agreed that Liechtenstein had improved tremendously since Loose took over. It turned out that Ernst used to coach the under-eighteen national team, having been quite a player in his day, and was the LFV press officer for a while as well as being the sports editor of the *Vaterland*. When Ernst and Romed got up to leave, Romed made to give me his LFV pin badge. 'Ah, thanks,' I said, 'but I bought one at the Austria game in Vaduz.'

'Oh,' said Romed, 'all the money from that stall goes to Ernst. He makes all the stuff and takes the money.'

I'd already decided that Ernst was the greatest sports journalist in the world. To fill five broadsheet pages with Liechtenstein sports news every day is an achievement in itself. It was also clear that he was quite an entrepreneur.

The rain began to fall as soon as I left the hotel for the stadium, a relentless drizzle that seemed to accompany every Liechtenstein game I watched. Twenty minutes later I was outside the Tivoli stadium, the new home of FC Tirol Innsbruck. Their ramshackle old stadium lies just across the road from the new one, and is still used for training. The new ground is mightily impressive. With a seated capacity of 15,000, more than sufficient for modern Austrian football, the Tivoli can be switched easily from all-seater to having standing areas behind the goals, something important to Austrian fans who can produce some of the most colourful and best-choreographed support outside Italy.

Having walked around the stadium to the press entrance, coming face to face with a man hanging upside-down from an artificial rock behind a plate glass window on the way, I entered the press room and was immediately handed a bowl of chicken curry from the left and a beer from the right. Now that has never happened at any British ground I've ever been to – you might be begrudged some curly sandwiches and a warm bottle of Budweiser if you ask nicely enough, but that's about it.

Inside the stadium, ear-splitting pop music thundered from the speakers and reverberated around the surrounding Alps. The programme bore the title *Der Gipfelsturm*, which my dictionary could only translate as 'The Summit-Attack'. Not, as I'd hoped, a call to arms to Austrian fans to join anti-globalisation demonstrations, but a reference to the fact that victory over Liechtenstein would take the Austrians to the top of Group Seven.

With each nation now having played four games, Spain topped the group with three wins and a draw. Austria, with two wins and two draws from their four matches, sat two points behind, with Israel two points behind them with six. Bosnia were fourth with four points, thanks to their win in Vaduz and the draw with Austria four days earlier. Liechtenstein brought up the rear with their four defeats in four matches. But they had conceded an average of less than three goals a game, easily their best defensive record since entering European competition.

I was distracted from perusing the programme when the Europop was interrupted by some whooping and shrieking. Two girls and a boy were marching towards the centre circle, each carrying one of those chunky portable microphone things. The bloke was wearing a cap-sleeved t-shirt and leather trousers, and the girls weren't wearing nearly as much. The blond one wore a small pink stetson.

According to the programme these people were something called Rimini Project, whom I deduced were a popular Austrian beat combo. Daddio. They were described (in English) as 'the rebirth of dancefloormusic'.

There was some more whooping and shrieking, and then some more identikit pop music thundered from the speakers. The trio, who by the look of them were having the best time they'd ever had in their lives, as if performing to about six thousand uninterested Austrian football fans was what they were put on this earth to do, leaped around in energetic synchronicity. During an instrumental break, one of the girls squawked, again in English, 'C'mon Österreich, gimme your hands.' I rather needed mine, and was not alone in not lobbing them on to the pitch. What would she have done with them anyway?

The record to which the trio had been expertly miming (the plea for hand removal was a dangerously individual piece of ad lib, for which the perpetrator hopefully received a dressing down from the management) ended in an explosive finale. As the final cadence bounced around the mountains the three sprightly young things held their final pose ready to receive the roaring adulation of the crowd, their teenage chests heaving and their grins fixed. There was a small ripple of applause.

'Woo! Thanks Österreich, we love you!' they bellowed as they left the pitch. If that was the 'rebirth of dancefloormusic', then I was suffering from post-natal depression.

In an attempt to follow that, the organisers sent out another trio, all male this time, carrying a bass, an electric guitar and, horror of horrors, a piano-accordion. Rather than flinging my arms around my face and screeching 'Aiiieeeeee!!!!' at this, I retained my dignity and escaped back to the press room, where I was handed yet more curry and another bottle of beer. Dubious musical acts notwithstanding, I was growing to like this place.

The teamsheets were just being distributed. Loose had Harry Zech at sweeper again, with Patrik Hefti partnered this time by Christof Ritter of FC Vaduz. Daniel Hasler was there to marshal the midfield alongside Jürgen Ospelt, Martin Stocklasa, Martin Telser and Frédéric Gigon. Thomas Beck partnered Mario Frick up front. This was arguably Loose's strongest starting eleven which, coupled with Austria's selection problems, was an encouraging sign for the forthcoming ninety minutes.

I returned to my seat as the anthems concluded, and before long the game was underway. I was distracted in the first couple of minutes by a fantastic tug of war between two Austrian journalists both trying to angle a large television set, screening the match and helpfully placed in the press box, to their own advantage. The result was a bitter compromise, but I noted throughout the game that whenever one of the combatants looked the other way, his opponent would edge it towards himself.

I looked up just in time to see Mario Frick running on to a long clearance from Jehle. Super Mario had slipped through the Austrian backline and was bearing down on the ruddy-cheeked Alex Manninger in the Austrian goal. Unfortunately the pass had just too much weight and Manninger was able to come out and smother the ball as Frick hurdled over him. It was an encouragingly positive start for Liechtenstein, and showed that they weren't necessarily going to pack everyone behind the ball. Indeed, the first few minutes were as open as any of the Liechtenstein matches I'd seen, with the ball swinging from end to end.

On six minutes, Peter Jehle was called into action for the first time, when Richard Kitzbichler sidefooted a ranging pass from Herzog towards the near post. Two minutes later Jehle was able to watch a shot from Alfred Hörtnagl, one of four FC Tirol players in the team playing on their home turf, fly harmlessly over the crossbar from distance, and then Liechtenstein came forward again. Little Thomas Beck was released down the right by Ospelt and won a corner, the first of the game. Beck himself took it, which was met by the blond head of Daniel Hasler. The big midfielder didn't make perfect contact but the ball flashed towards Mario Frick, unmarked on the six-yard line. With little time to react, Frick angled his body in an attempt to chest the ball over the line, but fortunately for the home side two defenders managed to scramble the ball away.

For the second time in the opening ten minutes, Liechtenstein had threatened the Austrian goal, and had already enjoyed more possession than they had in the whole of their last away game in Alicante. Gigon was having a fine game on the left, Frick and Beck were making nuisances of themselves up front and the Austrians were failing to exert any kind of dominance on the game. For the 13,000-strong Innsbruck crowd, this wasn't how it was meant to be. It was then I noticed something curious. When I first heard it, I thought it must have been my imagination. But no, it was true. Above the whistles of the home support I could definitely hear a chant of 'Liechtenstein (clap clap clap)!' My eyes swivelled to the other end of the pitch and there, behind Jehle's goal, was a knot of about a hundred people grouped around a large blue-and-red Liechtenstein flag. Not only had Liechtenstein brought some fans, the encouraging start to the game for the visitors had provoked them into audible support.

Having created the previous opening, three minutes later Thomas Beck himself was put through by Martin Stocklasa. Receiving the ball just inside the Austrian penalty area, Beck snatched at a shot which flashed only just over the crossbar. Manninger bawled out his defenders for allowing the youngster the room to swivel and shoot, but he was drowned out by the whistles of the disgusted home crowd. Barely a quarter of an hour played and Liechtenstein had now threatened to score three times. Austria, for all their talk of seeking an early goal, had managed merely a harmless cross and a wildly inaccurate effort from distance.

This was just what the visitors needed. With doubts already creeping into the minds of the home players, the reaction of the crowd was to the Liechtenstein players like suddenly having 13,000 fans of their own in the stadium. You could almost see the surge of confidence and belief permeate through the visiting players – incredibly, they were controlling the game.

It couldn't last, and any illusions that Liechtenstein might have been developing were put into perspective on sixteen minutes when Sturm Graz striker Ivica Vastic finished a neat, incisive passing move by shooting just inches wide of Jehle's left-hand post. Five minutes later a Herzog cross from the left evaded Jehle, and the rangy figure of Freddie Gigon just cleared the ball from danger as Vastic lurked ready to pounce.

But the lack of clear chances was visibly beginning to frustrate the home players as much as the crowd. For all their pre-match talk praising Liechtenstein's defensive capabilities, the Austrians surely could not have expected this multi-layered rearguard that snuffed out passes and hunted down poor first touches. Ospelt and Gigon patrolled the flanks, rarely allowing a cross to come over. Daniel Hasler was controlling the midfield, with Martin Stocklasa and Martin Telser snapping at the heels of their opponents. The sight of Werder Bremen's Andreas Herzog, Austria's most respected and experienced player winning his eighty-seventh cap, being harried into a misplaced pass into touch by the diminutive Telser showed that the Liechtensteiners were certainly not in awe of their hosts.

Anything that got through the midfield had then to face big Patrik Hefti and the lanky salesman Christof Ritter, with skipper Harry Zech lurking behind to mop up any stray attacks. And with Peter Jehle, one of Europe's most promising young goalkeepers, between the posts, Austria's prospects of topping their record score were already non-existent.

Liechtenstein's offside trap was better organised than it had been against Bosnia, a tactic that did little to improve the Austrians' temper. In addition, Gigon and Beck were making more frequent forays forward in an attempt to serve Mario Frick. The Austrians' frustration was demonstrated most effectively midway through the half when Hörtnagl clattered through the back of Telser in the middle of the field to earn the first yellow card of the evening.

It was nearly half an hour into the game before Austria really looked like scoring. A corner from the right flew across the six-yard box, only for Flögel to head over under pressure from Gigon, who was having a storming game. Thomas Beck then hared away down the right and crossed for Mario Frick, as the Liechtensteiner charged into the penalty area. Martin Hiden scrambled the ball away from Frick, and sent it forward for Edi Glieder on the right. Glieder ran into the area, where Harry Zech produced an excellent tackle to concede the corner. It was good stuff to watch, with Liechtenstein contributing to their most open game so far.

Shortly afterwards, Herzog lobbed a high ball to the corner of the penalty area. Vastic took it on his chest, swivelled and sent in a stinging volley that Jehle did well to beat away. At last the Austrians were starting to look like a team that wanted to go to the top of the group. Jehle was called into action again on thirty-six minutes when another corner was allowed to reach the far post, Michael Baur stabbed a low shot towards the near corner, which the young goalkeeper plunged to turn aside. A minute later, Herzog was finally allowed some space to manoeuvre. Receiving the ball wide on the right his run took him to the edge of the penalty area but, as danger loomed, he dragged his shot hopelessly wide of Jehle's right-hand post.

Austria were looking more threatening now, and Vastic should really have done better in the thirty-eighth minute when he shot across the face of the goal after a clever pass from Herzog. The home side forced a series of corners which woke the crowd a little, but if Liechtenstein could reach half-time at 0–0, the Austrians might start to become desperate and leave holes at the back for Frick to exploit.

Alas, it was not to be. After a neat exchange of passes between Herzog and Vastic, FC Tirol's Edi Glieder, played onside by Harry Zech, sent in a low shot from twelve yards that flew past Jehle's outstretched glove and into the bottom corner of the net. It was the first piece of real quality the Austrians had produced in the entire game. There was barely a minute left before half-time, and you could sense the relief all around the stadium. It was hard on the Liechtensteiners, who had defended superbly and looked more potent as an attacking threat than they had in the entire campaign so far. Despite being a goal down, however, the blue-shirted visitors trooped off the field knowing that if they played as well in the second half, there was still a chance of perhaps retrieving something.

Austria came out after the interval looking far more determined than when they had started the game. The comfortable stroll they had expected was turning into a considerable hike, and the increase in their application was tangible. Evidently Otto Baric had not minced his words over the half-time teapot. Roland Kirchler had a shot deflected over soon after the restart, and Herzog saw a searing, rising twenty-five-yard thunderbolt flash just wide of the post immediately afterwards. Hearts' Thomas Flögel was starting to cause real problems for Gigon on the Liechtenstein left and, having already been booked for a foul on Kitzbichler, the schoolteacher was having to watch his step.

Indeed, it was after Gigon had caught Flögel near the edge of the box that Andreas Herzog brought a fantastic diving save from Jehle, who flew to his right to tip away the Austrian captain's fiercely struck free kick. Having weathered the storm, Liechtenstein gradually began to look more comfortable. Gigon began to contain Flögel, and substitute Fabio D'Elia, a trainee mechanic from FC Schaan, began to look threatening after replacing Thomas Beck early in the half. The stocky eighteen-year-old was winning only his second cap, but unsettled the Austrian midfield as soon as he came on.

The Austrian onslaught gradually faded and Liechtenstein began to knock the ball around with confidence. With fifteen minutes remaining, however, the visitors were made to pay for their first real defensive lapse of the entire game. Herzog sent over a corner from the Austrian right. Nobody from either side attacked the ball and it bounced on the six-yard line. Thomas Flögel arrived at the far post and sent a looping header over Jehle and Harry Zech on the line to put the result beyond doubt. It was hard on Liechtenstein, but if one of the many blue-shirted players had taken the responsibility of hoofing the cross clear, they might have gone into the closing minutes still with a chance of causing an upset.

Instead, a revitalised Austria came forward again, with the crowd in fuller voice than they had been all evening. Glieder saw a stinging shot saved by Jehle at the second attempt, and shortly afterwards the Liechtenstein goalkeeper was again in action following some penalty-area pinball in the visitors' box. From a forest of legs somebody hoofed in a shot, it took a deflection, and it needed a fine reaction save from Jehle to prevent a third goal.

In the meantime, Mario Frick had been substituted. As Liechtenstein's star player trotted from the field, and handed the captain's armband to Daniel Hasler, I didn't know that it would be the last time I'd see him in a Liechtenstein shirt.

Austria had noticeably relaxed since the second goal, but there was still time for Herzog to send a scudding effort thumping into Jehle's chest and Hortnägl to sting his palms from distance in the dying minutes. The stadium was emptying fast, with the vacant shiny white seats glinting in the floodlights – once again, Liechtenstein had travelled abroad and the goal-fest expected by the home fans had not materialised. The final whistle sounded to widespread relief for everyone in the stadium losing 0–2 in Innsbruck was certainly a result of which Liechtenstein could be proud. The players shook hands with their opponents before going to the knot of ecstatic Liechtenstein fans behind the goal, lining up, joining hands and giving five emphatic cheers. It was wonderful to see some tangible support from the small travelling contingent. Indeed, the group of about a hundred fans making themselves heard among 13,000 Austrians was almost an allegory for the match itself. Little Liechtenstein may have been defeated again, but the reactions of the players and supporters demonstrated that this was more like a victory.

At the press conference, Ralf Loose was clearly the happier of the two coaches.

'We don't have players of the same quality as the larger countries,' he said, 'but with a little more bite, will-to-win and enthusiasm, maybe one of our three chances might have ended with a goal. To concede a goal so close to half-time made it difficult for us, but I was still hopeful that we could spring a surprise.'

Baric congratulated Loose on the way he organised his team before attempting to head off the looming torrent of criticism.

'The most important thing about this match was the victory, claiming the three points,' he said. 'Playing against such a defensively strong and disciplined opponent was difficult. I wasn't particularly concerned that it took us so long, because I knew that if we kept applying pressure, sooner or later we would break through and score.'

Liechtenstein's players were also pleased with the performance.

· 'At the beginning we had two good chances, which we couldn't convert,' said Mario Frick. 'Then at the worst possible psychological moment we went a goal behind just before half-time. All in all though, we can be pleased with the performance. Above all the defence showed further improvement.'

'Right at the beginning we missed two good scoring opportunities and a possible 2–0 lead. Who knows how the game would have panned out then?' asked Jürgen Ospelt. 'The Austrians looked a little under-prepared at the start of the match, but that was overturned by the goal just before half-time. The most positive aspect of the game was the performance of our defence.'

Peter Jehle, who once again stood out with a fine performance between the posts, also paid tribute to the defence. 'It was a good team performance, particularly defensively. I think we probably deserved to score a goal. We can certainly be happy with the scoreline: although Austria were missing a few players, that didn't necessarily weaken them as the new guys were keen to prove themselves.'

As I walked back to town through the drizzle, I realised I was coming around to how things work when you follow Liechtenstein. Curiously I felt proud. Proud to have witnessed the way that the tiny nation had thumbed its metaphorical nose at its larger neighbour. When Martin Telser harried Andreas Herzog into that misplaced pass, I'd wanted to cheer. As Mario Frick shaped to turn the ball past Manninger with his chest, I was starting to rise out of my seat without knowing it. And as I watched the team celebrate their latest fine performance with the travelling supporters, I felt both detached and a part of it at the same time. I felt a part of it because I'd come to support Liechtenstein. The players' individual styles and appearances were becoming familiar. The way Mario Frick held the cuffs of his shirt as he ran, Martin Telser's head-down, fists-pumping running, the slightly effeminate way that big Patrik Hefti held his arms when he ran. Freddie Gigon's tireless thunderous running up and down the left, and Harry Zech's deceptively quick stooping gait as he snuffed out another opposition attack. The pride I felt at the final whistle betrayed my growing affection for this plucky mixture of lower division professionals and part-timers.

Yet at the same time, as I watched the celebrations, I felt detached and alone. I wasn't a Liechtensteiner, and I never would be. The players and supporters were united by the red-and-blue bars of the national flag that billowed in the chill mountain breeze. The crown on the flag was the same crown that the players wore over their hearts. They may have lost again, but the team had struck another blow for their nation. It might just have been a football match for some, and one that had ended in another defeat, but the concept of defeat was taking on an extra dimension. After the previous matches, I'd been happy that Liechtenstein had acquitted themselves well but still disappointed at the loss. That night though, as I walked back to the centre of Innsbruck, I began to realise that success can be measured in other ways than goals and points. As Liechtenstein were beginning to demonstrate to me, it really isn't about the winning. It's about being there and giving your best. And when your best exceeds your expectations, that can be as good as a victory in itself.

The next morning, as the train left Innsbruck for its seven hour jaunt to Vienna, a middle-aged woman sat in the seat opposite me, pulled out a newspaper and opened it up. I looked at the front page, which contained a picture of Harry Zech and Patrik Hefti both converging on Ivica Vastic as he stretched to retain possession. Zech and Hefti both looked determined, eyes fixed on the ball. Vastic's features were set in a panicky grimace. It was a great picture. The headline read Only Two Goals Against The Football Dwarves!

I smiled wryly – this football team was becoming addictive.

Twelve

It was the end of May and Liechtenstein was sweltering. I had arrived two days ahead of the match with Israel, and for the first time since I had begun visiting the tiny country, it wasn't raining.

This time I wasn't staying at the Grünesholz. The saintly Martina had told me that they were full, but she'd find somewhere similar. Full, I wondered? On my two previous visits I'd been just about the only guest; how could they suddenly be full? I recalled that when I left the Grünesholz after the Bosnia game, there was a young girl whom I'd never seen before at reception. Martina had told me that the tourist board would make a hefty contribution to my accommodation costs but the girl didn't seem to know this, though I did my best to explain. In the end I paid my part of the arrangement and left for England. If I'd turned around would I have seen Anita chasing the girl out of the door with a broom, shouting about bankruptcy? Had she then taken her broom to the Tourist Office and chased the saintly Martina around the building? Had I completely misunderstood the situation and caused the biggest rumpus in Liechtenstein tourist history since ex-King Farouk's moonlight flit decades earlier?

Bravely, I decided not to mention it. Martina had arranged for me to stay further down the road from the Grünesholz, past McDonald's, at the family-run Gasthof Schäfle in Triesen.

It was similar to the Grünesholz in most respects – a bar and restaurant downstairs, rooms upstairs – but different in that I couldn't imagine the staff to have ever graced the pages of a gothic novel. I was joined on this trip by Matt the photographer, and we were greeted with a smile by the owners, a friendly couple called Burgmeier, and shown to not a room but an apartment, complete with kitchen.

Like a cat returning home and checking out its territory I went to do my usual circuit of Vaduz. Once again, despite only two months having elapsed since my previous visit, yet more new buildings were on their way up. I called in at the tourist shop to check that the piles of t-shirts and tea towels were just as I had left them. They were. The manager was engaged in conversation with the obligatory middle-aged overweight American couple.

'We've been married for thirty-five years,' they saw fit to announce, beaming around the shop in anticipation of a round of applause and people rushing up to them with flowers.

'My wife left after five minutes,' said the shop manager, a short man in his forties with dark hair, who had hit on the perfect manner to charm money out of middle-aged overweight American tourists. 'You couldn't blame her, because I was here in the shop seven days a week working until midnight.' Presumably he knew exactly when it was midnight thanks to the mass ululation from the dozens of cuckoo clocks of varying sizes that adorned the walls.

That evening I returned to the Crash Bar. It was a sultry night, and the tarmac oozed heat. Matt and I sat at the bar and had a couple of beers. After a while, I saw a familiar-looking figure approaching accompanied by a young woman. He wore a grey t-shirt, jeans and his hair was slicked down over his ears. They sat at a table outside and ordered beer.

'You know what,' I said to Matt, 'I think that's Mario Frick.' I wasn't sure, as this was the first time I had seen him not wearing full Liechtenstein kit. But he definitely looked familiar. The other difference was that in the bar, unlike when he played for the national team, when he needed service it arrived straight away. A couple more surreptitious glances, and I was certain.

'Why don't you go and speak to him?' said Matt, who had cut his own journalistic teeth on local newspapers in the Midlands, which frequently involved doorstepping the grieving relatives of murder victims.

I've never been one for aggressive reporting. I don't feel comfortable doorstepping and buttonholing. Or doorholing and buttonstepping for that matter. Hence I shrank back and shook my head. 'Nah,' I responded. 'Look, the guy's just out for a quiet drink with his girlfriend. The last thing he needs is some scruffy English bloke firing questions at him outside the pub. There's plenty of time, I'll arrange something with him when he'll be up for it.' Having finished their drinks, Mario and his companion strolled off into the evening.

The next morning I discovered that had 'Scoop' Connelly wandered over and spoken to the Liechtenstein star, he would have stumbled across the biggest controversy in the principality's football history.

We had had a disturbed night thanks to the tremendous thunderstorms rolling around the mountains: rain lashed down and the floor-length net curtains were captured in the lightning flashes as they billowed away from the open windows. Suddenly I was back at home months earlier watching Boris Karloff lumbering around the hills with bolts through his neck. At some point in the middle of the night, somebody had tried the door of the apartment. Not once, not twice, but three times. Eventually they gave up and as I heard their steps retreat up the corridor, I'm sure I heard the dragging of a clubfoot.

Walking into Vaduz the next morning, I picked up a copy of the *Vaterland* to see what the team news was, and discovered that the previous night's storms were nothing compared to the maelstrom raging through the national team that day. The coffee spilled from my open mouth as I read the front page of the sport section. Super Mario was involved in a huge club versus country row. It turned out that Frick's goals had helped his club Arezzo into the Serie C play-offs, with the opportunity to win promotion to Serie B. Arezzo had lost the first leg at home and were due to play the second leg on Sunday, the day after Liechtenstein played Israel. Arezzo and Frick had asked that the player be excused the Israel game, given the importance of the match to the Italian club.

Understandably, given the precedence of international over club football and the fact that Frick was Liechtenstein's key player, the LFV refused the request and the striker was instructed to report for the game as usual. He wasn't happy. The *Vaterland* carried a full-scale interview with Frick in which he made it clear where he would rather be. The interview began with a civilised enquiry after Frick's health.

Well, if you mean physically, then I'm fine. Otherwise, I'm absolutely bloody furious. I have not come voluntarily to Liechtenstein, because I wanted to play in the promotion play-off on Sunday for my employer AC Arezzo against Livorno and not in the international match against Israel. I am only here because the LFV threatened me with a ban if I didn't show up.

I wanted to play for Arezzo, but the federation called me up for the national team. I'd had long discussions with LFV president Otto Biedermann, and in my opinion I'd indicated early enough that I do not want to play for the national team against Israel because the play-off with Arezzo is important for my career. I have the unique possibility as a Liechtensteiner to perhaps play soon in Serie A – there will be scouts from several clubs at the game – and I want to use this opportunity to take a step closer to that. Therefore I absolutely wanted to remain in Arezzo.

There are people who are too egotistical in Liechtenstein, who want success at any price at the expense of other people's opinions and options. Therefore I am here in Liechtenstein, but it might be for the last time.

My point is that the LFV could have made an exception for this game and released me. Last year I decided to play for the LFV in the international match against Germany, when I would have preferred to play for my club FC Zurich. I am convinced, however, that if it was just down to Otto Biedermann, I would have been released. In my opinion, he was influenced by others.

I can say only that I will try on Saturday to play well. I hope that I do not hurt myself, because on Sunday morning I fly back to Italy and want to then play in the afternoon against Livorno.

It was raining again. Absolutely rodding it down. If the storms of the previous night had cleaned out the muggy air, this would have it squeaking in absolutely no time. Torrents of water swirled down the drains, and ghostly gusts of rain blew across the sky above the capital. I called in on Martina for a quick chat. As I dripped all over the carpet, I mentioned that I was thinking of going up to Malbun for lunch but was having second thoughts given the weather.

'Oh,' she said, 'you must go and see the Birdman!' 'Eh?' I replied. 'Norman, the Birdman at the Hotel Garni. He's married to an eagle, you know.'

A man married to an eagle. Now that had to be worth a bus ride up a mountain in the rain.

Malbun was as deserted as it had been when I'd popped in briefly with Sheila all those months before. The bus had heaved its way up the mountain, and Matt and I were so high now that the rain was below us. The ski lifts remained stationary, swinging gently above the grass.

We found the hotel and sat down at a long wooden bench while a trio of men sat at the far end laughing and talking over beer. We guessed that one of these must be Norman the Birdman. A poster in the window advertised a falconry display every day at three o'clock. It was now ten to, but there was little sign of action outside, where a three-row podium of seats had been set up and painted with birdy designs. Puddles had formed on the tiers. When one of the men passed our table on his way back from the bathroom, we asked if we could have a quick chat with Norman.

'Sure,' he said, sitting down and calling for three more beers. He certainly wasn't what I had expected from a birdman of the mountains. At the very least I thought he'd have long wild hair, perhaps with the odd piece of intertwined straw, and a beard to match. Norman was neatly shorn, clean shaven and dressed in t-shirt and jeans rather than an old overcoat and trousers tied at the waist with string. He was also looking at me expectantly.

'Not many people about,' I said cheerily, wondering how you begin a conversation with a man with an eagle for a spouse.

'It's always like this off season,' said Norman. 'Once the snows go there are only fourteen of us left living in Malbun. It does become a little like a ghost town. But at least it means we can relax a little as the winter is very, very busy here. We get a few visitors in the summer, because of the good weather. But at the moment it is not very busy because it's been raining all the time, and what can you do in the mountains when it's raining?

'When the weather's good we have a lot of walkers passing through, because up here is very good for walking. Down there,' he gestured in the direction of the valley, 'there's not much walking, it's too small, and too many houses. We have the biggest region of wild flowers in the whole area. There are about three-hundred-and-eighty different types, and there is even a flower police that watches for people picking flowers. If you take one . . .' He draws his forefinger across his neck and chuckles.

'I love it here. I was born in Malbun, but travelled around the world for eight years as a chef. I worked all over the place, but I was always going to come back here. For me it's the best place in the world. My family has always run this hotel, which was the first in the village. My great-grandfather opened it in 1908, so we've always been here. In fact from 1908 to 1996, we were the only hotel here. All the other buildings that are now hotels were just houses for cows, you know? It's funny, you see kids grow up here and when they get to sixteen or so they want to move away. Obviously there is not a great deal to do here in terms of discos and bars, so they go away, but almost without exception, when they want to have children they come back.

'When I travelled it was hard to explain that I came from Liechtenstein. I'd try to tell people that we are a country, but after a while I'd give up on that. I'd be talking to an American, say, and I'd tell him I'm from Liechtenstein and he'd say, "Oh yeah?" Then about an hour later he'd say to someone, "Hey, come and meet this Finnish guy!" and I'd think, oh, okay, from now on I'm from Finland. People don't understand. They think, what? A country of thirty thousand people? And it doesn't have an army? It doesn't even have its own money? That can't happen!'

As he hadn't made any move to introduce us to his wife (which he presumably did by donning a big leather glove and whistling), I asked about the birds.

'It's an interest I've had since I was a child. I've always tried to make friends with the birds. After all, my surname is Vögeli, which means "little bird". I am particularly interested by hawks and owls,' which he pronounced, endearingly, 'howks and earls', 'and you have to be careful because if you handle them wrong, that's it, they're gone. A hawk is strong enough to kill a rottweiler dog, and if you don't handle him right then you have many problems.

'Eagles are difficult to train too. With all birds of prey the hardest thing is to win their trust. With the eagle, first you must make, how do you say it in English, you must make a wedding with him. The eagle spends his whole life together with just one eagle. Only if one dies does the partner look for a new one. If I want to be friends with an eagle then I must make this relationship also. I have to go out in the forest at night and sleep where the eagle sleeps. You don't really know how long you have to do this – the eagle will decide and say that the wedding is here, now. It's sometimes a couple of days, often it can be two weeks, and that means being in the forest all that time.

'You have to go to the nest, where he lives in the mountains. Once he sees you near his home, you start to go out and familiarise yourself. You have to be very careful – if he gets used to seeing you dressed in black and one day you show up wearing yellow then he is scared and angry because it's unfamiliar. That can spoil everything. You gradually assimilate him, getting him used to people, children, cars, all that sort of thing.

'The first time you meet an eagle he is always angry with you; you're not a friend you are an enemy. But in time he sees that you are a good person and you fall in love, and that's when you can start training the bird. Eventually they fly with us. They will never be far from you, which means that you have made the wedding. They can fly a long way – we heard that one of my eagles was seen as far away as Bregenz in Switzerland, which is about one hour away with the car.

'An eagle doesn't forget anything; it will always remember the way back home. But if you upset him, he'll never forget it. If you do something he doesn't like it can be weeks before he'll forgive you. That makes him difficult to train.'

All three of our glasses were now empty, with lava lamp-like froth up the sides. Norman called for more beer, which arrived accompanied by shot glasses of a clear liquid. He wouldn't tell us what it was, but insisted that we drank it with him. 'Cheers,' he said, and the three of us threw the stuff into our mouths. It nearly blew my head off. Matt's startled expression suggested that he too was suffering from temporary decapitation. The drink had a similar effect to a blow to the back of the head with an Aga wrapped in a bedsheet. Not only had it caused me to forget where we were in the conversation, I was also struggling to remember my own name. Fortunately Matt managed to blurt out that international conversation kickstarter, 'Do you like football?'

I was still gagging and gurgling at this point, having swallowed what appeared to be a small quantity of petrol. Norman appeared unaffected, but suddenly I thought I understood him better. If I was knocking back this stuff on a regular basis, I'd probably end up thinking I was married to an eagle too.

'Do I like football?' he asks. 'Oh yes! I particularly like the English football! I am a fan of Manchester United.'

It just had to be so, really, didn't it? There we were, up a mountain in the heart of the Alps, in a ghost town whose population we had just temporarily boosted by a double-figure percentage, talking to a man who goes out into the forest and sleeps with eagles. And he's a flipping Manchester United fan.

'I don't really have the time any more, but I used to go at

least twice a year to England to see a soccer game. England has such wonderful stadiums, where you sit almost directly on the field without a track around the pitch. I was also a fan of Ruud Gullit, so I used to go to Chelsea when he was a player and a coach there. I also like the English game because they start running in the first minute and don't stop until the ninetieth. Germans, they are stupid, they only run when they must and then they stop. I like the English players. Kick and rush, that's what I like, not this psychological football, and players falling to the ground whenever they touch each other. I hate that. But I don't follow the Liechtenstein team because they are for us not interesting.'

Even in my meths-induced stupor this hit me between the eyes.

'Hnnngh?' I grunted.

'No, they play like, err . . .' He mimed flushing a toilet from an overhead cistern. 'The standard is no good. And the clubs play in the low leagues in Switzerland and that's nothing, you know? That's like baby soccer. It's fine for them, but anyone who wants to see good soccer wouldn't watch a game in Liechtenstein.

'There are a couple of good teams in Switzerland, like Grasshoppers, but you can also drive to Munich and Milan from here within two hours and see Champions' League matches, so why watch a team here? They also play on Sundays when there are big games on the television, so you watch them, not these stupid leagues.'

Yep, he's a Manchester United fan all right.

'People are more interested in the national team but they just follow it in the newspapers. I mean, it's interesting when Liechtenstein play a team like Portugal, but when people go to watch these games, they don't make a sound, they watch in silence. In England there is a lot of noise from the supporters. There are a lot of other nationalities in this area, so they come and support their teams and make lots of noise. When we played Portugal there were many Portuguese, who are fanatical supporters. The stadium was full mostly with Portuguese supporters. It's a problem for Liechtenstein. A Liechtensteiner isn't outgoing like you Englishmen, they only watch, they don't sing or cheer.

'Skiing is more the thing here, we have had skiers in the World Cup who have done very well – that is our national pride really. Now we have Marco Büchel, who won the silver medal in the World Championship skiing last year. It's one of the only ways in which we can beat the rest of the world. Team sports are not so good for us because we are only thirty thousand people. Germany has ninety million. So we can only do good in individual sports like skiing.'

Having attempted to get the feeling back in my throat by pouring beer down it, I was beginning to slur. This was as much to do with my tongue still being numb as the near-raw alcohol we had consumed. I managed to drawl something about the standard of living here, and how everyone seems happy.

'Yes, it's true. We're easy going, that's for sure. For example, in Switzerland, like in Germany, when you address someone you don't know, you use the formal "*Sie*" meaning "you". You don't get that in Liechtenstein. Here everyone just uses the informal "*du*", whether you know them or not. That's a good way of showing the difference. A Swiss guy is more reserved, and an Austrian guy is much more outgoing. He's a showman, he'll stand up on the table and sing. A Swiss guy won't do that, he'll just sit there quietly and drink his beer. A Liechtensteiner is probably somewhere in the middle.

'We do have a good standard of living. Here in Liechtenstein, you can be a really stupid guy and still make a good living, raise a family and be comfortable. Elsewhere, if you're stupid, then you're stupid, and that's that.'

My pickled brain was ringing bells somewhere. The bus back to Vaduz was arriving shortly, and if we missed it, it was an hour before the next one. Norman waved away all attempts to pay for the drinks and escorted us to the door. Which was handy, because after that shot of rocket fuel I was having trouble finding my own trousers.

We swayed to the bus stop waving to Norman. And to the hotel. And the ski-lift, the Peace Chapel and a cow up in the hills. Then, while we were waving to the bus stop, the bus arrived and so we waved at that too. Back in Vaduz we wondered what that clear liquid had been and where we might get a bottle of it. No one seemed to know, but when we told them that Norman the Birdman had given it to us, they just nodded knowingly.

That evening as we sat in Vanini trying in vain to recapture the feeling induced by Norman's spirit, and having thankfully stopped waving at everything, I hatched a plan for the following day. We would eat in three different countries: breakfast in Liechtenstein, lunch in Austria, dinner in Switzerland. It was a good plan. After a few drinks.

Thirteen

The first stage of our tri-national gastronomic odyssey was the most straightforward – breakfast in the Schäfle's surprisingly sumptuous dining room. From there it was to the offices of the LFV, where I had an appointment with Markus Schaper. Plenty had happened since our last conversation, so I was keen to hear the latest from the man on the inside.

I entered the office and was greeted by a slightly nervous young man with a prematurely receding hairline. My incredible luck with English speakers continued. 'Sorry,' said the man, who introduced himself as Ralf Wenaweser, 'today's my first day working here, so I'm not really sure how things happen.'

Nonetheless I was shown into Schaper's office which was somehow even tidier than it had been on my last visit. The needless clutter of the LFV pennant had been removed, so his desk was now entirely free of absolutely anything at all apart from a computer. No sign of any lucky gonks or Post-it notes: this was either the office of a man who was extraordinarily well organised or someone who had far too much time on his hands. When I put my dictaphone on the desk, I made sure that it was not at anything like a jaunty angle, but totally square on. I began by asking if he was happy with the way things were going in the qualification group.

'Yes, I can say we are happy. If we look at the points total, it's obviously not as good as the last campaign because that was our most successful and now we have no points; but if you're looking at the progress of the team then you just need to look at the results. We only lost 0–5 to Spain, one of the best teams in the world, and we have played 0–1 and 0–2 with Austria, so you can see that there is great progress. I have a wish that we would score a goal, and that's one thing we need to improve. The quality of our team means that we do not get many chances to score, but apart from that I am very happy.'

Given that the games with Austria and Bosnia in Vaduz had been attended mainly by supporters of the other team, I asked if he was as happy with the response of the people of Liechtenstein to the team's improvement.

'That's a good question,' he replied with a hint of a weary chuckle. 'At the home matches there are sometimes more fans from the away team than Liechtenstein. But you have to reflect on something here. I say always that we have the greatest stadium in world, because eleven per cent of the population of our country could fit into it. Now in England that would mean space for five-and-a-half-million people – I know football is popular there but I don't think even England versus Germany or England versus Brazil would attract that many people. The fact is that there are football fans in Switzerland and Austria nearby, and their national teams are on the television at the same time as Liechtenstein are playing, so we won't get the support from the local region either.

'But deep in my heart I have to say I am not happy with the supporters. I expect more from our fans because most of our players are amateurs doing their best against experienced professionals. To do their best they need support. It makes me wonder where the national pride is. Liechtensteiners should be proud that we can play in the World Cup and European Championships. Why don't they support the team? It's a whole different culture to other countries. To people here, playing football has always been a hobby, a pastime. Until now they haven't really considered that football could be a professional game, and a chance for good players to earn money. People still think of it as something you just do in your free time.

Combine that with the lack of national pride that surrounds the team, and that, I think, is why football here is not as popular as it should be.

'The draw for the qualifying rounds is very important. It's expensive to organise a match in Liechtenstein, and it's expensive for us to travel abroad. If you are playing teams where you're not going to attract many spectators, then it is not good in a financial way. Also, it's not so good for the players to play in an empty stadium. Football relies on the emotions of supporters, and I don't like to be in an emotionless stadium. It's not much of a motivation for our players either if there is nobody there.

'So the draw is important. Let's say, for example, we had a game with Iceland. Now you and I know that Iceland are a good team with professional players, many of whom play in England. But people here won't know that, won't come to the game and will look at the result and say, oh, look, Liechtenstein played Iceland and lost three nil, that's a terrible result.

'We have no fan culture here. We did have a fan club, but it died out. Now a few young fans are trying to start a new fan club, but it's not our culture. I hope that will change. I was pleasantly surprised at how many supporters were in Innsbruck – long may that continue.'

I mentioned to Schaper my conversation the previous day with Norman the Birdman who had scoffed at the very idea of watching football in Liechtenstein, especially when cities like Milan and Munich were so close at hand.

'But things are changing in that respect,' he said. 'Two or three years ago we had only one professional player, Mario Frick. Now we have five, six or seven professionals in the squad. Look at Peter Jehle: he's playing for Grasshoppers who won the Swiss championship this year, and will be playing in the Champions League. He's nineteen years old and for the last fifteen matches of the season was the number one goalkeeper at Grasshoppers. I suspect that next season he will be the number one goalkeeper at Switzerland's biggest club.

'Thomas Beck is also a professional at Grasshoppers; the Stocklasa brothers, Martin and Michael, are playing in the

Swiss second league. Our vice captain Daniel Hasler, who unfortunately has just sustained a bad injury, is also a professional. This was the aim of our youth programme, to train young players to strengthen the national team.

'Even though we're small, we're proving that if you're talented and prepared to work hard then the opportunities are there to play for your national team against the best in Europe. We don't have a big pool of talent to choose from, but we do our best. Peter Jehle five years ago was the third-choice goalkeeper for his youth team. But he realised that he had talent and a strong mind, so he changed his lifestyle to concentrate on improving his football. He changed his diet, and adopted a thoroughly professional outlook. The youth players also have a chance to play for the national team at youth level, against some of the best players of their age group in the world. That's the chance we have being a small country – there is greater opportunity. We don't have seven or eight goalkeepers at each age level, so three years ago Peter Jehle was the goalkeeper for the under-seventeens, the under-nineteens and the full national side all at once. There are tremendous opportunities here for young players, we just need to educate them to think of football as more than a hobby.

'Ralf Loose is the most important man on the technical side. His is the name that can be most associated with our success. When our youth programme began he was the youth coach, and since 1998 he has been the coach of the national team. He does an excellent job with great enthusiasm. He's the person who should get the most credit for our success on the field. The right man, in the right place, at the right time, in the right country.'

At this time, Sven Goran Eriksson was winning over the English press and supporters by turning a demoralised, tactically inept team into one actually capable of winning matches. The critics who lambasted the FA for appointing a foreigner had gone quiet, but there were still murmurings that a foreigner should not be in the job. I asked Schaper if there had been any opposition to Loose's appointment, which put a German in charge of the Liechtenstein national team.

'No. We don't have such problems here. First of all we don't have well-qualified coaches with the highest certificates and so on. But even when we do, there are other problems. When we started this programme, the Liechtenstein coaches weren't sure whether they should give up their jobs to concentrate on football. Also, because we are small, everyone knows everyone else, so everyone is a world championship level coach in their own mind. There wouldn't be as much respect for a Liechtenstein coach, as there would be for a well-known coach from abroad. We started with Dietriech Weise as our first full-time national coach. He's well-known for taking Germany's youth team to the World Championship. It was very important for our programme, because people thought, well, if Dietrich Weise is involved then it must be good.

'Ralf Loose was a well-known player at Borussia Dortmund and Fortuna Dusseldorf, and played under Dietrich Weise. Loose was coaching the German second-division team Mainz 05, and Weise advised us that he was the man to take over coaching the youth teams.'

Given the diminutive size of Liechtenstein, I wondered how the LFV is regarded in the corridors of European football power at UEFA.

'Well, I am on UEFA's marketing and new technologies committee, I am a UEFA referees' observer and also a UEFA delegate. I hope that UEFA is convinced about my knowledge and experience for these roles rather than it just being a token gesture to keep Liechtenstein happy. We have to improve football in general, and we need the best people in charge. There is so much money in football now, what with the Champions' League and everything, so we need capable people capable of producing the best footballing product. UEFA has begun looking for younger people, and I hope that UEFA looked at me and said, this Markus Schaper, he does a good job.

'At the moment I'm at the beginning of my UEFA career. As general secretary you have to go to a lot of UEFA meetings, and I'm involved in the licensing of the clubs so it's quite busy.

'Do international matches in Liechtenstein take a great deal of organisation? Oh, thank you for this question. People think that a small country will have only small things to organise. That's just not correct. Remember we have to obey the rules and regulations of FIFA and UEFA, which make no distinction between the small and large countries. They regard every country as a part of their product – football. Hence everyone has to obey the same rules and regulations. If there was crowd trouble in Liechtenstein, it would be regarded with the same shame as if it were in England or Holland, for example. I have to follow the same guidelines and logistical processes as a stadium that holds a hundred thousand people. If there are any crowd disturbances we would be punished as much as a big country – the size of the fine would be the same. Lazio, for example, can afford to pay this – we can't.

'FIFA's general secretary Michael Zen-Ruffinen came to our game with Bosnia, and I heard that he commented on how well organised everything was here. So if I don't hear anything negative, I think everything has been okay.'

Finally, I had to ask what was happening with Mario Frick. Schaper became tight-lipped.

'Mario Frick's club Arezzo is involved in promotion play-offs at the moment. Last Sunday they lost the first game 0–1, and now there is the second leg on Sunday, and we play tomorrow, Saturday. Mario Frick wanted to play for Arezzo rather than the national team, but there are clear regulations concerning this to protect the national teams. Otto Biedermann discussed the situation with him, and the fact is Mario Frick was here yesterday at our training camp and will play on Saturday. He says that scouts from Serie A clubs are intending to come and watch him play for Arezzo, and he thinks playing for Liechtenstein might ruin that chance. But if a club is really interested in Mario Frick, they'll come and watch him regardless of when or where he is playing. It doesn't depend on just one game. If a club is that interested in Mario Frick, we'll see who he plays for next season.'

Was it just me, or was the fur starting to fly a bit over the Frick situation?

From the LFV office, we walked back through Vaduz to take the bus to the Austrian border town of Feldkirch for the next step in our tri-national meal mission. To reach the old market town we had to pass through Liechtenstein's main border control. As we reached it, a guard climbed aboard the bus and checked everyone's documents. The upper arm of his jacket sleeve bore a Swiss flag.

Happily for Feldkirch, the sun was shining. This meant that we were able to see the town at its best. Impressive gothic buildings surrounded the market square, in the middle of which was a colourful flower market. Trays of yellows, reds and greens spilled across the cobbles, as Austrians strolled through the cloisters that lined the square.

Our hopes of dining on classic Austrian fayre were frustrated by not managing to find anything open. Instead we had to make do with an overcooked slice of pizza from a bakery, consumed alfresco amongst a bunch of skateboarding schoolchildren whilst fighting off wasps. Norman the Birdman had told us that a good chef needs to sample cuisine from around the world – we'd barely crossed the border into Austria and already failed to locate anything more adventurous than some doughy bread topped with a thin layer of crispy cheese and tomato.

The charm of this pleasant town failing to have been matched in the gastronomy department, we caught the bus back to Liechtenstein and on to Buchs, just the other side of the Swiss border. No passport checks this time, and no open restaurants either. Except one. An American place on the main street. So our mission to dine in three countries in one day had been successful, but our menu had consisted of overcooked pizza and McDonald's.

We cushioned our disappointment in the best way we knew how. We joined the regulars in the bar at the Schäfle, parking ourselves at one of the bar's long pine tables and called for beer. There was a wedding reception going on in the main room, and every time the doors opened, a wave of laughter, clapping and accordion music washed into the bar.

Frau Burgmeier came over for a chat. When she discovered why we were in Liechtenstein, she told us that the Schäfle was the clubhouse of FC Triesen. She produced a book, *Sixty Years of FC Triesen*, which contained numerous photographs of old football teams taken outside the back of the hotel. The team's first ground had been the guesthouse's back garden.

'My sons play football. My youngest has just joined FC Vaduz. He's eighteen and hopes one day to become a professional. He's a good friend of Peter Jehle, the goalkeeper of the national team. Ralf Loose has a high opinion of him. My eldest, Patrick, he plays for the national team, although he has been injured recently.'

She tells us that it is unusual for foreign visitors to stay at the Schäfle; most of the guests are friends and family. Looking around at the packed bar, I imagine that most of the income comes from down here rather than upstairs.

'We normally close for a couple of weeks at the height of the season and go on holiday. It's funny, wherever we go, we always bump into somebody from Liechtenstein. We were in Cape Town last year, went into a restaurant and bumped into a family we know from Vaduz.'

Back in the apartment I switched on CNN to find devastation. Ambulances screeched backwards and forwards, ferrying bloodstained passengers away from a scene of carnage. A suicide bomber had walked up to a nightclub queue on the seafront in Tel Aviv and blown himself to pieces. Nineteen people were dead, and around sixty more injured. The sleeping Israeli team would wake on the morning of the match to news that the worsening situation in the Middle East had spilled yet more of their compatriots' blood.

Fourteen

As matchday dawned Mario Frick was on his way back to Italy and Markus Schaper's confident assertion that Frick would be lining up for Liechtenstein against Israel had proved to be incorrect. Apparently Frick had been less than committed at training on Thursday night and Loose had told him that if he didn't buck his ideas up, he'd be on the bench. Frick's reaction was, apparently, not to Loose's liking and he told the player to go and get changed. Frick walked out of the Rheinpark Stadion and, possibly, out of Liechtenstein football for good. In the *Vaterland* the previous day, Loose had given his response to Frick's interview.

> I am a little surprised by his comments. We had already had a conversation about this before the Austria game. The decision was that he must come. For me it is also not as straightforward as to say that a player must come whether he wants to or not. I gave my opinion, but the decision was not mine. That was down to the executive committee.

Arezzo had asked whether Frick might just play half a game, in order that he be fresh enough to play for them the following day. Even that compromise seemed unlikely now.

This was not Loose's only selection headache. Daniel Hasler, the influential defensive midfielder, had sustained a cruciate ligament injury and would be out for several months. In addition the yellow card picked up by the experienced Patrik Hefti at Innsbruck meant that he would sit out the game through suspension. Patrick Burgmeier, the elder son of my hosts at the Schäfle, was also injured. With such key players missing, Frick's absence was the last thing that Loose needed.

During the day we killed time by visiting the new Kunstmuseum. As someone who is living proof of the old cliché 'I don't know much about art, but I know what I like', my reaction was mixed. There were some impressive names on loan from the Prince's collection that even I had heard of. Van Dyck, Rubens, Constable, Dali, Rembrandt, Klimt and Paul Klee all shared wallspace in the heart of Vaduz. There was also a lot of utter crap – in my expert opinion. A six-foot square piece of black material was set behind glass, with the word '*Mensch*' (people) written at its centre. At the foot of this was an old telephone in a bucket. In the next room a plastic relief map of Italy hung upside-down from the ceiling near a huge canvas scattered with tomato seeds, each of which had been circled and a number written next to it. There were apparently more than nine thousand tomato seeds, all of which had been circled and numbered. Which is surely the sign of someone with far too much time on their hands.

An underground, windowless room contained thirty old-fashioned school desks, each lit from above by a dim, bare bulb suspended from the ceiling. On each desk was a book of black-and-white photographs of the Auschwitz concentration camp. But these were not the more commonly photographed aspects of the camp that you might expect. The artist had instead used the functional parts: direction signs, close-ups of the symbols from the doors of the gents and ladies toilets, air-conditioning ducts. All this was set to a soundtrack of an old-fashioned typewriter coming from a speaker on the floor. If that was a statement of some kind it passed some distance over my head.

I could see what the curator was complaining about back in October. There really wasn't much room to do anything.

The building had a kind of reverse Tardis effect: it seemed smaller on the inside than it looked outside. Still, I thought, for an admission fee of £2.50 you can't complain. And there was not a chainsawed animal anywhere to be seen.

By the time the match came around in the evening, the drizzle had recommenced. Three quarters of an hour before kick-off, there was only one person walking up the road to the Rheinpark Stadion, and it was clear the match was some way short of a sell-out. There was a contingent of Israeli fans, not as numerous as the Austrians and Bosnians in previous games, but noisy nonetheless. Several Borussia Mönchengladbach banners were hung on the fence behind one of the goals, whilst a Star of David hung over the front of the *Gegentribune*.

Once the teams had entered the field, all wearing black armbands, it was announced that there would be a minute's silence in respect of the previous night's suicide bombing in Tel Aviv. Harry Zech, captain in place of Mario Frick, and Eyal Berkovic exchanged pennants and the players began to gather around the centre circle for the silence. The Faroese referee had other ideas, however. He summoned strikers Ronny Büchel and Frick's replacement in the side Hanno Hasler to the centre spot, and blew his whistle to start the game. Büchel tapped the ball to Hasler, who played it back to Jürgen Ospelt. Then the referee blew his whistle again, apparently to start the minute's silence. The players, assuming the match had started, took a few seconds to cotton on, whilst the Israeli fans, thinking the whistle was to signify the end of the silence, cheered wildly. After a few seconds, everyone realised that, possibly uniquely, the minute's silence would take place during the game.

Finally the whistle went again and the cheers recommenced with the ball at Ospelt's feet. The stadium announcer, who had been thrown by all this, then started to read out the Liechtenstein team. Meanwhile Israel had won possession of the ball, Oren Zitone had broken away down the left, and just as the announcer had reached Liechtenstein's number six, Haim Revivo slid in to turn Zitone's cross into the net. It was the second minute of the game. Or possibly the first, because no one really quite knew where the minute's silence fitted in. As the Israelis celebrated with their supporters, the Liechtenstein defence stood looking at each other. Jehle picked the ball out of the back of the net and punted it upfield, and Liechtenstein were a goal behind. It was almost an exact repeat of the match in Tel Aviv.

Büchel and Hasler renewed their acquaintance on the centre spot and must have considered asking the referee to start the game all over again. That was just a warm-up, right?

Four minutes later it got worse. Avi Nimny cut inside from the right and unleashed a rasping shot that had Jehle arching his back to palm the ball over the bar. From the corner, however, Everton's diminutive midfielder Idan Tal was allowed to rise unchallenged and head past Jehle for the second goal. Six minutes played, 2–0 down. The defence, minus the dependable Hefti and the influential Daniel Hasler, was a shambles. This was more like the old Liechtenstein, the porous Liechtenstein of yore, not Loose's well-drilled defensive unit that had restricted Austria, Bosnia and Spain to such modest victories.

Liechtenstein attempted to regroup in an effort to limit further damage. Jürgen Ospelt was trying to get things moving on the right, threading passes through and sending over a couple of crosses. Little Thomas Beck battled hard down the left, trying to make inroads into the Israel half, twisting and turning but not getting the run of the ball. The vulpine figure of skipper Harry Zech, the most capped player in the side, set about shoring up the defence, cutting out passes and using all his experience to ensure that no further sloppy goals would be given away. Indeed after a quarter of an hour Zech produced a fantastic double challenge to deny first Nimny and then Haim Revivo as both looked certain to score. With his floppy hair, stoop-shouldered gait and heavy footfall, Zech rarely looks anything less than thoroughly shagged out. When he arrives seemingly from nowhere to make a saving tackle, it's almost as if he's just put his pint on the bar and stubbed out a cigarette.

Freddie Gigon , the dark-haired, leggy wing-back, thundered up and down the left touchline attempting to trouble the Israeli back four, but with everyone back in defence Liechtenstein remained under the cosh. And in the eighteenth minute they conceded a third goal. Jehle had done well to beat away a stinging twenty-yard effort from Revivo, but the rebound fell to Nimny. As the young keeper scrambled to his feet, the Israeli midfielder unleashed a rising shot that Jehle somehow got his fingertips to, but couldn't prevent going in just under the crossbar.

It was a disastrous start for Liechtenstein. Even the most optimistic spectator could have seen this turning into a rout, and it even crossed my mind that we might see a repeat of the Macedonia massacre of five years previously. The Israeli fans opposite danced with delight as their white-shirted players huddled in a congratulatory knot for the third time in a quarter of an hour.

Liechtenstein needed to delve into their reserves of character and have a good rummage around. It would have been easy for their heads to drop at this point and risk losing by a score pushing double figures. But instead, led by the inspiring Zech who had played in the 1–11 against Macedonia and clearly didn't want to be part of a repeat, Liechtenstein knuckled down and fought for every ball in an attempt to salvage some pride. Admittedly Israel might have eased off a little after the third, but that should take nothing away from Liechtenstein's spirited response.

Three minutes after the third goal, Martin Stocklasa embarked on a surging run down the right, played a one two with Ronny Büchel but saw his cross pass harmlessly over the crossbar. At least, however, the ball had passed over the Israeli goalline for the first time in the match.

On the touchline Loose was as animated as I'd ever seen him. Dressed in a dark suit, he normally stood impassive on the corner of the technical area, one hand in his trouser pocket, calling out the occasional instruction. When Zitone couldn't control a Revivo pass into the area when unmarked, allowing Jehle to thunder from his goal to claim the ball, the tall Liechtenstein coach was absolutely doing his pieces at the defence for allowing the Israeli such space in the penalty area.

Liechtenstein attacks were virtually non-existent. Hanno

Hasler made his first significant contribution near the half-hour, dipping his shoulder and making for the goalline. His cross was low towards the penalty spot but there was no one in support.

This move aside, play was concentrated around the edge of the Liechtenstein area. Israel's short passing game was causing problems for the defence, and if it wasn't for the wily Zech hoovering up any potentially incisive passes, the damage could have been a lot worse. With half an hour gone, some beguiling passing between Revivo and Ofer Talkan produced an opening for Revivo but the Fenerbahce midfielder placed the ball just the wrong side of Jehle's right-hand post.

The Liechtenstein defence was battling hard. Gigon was playing well, fighting for everything and winning some fierce tackles and, on thirty-five minutes, had a hand in Liechtenstein's best opportunity for many games. After a flurry of passes, Gigon set up Martin Telser, who hit a skimming twenty-five-yard shot low towards Davidovitch's left post. He'd struck it well, but the Israeli keeper plunged full-length to his left and turned the ball around the post for a corner. It was a superb chance, certainly worthy of being Liechtenstein's first competitive goal for three years. Telser looked at the sky, his hands clasped on top of his head as he replayed the chance in his mind. Zech clapped his hands and urged his team on to greater things.

The opportunity also woke the spectators a little, drawing a combined bark of disappointment and a warm round of applause from the Liechtenstein fans in a disappointing crowd that barely topped 1,500. There was further encouragement three minutes later when Gigon curled a delicious cross in from the left. The ball moved tantalisingly away from the leaping Davidovitch, but the big Israeli keeper just managed to get a crucial fingertip to it as Hanno Hasler leapt, ready to pounce.

Liechtenstein were making a fight of it. Where twenty minutes earlier they had looked thoroughly demoralised and heading for an inevitable hammering, the home side were beginning to take the game to their opponents. As half-time approached

Ospelt was disappointed to see the ball spin harmlessly off his shin after Beck had found him. Ospelt then sent a rising twenty-five-yard effort over the crossbar as Liechtenstein enjoyed easily their best period of the match.

Israel had to cope with further sticky moments as the interval drew near, with Beck causing problems down the left. Two crosses were scrambled clear, the second falling to Telser on the edge of the area. Unfortunately his connection wasn't as clean as his earlier effort and the ball thudded into the advertising hoardings well wide of the goal.

As the teams left the field at half-time, Liechtenstein could be content with their response to the calamitous opening quarter-hour. Indeed they finished the half on top in terms of possession. It was practically impossible for them to hope to claim a point, but the way they had set themselves to play with such determination and passion despite the disastrous start would have been encouraging for Loose as he gave his half-time team talk.

During the interval Martin Frommelt, the LFV press officer, moved along the press box dishing out sandwiches to the journalists. I was sitting among the Israeli press. 'Would you like a sandwich?' Frommelt would ask. 'What's in them,' would come the reply. 'Ham or cheese.' Surprisingly, every Israeli journalist took the cheese option.

Liechtenstein began the second half in the same positive style in which they had finished the first. Indeed, had Hanno Hasler produced a better cross on fifty-three minutes than his mishit effort straight into the arms of Davidovitch, they might have had the first clear chance of the half.

Indeed so well were the home side playing that the hour mark had almost passed before Jehle was called into action again, diving to smother a Nimny header at the foot of the near post.

But the team was battling well. As the match passed the hour mark the perpetually-in-motion Thomas Beck, his socks around his ankles, cut in from the left and sent in a rising right-foot shot from twenty-five yards. It passed way over the crossbar, but it was further evidence of Liechtenstein's positive attitude. Clearly the home side was going to fight until the final whistle.

Shortly afterwards the stocky Hanno Hasler, bursting with enthusiasm and commitment after his late inclusion in the side, battled down the right and crossed low to the near post. There was a mix up between Davidovitch and David Ben Dayan, and the ball was hacked clear as Ronny Büchel threatened.

On sixty-eight minutes, Liechtenstein produced their slickest move of the match so far. Ospelt overlapped down the right and sent a dangerous cross towards the penalty spot. Büchel stretched every muscle in his neck, and flashed a header just wide of the post when in fact the incoming Fabio D'Elia might have been better placed. This was great stuff from Liechtenstein, and the fact that there were two players waiting to receive Ospelt's cross illustrated their positive approach to the game. It was all rather different from Frick's lonely pacing of the centre circle of previous games.

Israeli threats on the Liechtenstein goal were rare, but despite the home side's good performance, Israel knew that the match was won and were content to sit back and soak up the pressure.

But with six minutes left, something incredible happened.

Martin Stocklasa broke down the left and sent the ball into the area. Martin Telser picked it up near the penalty spot and slipped the ball forward to Fabio D'Elia who found himself with only the goalkeeper to beat. As Davidovitch bore down on him, D'Elia unselfishly rolled the ball right to the unmarked Matthias Beck who passed the ball into the empty net as the goalkeeper floundered helplessly on the turf.

Liechtenstein had scored.

Israeli defenders stood with their hands on their hips. The electronic scoreboard in the corner went dark for a fraction of a second and then flashed up 'LIE 1 ISR 3'. Liechtenstein had scored their first competitive goal in three years. Peter Jehle had tried four different hairstyles since the last time Liechtenstein had hit the back of the net in a competitive game, for goodness' sake. As delighted blue-shirted players converged on Beck, I was out of my seat. Pens and paper went flying as my chair flew backwards and I pummelled the air, screaming incoherently. Incredibly people in the stand in front of me were doing likewise. Arms that were normally folded demurely were punching at the sky, silhouetted against the floodlit pitch. Programmes were hurled skywards, and flags waved. The roar would have had the Prince rushing to the castle window and peeping through the curtains, fearing popular rebellion. Liechtenstein had scored.

Then I felt someone tugging at my sleeve. It was the Israeli journalist next to me. I looked down and saw him mouthing something at me. It appeared to be 'no goal, no goal'. He pointed towards the near corner of the field. I followed his gaze and my knees almost buckled under me. The linesman was standing on the touchline, one arm by his side, the other, the one with the flag, straight out in front of him. The referee was back-pedalling towards the centre circle, his right arm raised vertically. Offside. The goal wouldn't stand.

I felt crushed, absolutely crushed. My hands flew to my head and I wailed wordlessly at the injustice. To be honest, I couldn't even tell you if it was actually offside or not, although it was apparently a dubious decision. All I can see to this day, in my mind's eye, is that ball rolling slowly over the line and coming to a stop in the back of the net. It's in slow motion.

I remember nothing of the last few minutes of the game, and sat with my head in my hands, my mouth hanging open. But as the whistle sounded, even though they had again failed to score, Liechtenstein could be proud of the way they had played. Such a horrendous opening would have seen teams of greater talent but lesser resolve give way completely. Skipper Harry Zech, who had been outstanding at the back, had simply got the team to start all over again, to knuckle down and play to the best of their ability. They had gone beyond that. Admittedly Israel had not exactly gone hell for leather after going three up, but the home side had not only repelled the barrage, they'd actually threatened the Israeli goal on several occasions. And if it hadn't been for a Faroese linesman with a heart of basalt, they might even have pulled a goal back.

This time there was no press conference as such, rather a

'mixed zone' for journalists, players and coaches to mingle down by the tunnel. Predictably it was chaos. I saw Ernst in the corner scribbling frantically as Loose gave him his version of the match. Happy Liechtenstein players emerged, showered and fragrant, their hair wet and shining and their bags over their shoulders. As the sullen Israelis moved between them on their way to the coach, you'd have been forgiven for misidentifying the winners and losers. Standing by the tunnel was Ralf Wenaweser, the LFV's new recruit we had met at the office the previous day. He looked relieved that it was over. Gesturing at the melee in front of us, I mentioned that Matt and I were going for a beer if he fancied one. He certainly did fancy one, he said, and even though he was supposed to be going to the official dinner with the Israeli officials, he'd meet us in Vanini's. As we made our way out of the stadium I spotted the grey-topped figure of Ernst Hasler bustling towards the car park.

'Ernst, we're going for a beer,' I called out.

'I have to go to my newspaper and set up the pages,' the greatest sports writer in the world called over his shoulder, his tie flapping in the same direction. 'I'll be in the Schwefel in about an hour.' He disappeared into the darkness.

Ralf joined us at the bar after a few minutes looking thoroughly worn out. He was certainly in at the deep end, starting a job at the national association the day before a World Cup qualifying fixture. Ralf, it turned out, had been the national squash champion of Liechtenstein on five occasions. Wherever you go in this country, you'll find a sportsman or woman with a claim to greatness. In the Schäfle a couple of nights earlier, Frau Burgmeier had pointed out a man of late middle age squinting myopically in an attempt to locate his beer on the table in front of him. 'He used to be the Liechtenstein rifle-shooting champion,' she said.

After a while I mentioned that we were heading down to the Schwefel to meet Ernst. 'Oh, he's quite a character,' said Ralf. 'He has a rare talent for a journalist. He can fill two pages and not actually say anything at all. I phoned him once from a tournament. I was sniffing a little, and after I gave him the news I apologised for my sniffing, saying that I had a little cold. When I got home, someone showed me the *Vaterland*, which had as a big headline Wenaweser Has A Little Cold.'

When we reached the Schwefel, the large upstairs bar between Vaduz and Triesen where Claudia had unburdened herself of her doomed love affair, it was busy. There was a deejay in the corner, and at a table nearby sat Ernst, Romed and an Ernst doppelganger who had to be his twin brother. They sucked on tall glasses of beer, thumped the table in time to the music and sang along.

'Hey,' said Ralf, 'there are some of the players.' Standing nearby laughing and drinking were Jürgen Ospelt, Hanno Hasler, captain Harry Zech and the suspended stopper Patrik Hefti. Ralf went over and explained that I was travelling from England for every game, and four jaws dropped towards the floor. 'Were you in Spain?' asked Zech. 'Yes,' I nodded. 'And Innsbruck?' said Ospelt. 'Mm-hmm,' I replied with a growing sensation that I was a really, really sad bastard.

Patrik Hefti came over, towering above me. A huge slab of a man, with his chiselled features and swept-back hair, he put me in mind of Dennis Bergkamp on steroids. 'Where will I be able to buy this book?' he asked.

Patrik was open and friendly. He spoke slowly in a booming voice with a hint of an American accent, a relic from the three years he had spent as a professional in the USA in the mid-nineties. In fact, thinking about it, he sounded a little like Arnold Schwarzenegger.

'I'm just going to find my drink. I'll be back,' he said, as if to prove my point.

Patrik had played for Greensboro Dynamos, who won the last US league title in 1994, the year before Major League Soccer began. He'd met his wife there, and she had returned with him to Liechtenstein. Although he was now playing in a lower division with Schaan he hoped, he told me, to rejoin FC Vaduz the following season. Vaduz had just won promotion to the Swiss second division, the first time that any Liechtenstein club had risen so high. The only problem was that he was studying for banking exams, which were taking up a lot of his time. Vaduz train more often than Schaan, and the lighter football work-load suited his banking career.

Harry came over dressed in jeans and a checked shirt with the sleeves rolled to the elbow. 'Well played,' I said. 'I thought you were the Man of the Match. 'Sank yew,' he replied, pleasantly surprised. I tried to shout a few comments about the game into his ear over the music, but the nods and smiles I received in response demonstrated that he didn't have a clue what I was on about. He told me that after the qualification round was finished, he and a few of the players were coming to London for a weekend. 'Great,' I said, 'you'll have to let me know and we can meet for a beer.'

'Yes,' he replied, looking from side to side conspiratorially, 'but do you know For Your Eyes Only?'

'Um, yes,' I replied, a little flummoxed. 'I've seen it a couple of times. That was when Roger Moore was really starting to look too old for a secret agent.'

A flicker of confusion skittered across Harry's brow.

'Er, the James Bond film?' I said, raising an eyebrow.

'No, no,' he said. 'For Your Eyes Only, it is a striptease club in London.'

Clang went the penny as it dropped. 'Oh, right,' I said with an embarrassed chuckle and admitted that no, I'm afraid I didn't know For Your Eyes Only. Harry wandered off, disappointed that he had not found a knowledgeable guide to London's sleazier nightspots.

'How do you feel about marking Raul in the next match?' I asked Jürgen Ospelt. He shrugged, took a swig from his bottle of beer and said 'Okay. I mean, I've marked Figo before. In Spain I marked Mendieta and it was a piece of piss. He did score two goals though.'

Harry came over and joshed with Ospelt about him appearing at left back during the game when he was supposed to be on the right. A five-minute discussion in dialect ensued, complete with gestures and, eventually, the use of empty bottles and glasses on a nearby table to represent players.

As I watched this post-match post-mortem, I reflected on how a similar scenario would be received in England. Imagine if England had lost 0–3 at home to Israel, and immediately afterwards Messrs Beckham, Owen, Ferdinand and Neville were seen in London's premier nightspot throwing beer down their throats and generally having a good time. The papers would go ballistic.

After a couple of hours of shouted drunken conversations with squiffy international footballers, Ernst staggered over to tell me the goal was never offside, never in a million years. A familiar record came on, a track by an Elvis impersonator from Belfast who sings cover versions of songs by other dead artists. Two friends of mine played in his backing band. As the strains of Elvis singing 'Twentieth Century Boy' thundered from the speakers, I saw Ernst's brother stand up, raise both hands in the air and headbang along to the music.

'I know a couple of the blokes playing on this record,' I said. Ernst's eyes widened, and the news went around the bar like a bushfire. I felt almost like a celebrity. The next record came on. 'Ohhhh,' said Ernst, 'I requested this one. "Cry Baby" by Janis Joplin.'

As the record started he told me once again that the goal was never offside, never in a million years. As he was telling me this, he suddenly screwed up his eyes, bared his teeth and bellowed, 'CRRRYYYYYYYY, CRRRYYYYYYYY BABY!!!!!' along with the music, announced that he loved this song, raised his arms above his head, began headbanging and moved off between the tables to join his twin brother who was still doing the same thing.

The rest of the evening is a bit of a blur. I can remember telling the players that I'd be back for National Day in August, and them telling me that they had a friendly match away at the Austrian club Austria Lustenau the night before. I have a vague recollection of thumping the table and telling them that I would bloody well be there because they were not only the best bloody football team in the world, they were also the best bloody bunch of bloody blokes in the bloody world too. I can remember Ernst clapping me on the shoulder, looking me in the eye and crooning 'Let It Be'.

Then there is a fleeting memory of the police arriving and

shutting off the disco in mid-song and telling everyone to drink up and leave.

Then there are a lot of hugs, back slaps, firm, lengthy handshakes and promises of accommodation and lifelong friendship in London and Vaduz. And after that everything really does go blank.

'. . . let it beeeee . . .'

Fifteen

Whenever I arrived back in London after Liechtenstein matches, the principality soon seemed a long way away. Not least in terms of transport: after the Bosnia game, for example, I landed at Heathrow to find the tube station locked shut by a strike. It took me longer to get from one side of London to the other than it did to get from Vaduz to London. I also used to return having become accustomed to Liechtenstein's friendly ambience. I'd arrive in England and smile at people as I passed. They, of course, would regard me as a dangerous lunatic. Walking the streets of London was the biggest contrast – noisy, dirty, crowded and dusty, there was little chance of bumping into a cow in Tottenham Court Road.

Returning after the Israel game was even stranger than usual. That last night in the Schwefel took on an almost dreamlike ambience, which might have been due to the effects of the Calandabraü lager, but was equally to do with suddenly meeting and drinking with the players I'd been following for six months. As I returned to the disorganised mess that is my office, I began to wonder whether it had all actually happened. Had I really been getting drunk with international footballers barely an hour after a World Cup match? Were they really asking my advice on London's premier strip joints?

As the days passed I began to convince myself that it had been my imagination after all. Until, that is, an e-mail popped into my inbox about a week after the match. It came from the LGT Bank in Liechtenstein, and was titled 'Liechtenstein!!'

> Hello Charlie,
>   I hope you still remember me, we met briefly at Schwefel bar after our game against Israel. You told me about the book you are writing. It is very interesting that you are going to publish a book about our team. If you need any more information just send me an e-mail. When will you be back in Liechtenstein? I'm sure you are going to come for the game against Spain. That will be a nice experience for all of us to have Raul, Mendieta and all the other stars here in Liechtenstein.
>   Take care and best regards,
>   Patrik Hefti

So, I hadn't imagined it after all. Indeed I now remembered dishing out business cards to just about everybody in the bar. I dashed off a reply telling Patrik that I would be returning for National Day and the friendly at Austria Lustenau. He replied:

> Hello Charlie,
>   That's great that you are going to come to Liechtenstein on August the 15th. It's always a nice occasion and there will be many people in our little country. I didn't sign with Vaduz because I'm going to start at a new banking school in St Gallen this October. It was a difficult decision to make, but I will be 32 in November and I think my banking career is more important than football. I even spoke to Loose about retiring from the national team next year, but that decision doesn't have to be made right now. I'll be playing next week against Lustenau and for sure against Spain in September. We can meet each other when you're in town, just give me a call.
>   Best regards,
>   Patrik

I knew that National Day on 15 August might hold the key to my curiosity about what gives Liechtenstein its nationality. If any day was going to demonstrate what Liechtenstein was all about, this had to be it. I e-mailed the saintly Martina and asked if there was a programme of events. There was, she replied. I opened the attachment to find a timetable in English. '0930,' it began, 'mess on the field outside the castle.' A quaint but curious tradition, I assumed. After that there were speeches from the Prince and members of the government, before everyone moved into the castle grounds to be served beer and snacks by the Prince and his wife. In the evening there was to be a huge street party capped by a firework display.

I would arrive a week in advance of National Day because FC Vaduz were playing in the qualifying round of the UEFA Cup, a berth earned by narrowly edging FC Ruggell in the Liechtenstein Cup final by nine goals to nil. Their opponents would be Varteks Varazdin from Croatia. So, on the morning of the match, 9 August, I presented myself at Swissair's Heathrow check-in desk at the crack of dawn. 'Ah, I see you've been upgraded,' said the clerk. Now I had heard about airline reps scanning check-in queues for people they deemed suitable for upgrade, and had never experienced this privilege before. I looked down at my scuffed trainers, baggy green combat trousers that were frayed at the back where they were too long for me, my grey casual jacket with the blob of black grease on the forearm courtesy of a train door, stroked my unshaven chin and said, 'Um . . . why?'

The check-in clerk had no idea, certainly now that she'd seen me. But I wasn't complaining and snatched my boarding pass from her hand before she could change her mind and flounced off to the business lounge. Boarding the plane I made a big show of walking through the door and plonking myself on to the first seat on the left. None of that tedious queuing in the aisle, craning your neck to see someone removing several layers of clothing, heaving their hand luggage into the rack, remembering that their newspaper was in their bag, unzipping and rummaging through it for a full minute and then remembering that their newspaper is actually on the seat where they'd put it.

When I said I plonked myself on to the seat, that wasn't exactly true. It was more a case of landing somewhere in it. It was huge, one of those seats that converts into a full-length single bed, all plush leather and enough leg room for the Harlem Globetrotters basketball team to be placed end to end. To the right was a console of buttons, all of which I was dying to press but couldn't, because first I had to nonchalantly read a book while the economy class plebs filed past, in order to give the false impression that I do this all the time.

Once everyone had boarded, and after I had instructed a stewardess to pull the curtain that separated business class from economy so I might not catch tuberculosis or nits from the riff-raff, I set about playing with the buttons.

Depressing one I heard a whirring noise but at first couldn't work out where it was coming from. Then I noticed movement in front of me. Gliding towards me with the effortless grace of Metal Mickey was a leather pouffe, or 'Ottoman' as the button called it. Unfortunately, blessed as I am with legs whose length would have prevented Eric Morecambe from ever lampooning Ernie Wise's, it stopped too far away for me to reach. This added another dimension to the upgrade mystery – not only was I a scruff, but a shortarse too. I was careful, however, not to try too many buttons in case I was suddenly catapulted into the wall in front, like Penry the mild-mannered janitor in the opening titles of Hong Kong Phooey.

As breakfast approached I took a chance and pressed a button with a picture of a table on it. From my right a huge mass of hydraulics sprung into action and a giant plastic table unfurled itself from a hidden cavity and opened out across my lap. It was so big I almost felt obliged to challenge my neighbour to a game of table-tennis. Typically though, my seat had a defect. As breakfast was served, the headrest suddenly slipped downwards to shoulder blade level, almost pitching me face-first into my scrambled eggs. This happened several more times during the flight, and I'm sure the man to my left was convinced that I was attempting to perform some kind of solo Heimlich manoeuvre to dislodge an errant tomato skin.

After another relaxing train ride, I arrived at the Schäfle to be greeted like an old friend. Herr Burgmeier hailed me as I entered, and the waitress gave me my key and said with a smile, 'I think you know where to go.' For the first time I felt like I actually belonged here.

I had arrived in good time to reach the stadium and, just for a change, as I set off for the Rheinpark Stadion it chucked it down. FC Vaduz had raced to the top of the Swiss second division, their first season at that level and the pinnacle of achievement for Liechtenstein's seven clubs. This was the strongest Liechtenstein club side ever assembled, and the UEFA Cup would provide an important test of their progress.

Liechtenstein clubs do not have a good record in European competition. Of the twenty-two UEFA and Cup-Winners Cup matches played prior to this Liechtenstein's only win had been when FC Balzers overcame Albania's Albpetrol Patosi 3–1 in 1993–94. FC Vaduz had their moment of cup glory in the 1996–97 Cup-Winners Cup. Having overcome Latvia's Universitate Riga on penalties after two 1–1 draws, Vaduz equalising in the last minute of the second leg, the Liechtensteiners were drawn against the then holders Paris St Germain. In the first leg in Vaduz the Parisians, who fielded players of the calibre of Bruno N'Gotty, Patrick Mboma and the Brazilian Edmundo, won 4–0, whilst in the return Vaduz, with Patrik Hefti and Harry Zech in the side, battled bravely in the Parc Des Princes to go down 3–0.

The current Vaduz squad contained four Liechtenstein internationals: Christof Ritter, Thomas Beck, Martin Telser and Andreas Gerster. Franz Burgmeier, the younger son of my hosts at the Schäfle, had made an explosive contribution to his last two league games, coming on as a substitute ten minutes from the end and scoring twice on both occasions. Vaduz officials were already mooting his inclusion in the full national side. Varteks would be tough opponents, however. The former textile-works team from Varazdin led the Croat league ahead of big names such as Dinamo Zagreb and Hajduk Split. They were clear favourites to go through.

The rain stopped as the teams emerged on to the field, Vaduz in their change colours of all red, and Varteks in a snazzy light blue-and-white combination. Polite applause from a healthily sized crowd of around 1,500 welcomed the teams on to the field. Vaduz began well and passed the ball around with confidence. Lithuanian midfielder Vaidotas Slekys, representing one of the seven different nationalities in the Vaduz squad, produced the first clear effort of the match when he almost knocked Varteks' keeper Danjel Maderic off his feet with a fierce drive from the edge of the area. When Marius Zarn was allowed a free header on twelve minutes, you could sense the fragility of the Varteks defence. Their marking was non-existent, and Vaduz began to attack with increasing confidence. When André Niederhäuser headed wide when well-placed the crowd began to sense that Vaduz might not be on their way to the expected defeat, and began to clap rhythmically like an athletics crowd responding to a long jumper at the start of their run.

Three minutes before the break, Niederhäuser was left untended again, and when Madaric dropped the ball the defender was able to nod it into the net without a Varteks player near him. The crowd erupted; it was nothing more than Vaduz deserved. Five minutes after half-time, however, the visitors got back into the match. When Varteks' mightily impressive midfielder Milenko Mumlek crossed from the left, the Vaduz defence just stood and watched as Sasa Bjelanovic headed the ball past Javier Crespo and into the net.

Vaduz bounced straight back, however, thanks to yet more slack marking. Martin Telser crossed from the right, and Vaduz's burly striker Moreno Merenda thumped a header under the diving Madaric to restore Vaduz's lead.

The crowd came to life as the rain again began to fall out of the darkening sky, and the home side responded by turning on the style. Slekys skipped through two challenges just before the hour and curled a forty-yard ball with the outside of his boot that just evaded Telser's lunge. Varteks were beginning to panic, but on sixty-eight minutes they produced their best move of the match when Devis Mukaj beat two challenges on the left and placed an exquisite cross on to the forehead of Veldin Karic. The striker's header was athletically plucked from the air by the diving Crespo in a wonderful piece of football.

Shortly afterwards, both FC Vaduz and the national team suffered a major blow as Christof Ritter was stretchered off with what later turned out to be a broken ankle, an injury that would keep him out of the rest of the World Cup campaign. With a quarter of an hour remaining, the lumbering, barrel-chested Merenda found himself through one on one with the goalkeeper, slipped the ball past him and notched his second to put the home side 3–1 up. The Liechtenstein crowd went mad – Vaduz surely were set for their first ever win in European competition, and certain now to register the first victory by a Liechtenstein side in Europe for nearly a decade.

Varteks responded by bringing off Mumlek, easily their most creative midfielder. As I suspected, rather than responding to Mumlek's subtle promptings they would now resort to humping the ball forward in an effort to salvage the game. With five minutes remaining Varteks pulled a goal back. A cross from the right wing was met at the near post by the head of Bjelanovic, who offered a glimmer of hope to the visitors. Two minutes later, disaster struck. Another cross from the right was met once again by the head of Bjelanovic. The striker had an all-headed hat-trick and Varteks were level. Their supporters shrieked and yelled with disbelief, leaping around the *Gegentribune* as if a swarm of hornets had suddenly descended on them.

In the final minute, Bjelanovic was presented with his easiest chance of the game but somehow managed to heave a shot over the crossbar from six yards. From being dead and buried five minutes earlier, Varteks were now ruing a miss that could have won them the game. At the final whistle the Vaduz players fell to the ground, shell-shocked. Player-coach Uwe Wegmann pursed his lips with disappointment afterwards, but rated his side's chances in the return leg as an optimistic fifty-fifty. However, having conceded three away goals it would be a difficult task, particularly without Christof Ritter. Indeed in the return leg a fortnight later, Varteks would hammer the Liechtesteiners 6–1 and go on to beat Aston Villa over two legs in the next round.

In the lounge afterwards I bumped into Ralf. I hadn't heard from him since that night in the Schwefel, and wondered whether he had blundered by ducking the official dinner and going to the pub with Matt and I. I had in fact worried that Markus Schaper, a bit of a stickler for bureaucracy, had given him the heave-ho as a result of the empty place at the table, but Ralf laughed and said no, he was still in a job. He'd had his wrists slapped, but nothing more. As Christof Ritter limped into the room on crutches and the Varteks coach vroomed away from outside the window and into the night, Ralf said, 'I need a beer. Let's go to Switzerland.' So we went abroad for a quick pint before bedtime.

The following day I woke early and pulled open the curtains. Outside the window was a small boy in swimming trunks peering through the glass. Neither of us was particularly fazed by this, and the boy calmly walked off back to his room.

I had no time for surreal balcony encounters, however, for I had an important date in my diary. Today was the *Malbuner Eselfest* – an annual donkey festival up in the mountains, featuring races and a donkey beauty-contest. I was looking forward to the bikini round. I had managed to persuade Ralf to accompany me, and we were soon driving up through the mountains in the late summer sunshine. Fast. Very fast. Very fast around some very tight bends with sheer drops below them. We arrived in Malbun, where I unpicked my hands from the underside of the seat finger by finger.

The pure mountain air was filled with the honking and braying of donkeys. There were horseboxes wherever you looked, and men, women and children of various shapes and sizes wearing numbered gymkhana bibs wandered around. In front of the Peace Chapel was a large fenced-off area where a substantial crowd had gathered. This was the arena around which the owners would lead their donkeys. There were some taxing obstacles to overcome. Once through the starting gate there was a small fence to step over. Then a bridge, then a see-saw arrangement where the donkey had to walk up one side until its momentum pushed the other end of the see-saw down and it could continue down the other side. After that was a chicane of two parallel panels of fencing side by side, then a doorway affair draped in polythene, a low trough of water, and finally a trailer to pass through, in the back door and out of the side.

Unsurprisingly for Liechtenstein, the event was meticulously organised. There was one of those digital clocks you see on top of cars at marathons suspended from a fence and a small PA system relaying the competitors' details. There were even advertising hoardings, although I couldn't really see how the Silberhorn Fitness Centre saw a donkey race as an ideal opportunity for product association. Nevertheless I went on to spend one of the most enjoyable sporting afternoons of my life.

Now this was entertainment. It topped even the German version of *The Weakest Link*, which was presented by a woman exactly like Anne Robinson in every way except that she was actually scary. You felt that, unlike Robinson, she actually knew the answers and would shoot you in the leg for every incorrect one given. One of the contestants was the magnificently named Ufuk, whose appellation I had found myself coining many times as I clung on for dear life while Ralf negotiated the twisting bends of the road to Malbun at breakneck speeds.

One by one the donkeys were led around the course. There were more than sixty competitors, and it made for entertaining viewing. Small children led enormous donkeys, great big burly adults led tiny mules, and each had their own tactics. The afternoon was filled with a mixture of tearful children trying to coax their charges over the first obstacle, pulling the halter in vain, and stocky grown-ups practically able to carry their charges around the course. I noted a number of tactics used to persuade reluctant animals into movement. There was good old-fashioned brute force, where the owner would heave on the halter like a tug-of-war competitor. Others would go around the back and give the beast an almighty open-handed slap on the arse. Another method was to put your shoulder against the donkey's rear and shove.

A more subtle approach was to stand on the other side of the obstacle and produce a treat from an anorak pocket with which to tempt the animal across. These ranged from the humble carrot, right the way up to a bar of chocolate. The crowd, which stood three deep around the course, lapped it up. There was, apparently, nothing funnier than the sight of a pre-teen girl with tears of embarrassment running down her cheeks trying hopelessly to pull her donkey over the water jump. When she fell on her backside into the water, the crowd as one doubled up with laughter. A fat man near me laughed so hard that the upper plate of his false teeth shot out of his mouth and bounced across the course.

Almost as funny was the small girl whose donkey was followed by a foal, attempting to drink its mother's milk as it negotiated the course. The girl's tears were welling up as she pleaded with the younger donkey to just piss off, but the fat man's tears were already streaming down his face as he spat bits of grass from between his dentures.

Entertaining though it was, you had to feel sorry for the kids. They'd spent ages practising and grooming, investing all their spare love and attention in a beast that would blatantly and ungratefully show them up in front of hundreds of people.

About a quarter of the way through the competition a middle-aged man approached the start, leading a small grey donkey. A murmur went through the crowd. This was one of the favourites. Now most of the speedier donkeys had completed the course in two or three minutes, but this guy looked keen and able enough to come in well under that. The crowd went silent. The word had got around and people were running out of the beer tent and nearby hotels to watch. The man adopted his ready pose. The atmosphere was like the Olympic hundred metres final just after the starter had said 'on your marks'. The only sound was the breeze rustling the long grass when, after what seemed like an age, the starter honked his claxon and the man sprinted away. As the slack on the halter was taken up, his donkey, which had just found a nice tuft of grass to chew on by the starting gate, was yanked into action. The man had worked up such a head of steam by this point that the poor animal didn't have much choice but to follow, and galloped in his wake. Over the fence they went, and across the bridge they flew, barely touching the wooden slats. The see-saw presented no problems, and the crowd began to urge the duo onwards. They scampered through the chicane, through the doorway draped with plastic and were across the water jump before the beast even knew it was there. Into the trailer they went and out the other side, sprinting across the finish line to a massive ovation. Hats were thrown in the air, and the fat man near me was clapping and cheering wildly, pausing only to thumb his denture plate more firmly into the roof of his mouth.

The dynamic duo had been extraordinarily fast. The digital clock showed an incredible twenty-five seconds, well over a minute and a half faster than the previous leader. I could do little else but stand agape at an extraordinary sporting perform- ance. I knew how people who had been in Mexico for Bob Beamon's record 1968 long jump, or in Sarajevo for Torvill and Dean's perfect 'Bolero', must have felt. I had witnessed a truly great sporting occasion. I wanted to go over to the man, grab him squarely by the shoulders, and tell him, 'Look, it's just a bit of fun, don't take it so seriously, you humourless twonk.'

As the hubbub subsided, the single bell in the tower of the whitewashed Peace Chapel began to ring. There was a commo- tion at the bottom of the field and an open-topped sports car purred up the lane; a bride in full wedding dress sat in the back seat looking, it must be said, a little bit sheepish. Presumably when the happy couple had booked the chapel, they'd envisaged a peaceful summer day in an idyllically quiet village, without an audience of several hundred people eating bratwurst, without a soundtrack of braying and honking, and certainly without the tangy whiff of donkey dung among the incense.

Once the wedding party had gone inside, the fun began again. The wind was gusting up a little as the afternoon wore on, so we went into a nearby hotel to warm up with coffee and *Käseknopfe*. *Käseknopfe* is about as close as you get to a traditional Liechtenstein dish and is basically doughy dumplings covered with cheese. Our plates arrived and Ralf sniffed at his tentatively and announced with disappointment that it wasn't smelly enough. He had an aunt who made *Käseknopfe* so good, you could smell it for days afterwards. Sounds mouthwatering, I thought.

As we moved on to coffee and Black Forest gateau, who should walk in but the saintly Martina. Of course, this being Liechtenstein, Ralf and Martina knew each other well. Indeed they used to be next-door neighbours. It turned out that one of Martina's young relatives was a competitor in the race and his turn was coming up shortly, so she was armed with a fearsome-looking camera. She gave us one of her saintly smiles and disappeared out through the door.

We moved outside again just in time to hear the commentator make a spectacular Freudian slip as a boy with blond spiky hair had enormous problems controlling his charge. Having refused to be coaxed over the water jump with the offer of half a loaf of bread, the donkey decided to bypass the rest of the course altogether. Off it went, heading straight for the finish line. The boy tried valiantly to arrest its progress by tugging on the halter and digging his heels into the turf, but merely ended up being dragged along like a waterskier.

'Ohhhhh,' purred the commentator over the tannoy. What he meant to say next was '*das war Schade*' – that was a pity. But what he actually said was '*das war Scheisse*' – that was shit. As the boy and his donkey disappeared down the road and down the mountain, destined for who knows where, the final competitors went round the now worn and slippery course. No one could come anywhere near the winning time of twenty-five seconds.

Once the race was done with, the beauty pageant could start. All the contestants paraded around the course, which, given the uncontrollable nature of the animals, led to some predictable and amusing tangled-halter episodes. After about fifteen minutes, the small blond boy reappeared, still skiing behind his donkey, passing the arena altogether and disappearing up past the chapel and heading for the upper ski slopes.

We all wrote down our vote on a piece of paper and dropped it into a bucket. I plumped for a little grey mule, purely on

the grounds that it had fluttered its eyelids at me in a particularly flirty way on its way around the course. As it turned
out I hadn't picked the winner, but I did consider asking the
grey mule out for a drink and maybe some dancing later.

Ralf drove us back down the mountain as if he were trying
to outrun gravity, pausing at Triesenberg to have a look at their
remarkable football ground. As Triesenberg is set on a steep
hill, there wasn't a piece of land flat enough for the football
ground, so the town constructed a concrete platform and put
a football pitch on top of it, making a car park underneath.
To the side of it was a flat-roofed clubhouse, on top of which
was a full-size tennis court. We walked on the pitch for a while
marvelling at the ingenuity of it all, when suddenly we heard
a commotion from the road. A chunky brown donkey passed
by dragging a small boy with spiky blond hair behind him.

We called in at Ralf's family home, where he said there were
several books of old Liechtenstein traditions and history that
I might find interesting. After a few minutes poring over old
tomes, his parents arrived home with some relatives over from
England and the US.

Ralf's uncle John hailed from Amersham. He'd played in
goal for FC Schaan for three seasons in the late sixties, and
now spent his weekends watching Wycombe Wanderers. As
we sat around the table on the balcony, I admired the magnificent view to the south. The evening sun was just catching the
top of the mountains and made a small patch of mist around
one peak glow deep orange. I asked what people around the
table thought made Liechtenstein what it is. Everyone agreed
that the Prince made a huge difference. There was some discussion over whether he would actually leave the country in the
event of his constitutional proposals being rejected. This would
be a disaster, it was decided, and anyway, wouldn't the country
have to change its name if the family whose name it bore
deserted the nation?

The conversation then turned to the shortcomings of the
Swiss, which seemed, on the face of it, rather unfair given that
the Swiss patrolled the border with Austria and allowed the
Liechtensteiners to use their currency. But no, there are

apparently numerous examples of the Swiss invading Liechtenstein in less generous and diplomatic ways. Apparently a few years ago a Triesenberg grandmother answered a knock on her door one afternoon to find a group of Swiss soldiers demanding to occupy her cellar as part of an exercise. As it turned out the soldiers had spectacularly misread the address, and Switzerland was obliged to issue a formal apology to Liechtenstein for the incident. But not before the grandmother had chased the soldiers away with a broom.

Another balls-up that brought an official Swiss apology was when a mortar shell landed in Liechtenstein. There was a Swiss military exercise going on in Sargans, one of the mortars was pointing in the wrong direction, and boom, clods of Liechtenstein earth were blown skyward. Given Liechtenstein's diminutive stature and lack of a military, it's no wonder the residents get touchy about being shelled and occupied by their larger neighbour.

Not wishing to interrupt the family reunion any longer, I bade farewell and made my way back to the Schäfle for German football highlights and an early night.

Sixteen

Sunday was blessed with beautiful weather, and I spent the morning sitting in Vaduz watching the tourists pass by. It was blissfully peaceful, with occasional churchbells, the hubbub of conversation and the tinkling of the cowbells on the tourist-shop racks the only disturbance. As I read a book in the shade of a tree, an elderly couple came and sat next to me on the bench. '*Was lesen Sie?*' said the man with a smile, asking what I was reading. '*Interessant?*' Unfortunately my German didn't stretch to describing the book, which reconstructed London life in the late sixteenth century, let alone the passage I was reading which dealt with the removal of gallstones without anaesthetic.

'English,' I said, turning the cover of the book towards him. 'Ah,' he said nodding and smiling.

I love this place, I thought to myself. Much of the architecture might be awful (Ivan the Terrible put out the eyes of the architect of St Basil's cathedral so that he wouldn't create anything as beautiful ever again. I wanted to do the same thing for different reasons to whoever designed the Vaduz Post Office), but the ambience on a Sunday lunchtime, without the roar of traffic and clank of construction, when the sun's out and the sky's blue, is just unbeatable. And in the afternoon there's more football to watch.

FC Vaduz had a Nationalliga B fixture against FC Locarno

at the Rheinpark Stadion, and I'd arranged to meet Patrik Hefti there. The approach to the stadium had never looked better. It was just like the Sunday after the Austria game on my first visit – the Alps were sharp and clear in distance, the goats bleated and their bells tinkled, the maize grew to six feet in the fields and all seemed right with the world.

Vaduz seemed certain of a home victory too. They sat at the top of the table, Locarno were three points adrift at the bottom.

I met Patrik and we took up seats in the *Gegentribune*, looking across Vaduz to the tree-smothered mountains and the castle. Vaduz took the lead in the first half, and at half-time we walked around the ground to get a drink and bumped into Peter Jehle in the queue. Dressed in a snazzy pair of white trousers, a grey cap-sleeve t-shirt and with a pair of sunglasses on his head, he looked every inch the young international footballer. The Swiss press was after him, however, despite some solid performances, not least in Porto the previous week when Grasshoppers earned a creditable draw in the Champions' League. He'd made a couple of errors in recent games which led to the Swiss tabloid press calling for him to be dropped. The previous day he'd spilled a cross that led to the equaliser in a 1–1 draw. Patrik commiserated with him, not letting on that he'd seen a particularly virulent tabloid attack on the young keeper that morning.

The second half was not so good for the home side, Patrik's former club. Midway through, Locarno equalised with a glancing header at the near post. Straight from the kick-off, a misunderstanding in the Vaduz defence allowed a visiting forward to nip in and stroke the ball past Javier Crespo. Two goals in thirty seconds. It was like the Varteks game all over again. Player-coach Uwe Wegmann brought on Franz Burgmeier for the last few minutes, but the goal machine could muster only a couple of half chances. Vaduz's fate was sealed when a Locarno forward broke away in the dying seconds to beat Crespo from the edge of the area.

The final whistle blew, and the dejected home players trooped from the field. Locarno couldn't believe it – they'd gone to the league leaders without a victory all season and come away with a convincing 3–1 win. At the whistle they whooped and embraced each other in disbelief. Vaduz had faded in the second half, the Herculean efforts from the Thursday night clearly taking their toll.

Patrik and I wandered back into Vaduz for a drink. We went to a new bar called Nexus, owned, as it turned out, by the president of FC Vaduz, and sat outside in the sunshine talking about football in the principality.

'I played in the junior teams at Vaduz, joining when I was seven years old,' said Patrik. 'I played one year in Triesen, and after that when I was seventeen I got into the first team at Vaduz. I played there for a couple of years but hurt my knee. After that I went to Schaan, where I play now, for one season before going back to Vaduz for four years. Then I moved to America and played there, then came back to Vaduz, went back to America again, and then came back to Vaduz and now I play in Schaan. Which actually all sounds a bit confusing, come to think of it.'

I asked about his time in the US where he had played for Greensboro Dynamos, alongside Robert Rosario.

'In America soccer doesn't have such a high profile, it's not so popular. But it was nice to be a professional and just play football. I enjoyed that. I was out there just before the MLS started and in 1994 we were the national champions, the best team in the US at that time.

'But my first game for the Liechtenstein national team was in 1990, a home friendly against the US strangely enough. I played for all the youth national teams as well, which means I've been playing the longest out of all the guys in the national team. At first it was just friendly games, but in 1994 we entered the qualification rounds for the 1996 European Championships, and the opportunity for us to play against some great teams was wonderful. People in other countries who play at our level would never have opportunities like that. I mean, next month we'll be actually playing against Raul and Mendieta again instead of just watching them on TV.

'I was in the US in 1994, so I missed the first game in

Northern Ireland. But I came over for the rest, because they were so important to us. I missed the 0–0 with Ireland because I was injured. I played in the draw with Hungary a couple of years ago, which was a good performance. It's hard to judge which are the best performances, because although we lost 0–3 to Romania, we played really well against a much better team than Hungary. So it's hard to compare games.

'But one thing is for certain: we've improved immensely since Ralf Loose took over. He's helped us cut down how many goals we let in; he's organised the defence well and knows what it takes to be successful. That's success in our terms, by the way. I mean we were on the end of some very high scores like 0–8 to Romania, and that wasn't too much fun. When Ralf started he put a stop to that and our games now are much closer. I mean, nowadays we can get to the eightieth minute and be only one goal down. It's still tough because we don't get many chances to score, but as long as it's 1–0, the other team still has to watch out and not make a mistake.'

I mentioned how the Austrian newspapers had printed Austria's record scores on the day of the match in Innsbruck, and asked whether that sort of thing affects the players.

'No, it happens pretty much everywhere. That's just how it is. They need to know that we have improved. I think all the little countries in Europe have improved. It's not like a few years ago when there were some very big scores; now the small teams are better and don't concede so many goals. They're more experienced and I think the training and coaching have improved everywhere. You can do a lot with a good defence.

'Loose is the best coach I've ever played under, and I've had a lot of coaches in my career. It's not always easy with him, but he knows what it takes to be successful. We'd done well in the Euro 2000 qualifying group, but this time we are in a group with five teams rather than six. With six teams we know that there will be another of the weaker teams, so we'll have a chance – like when we beat Azerbaijan in 1998. In a group of five it's harder for us to get a draw with anyone. So when we saw that we were in a group of five, the first aim was to let fewer goals in than we had before. I didn't play in the 1–11 against Macedonia, but it was a nightmare to watch. We certainly don't want a game like that ever again. The whole week before the coach had been talking about winning that game or at least getting a draw, but they really screwed up. The players were thinking that they could beat Macedonia pretty easily because they weren't a big name, so that was a really disappointing moment for us. I was only watching from the stands, but I was hurting watching the guys out there.

'We also want to score a couple of goals, maybe even three or four. The big one would be to score a goal in a 1–0 win over Spain next month! Although I think I'd probably settle for a draw . . .

'Loose has really made a big difference with the youth teams as well. The under-seventeen national team won the Swiss championship last year. When that happens, people start to realise what a great job he does, because they think, hey, what does Liechtenstein do differently to, say, Grasshoppers, or another big Swiss club that they finished ahead of? Loose is the reason that we have so many guys who are professional now.'

I wondered whether, as a non-professional, Patrik's job had ever interfered with his football or vice versa?

'No, not really. My bank is pretty good. They support quite a lot of sport here in Liechtenstein, and if I did ever go back to FC Vaduz I'm sure the bank would let me reduce my hours.

'It's in my mind right now to retire from international football, because I'm starting a course at banking school in St Gallen. It's a tough decision because you can't come back once you've retired. But I'm nearly thirty-two, and I really want to make a good career and put soccer behind me. I'll always help out the national team because being so small we don't have as many players as other countries. So I'll still be around even if I retire. If I decide not to retire, then I'll have to co-ordinate the national team with my school and my work which could be tricky.

'There are a few young guys coming through in my position like Andi Gerster at Vaduz, he's only twenty, and Ritter. I've got a good relationship with Loose, fortunately, and he thinks at the moment that I'm better than they are, so maybe I'll play as long as that's the case. I wouldn't want to travel to all these places and just sit on the bench and watch the games.

'Who is the best team I've played against? Spain, in Alicante, without a doubt. Having played against Germany as well, if you compare the way those two teams play, Spain don't force the game, they pass it around. But the Germans just want to hit long balls and so on. Technically they're not as good as the Spanish players. They hit a long ball and just run and run and run. Spain's movement and ability are fantastic. If they hit a long ball across you, it lands right on the foot of the other player and you're already too late.

'Mendieta is probably the best player I've played against. We had a big night there in Alicante. Raul is an incredible player but didn't have such a good night against us. It didn't matter so much for them though because it's not important who scores the goals as long as they win. Niall Quinn was real fun to play against, he's tall and awkward, and he's a nice guy as well.

'Toni Polster was good too. We played one game against Austria, a friendly, and I was in America at the time. I flew over just to play in this game, and I was sent off after seven minutes, a second yellow card. I made a foul after about four minutes and got a yellow. Then, two minutes later, one of our defenders had the ball and tried to play it across to me, but he didn't hit it right. Polster picked it up and played it to Harald Cerny, who plays for Munich 1860 in the Bundesliga, and we both chased it. I ran into his legs, he fell, and the referee gave a penalty and showed me my second yellow. Great, I thought. All the way from America for seven minutes. That was awful.

'My only other bad memory was a game in Ireland. I was marking David Connolly and he scored a hat-trick in the first half. Two of the goals I couldn't really have done anything about, but the final one, he tricked me pretty well. So we'd been playing forty-four minutes, they were three-up, I was lying on the ground and he was in front of the stand with his arms out celebrating a hat-trick with thirty thousand people. That was a tough moment. But you have to get over these things and put them behind you.'

Patrik rated the Hungary game as a turning point for Liechtenstein, and also one of his greatest moments.

'Yes, drawing with Hungary was good, and so was beating Azerbaijan. Even though I wasn't in the team for those games, you're still part of the squad. Loose introduced a lot of young players, and also Freddie Gigon arrived on the left. He is a key player, someone we had been missing before because he only got a Liechtenstein passport recently.

'When he first arrived we went to Germany and played in a small tournament and won. Then we drew with Hungary, drew with Bosnia in a friendly and beat FC Zurich, who had some great players like Shaun Bartlett of South Africa. And Freddie was saying, hey look, since I arrived we've done really well, it can't be coincidence!

'Look at the game in Freiburg against Germany. After eighty minutes Gigon got hurt and had to go off, and it was 3–2. Christof Ritter came on to replace him, but he'd pulled a muscle and couldn't even run, could hardly move. But he hadn't told Loose. So Germany scored five goals in the last eight minutes and I was freaking out, I could have punched the guy. I was saying, why didn't you tell the coach you couldn't run? Loose was really mad about it. If Frédéric had stayed on, we might have only lost 2–3 or 2–4 instead of 2–8.

'But that game made us more confident going into this World Cup. In the past the question was always how quickly are we going to be three or four behind. But now our aim is to keep it close for as long as possible, to make the opposition work as hard as we can, to really make it difficult for them to score.

'We had a disastrous start against Israel, with the goal after sixteen seconds, but that turned out to be one of our best games. After that goal Israel were thinking, hey, this will be really easy. Then we got back into the game and they didn't score again until the last ten minutes. We played very well, and Mario had a huge, huge chance. A cross came over, and he was unmarked in front of the keeper, but he didn't head it right.

'Mario's probably the best Liechtenstein player I've played with, but it's hard to say, really. It's hard for him to play with us because we're not an attacking team, we're always defending. Peter Jehle in the last five or six games was a big help, and Daniel Hasler as well. Those three are the spine of the team, with Harry Zech too. Harry and I have played together for many years, for Vaduz and the national team.

'After Israel, Austria at home was a great performance. The goal was a bit unfortunate: we tried to catch them offside but it didn't work. Then we had a big chance for Martin Telser, but he chipped it over. They didn't actually have many chances. When we get so close like that, that's when we should really think about getting a point.

'But Spain in Alicante, that was a great night. People will look at the result and think it was easy for them, but it wasn't. To be 0–2 at half-time was good in Spain. But then straight after half-time was the penalty kick. It's tough to play against Spain, because their players have such incredible technique. It's not like playing Ireland, who are a great team, but it's easier to play against them than Spain.'

While we have been sitting outside the bar, several people have come over to say hello and ask about the forthcoming Spain game. Yet the interest doesn't seem to extend much beyond polite enquiry. Does the team receive the support it needs from the people, I wondered?

'It's not a football country,' said Patrik. 'It's sometimes hard for us, but that's the way it is. The people just aren't as interested or supportive as they are in many other countries. We're not as strong, we can't go to the European Championship finals, and the people's mentality here is different. It's not disappointing for me really, because I understand. I grew up here, I know the people, and I understand what is and isn't important to them. Other players do get a bit disappointed, like after the Bosnia game. We thought we were in Bosnia! When we arrived at the ground in the coach, their fans were gesturing and spitting at the windows and I thought, am I in Liechtenstein? Is this really a home game? The Bosnians are real fanatics, that's just the way it is, but they were really obnoxious. But, you know, it's motivating in a way.

'We had a few fans in Innsbruck, which was really good for us. But there are not many people in this country, and few are football fanatics. I've lived here for many years and I know that there are other things more important than football in Liechtenstein – banks, money, stamps, whatever.'

Despite the lack of support from their compatriots, I was curious as to the level of pride the players feel when representing Liechtenstein. What does it mean to play for your country, particularly one so small and, in terms of results, unsuccessful on the field?

'I've been proud to play every game for my national team, and I still am. I'm proud to have played so many games, representing my country all over Europe. It's a nice feeling to stand out there with the crown on my shirt, listening to the national anthem and think, hey, I'm doing this for my country. It gives you chills down your spine, when you're already nervous enough anyway!

'The football team does help to get Liechtenstein known around the world. I was in America while the 1994 World Cup was on. I was injured at the time so couldn't play for Greensboro and travelled around to some of the games. I got talking to some guys from Ireland, and told them I was from Liechtenstein. They said, 'Ah, Liechtenstein!' and knew all about it because of the football team. When I told them I was a player on the national team, they said, are you sure? Is that possible? And they paid for all the beers! Maybe they wouldn't have done after we drew with them in Eschen the following year though . . .

'So it's important in that way, but it's not so important for the people here. Some even think it's bad to have a football team. They say, hey, you always go away and bring back a bad result, but I think that we're representing our country and doing the best we possibly can.

'I don't think we can regard ourselves as particularly special. Yes, we're a rich country, and you can have a good life here, but that doesn't make us better than anyone else. I don't think anyone is better than anyone else. Football fans in Spain are real fanatics and they worship players like Raul. But, you know, when he stands next to me on the field, he's just another human being. Okay, he's a little more talented and he makes a lot of money, but he's just a person like I am.

'I told Sergej Barbarez after our game against Bosnia here, "I think how you act on the field is not nice." He wanted to have a fight with one of our guys and I told him, "You're a good player, you've scored twenty goals in the Bundesliga, but against Liechtenstein it seems you have to act like the biggest jerk." For me, it's a sport not a war. Maybe it's because he's from a country where there's been a lot of war, but I'm not going out on the field to hate the other team. Sure, I'll do things in a rough way, anything that's possible to win or draw, or keep the scores down, but I'm not out to hate anyone. To be a good player doesn't mean you automatically have to stop being a good person.

'Some players try to intimidate you. Not too many, but you have a few comments. The Spanish guys were really, really nice, not arrogant or anything, real gentlemen. The Germans are really cocky – when we played in Freiburg one of the German players was knocking on the dressing-room door and shouting, "Hey little guys, are you going to come out now, or are you too scared?" He was saying, "You guys shouldn't be on the same pitch as us," and I was thinking, well, let's see where we are in twenty years when your professional career is over.

'But generally this is a good time to be playing for Liechtenstein. I don't like what happened with Mario, but we have a good combination of older guys like Zech, Daniel Hasler and myself, and younger guys with lots of potential. The next couple of years might be tough. We don't know if Mario is ever going to play again, Zech and I don't know how much longer we're going to be around, so it's hard to set targets. It would be nice to score a goal and maybe get a draw once in a while; that would be a realistic and positive aim. It would be nicer maybe to lose 2–5 than 0–3. You know, I'm a defender and I like only losing 0–3, but as a football team you should score goals too.

'But as long as we keep improving and get more professionals out there, then sooner or later we'll see results. I don't think it's realistic for a country of thirty-two thousand people to have ambitions much beyond that.'

Seventeen

The following evening saw the Liechtenstein squad training at the stadium. I'd spent a leisurely day soaking up the sunshine in Vaduz and attempting to eavesdrop on a conversation between a sobbing American girl and her friend. I'd noticed the two of them sitting on a bench outside the town hall, one with her hands over her face and her shoulders heaving with sobs. Her friend had an arm around her, and was evidently attempting to console the stricken girl.

I sat at an adjacent bench and, uncharitably in hindsight, tried to earwig. From what I could gather, the girl had had a romantic tryst with a boy from their coach party, only to be dumped from a great height immediately afterwards because he actually fancied someone else. Now the poor girl had another ten days of traipsing around Europe cooped up in the same coach as this outrageous cad. Unfortunately a coach pulled up at this point and sat there with its engine thrumming, drowning out the conversation just when it was getting to the juicy bits. I considered leaning over and asking the girls to speak up, and even pulling out my tape recorder, miming an elaborate jaw-cracking arm-stretching yawn and depositing it next to them, but thought better of both, fortunately.

Hence all I could pick up was the occasional 'he's not worth it' and 'it's his loss' before the coach finally pulled away. At that point the girls stood up and walked off. 'Look, if there's ever anything I can do, even if you just wanna talk, whatever, I'm always here for you, okay?' said the girl. I had an urge to call out, 'She doesn't mean it, you know, she'll have forgotten who you are by Christmas,' but suppressed it just in time. The rest of the day was spent admonishing myself for harbouring such beastly thoughts and pondering how, to one girl from somewhere in North America, the name Liechtenstein would always be associated with heartbreak. You'll be glad to know that I did suffer some payback for my awfulness: sunburn, which tightened my face to such an extent that for the rest of the week I looked like I'd had a very bad facelift.

I arrived at the stadium to watch the team train, but found it locked. I walked around and peered through the fences, but the place was deserted. Hearing voices from behind the ground, I walked along the footpath and found Liechtenstein's finest footballers gingerly warming up on a pitch striped with ruts a foot wide and a good three inches deep.

Ralf Loose was standing there with a face like thunder. Ralf Wenaweser was with him, looking paler than usual. It turned out that the LFV had an agreement with FC Vaduz over use of the stadium. To preserve the pitch, they could only use it a certain amount of times each month. So when Loose and the players turned up this evening they had found themselves shunted to the park behind, whose surface had recently been dug up for a new drainage system, hence the grid-like trenches that criss-crossed the grass. Evidently no one had thought to tell the LFV about this in advance, so where Loose had quite naturally assumed that the national team would be able to train at the national stadium two days before a match, albeit a low-key friendly, the stadium management thought otherwise.

At that moment Ernst bustled up, wiping his eyes with his handkerchief, lugging his laptop, his sandals slapping across the tarmac of the car park. 'Hasler!' barked Loose, and let off an irritable tirade of which I understood not a word, but which probably contained the words 'tin-pot', 'two-bob', 'bureau-crats' and several swearwords. Ernst laughed nervously and scribbled on his notepad. It was a bit like England turning up for a workout at Wembley and being redirected to Neasden Rec.

White t-shirted players stretched and limbered up, nervously eyeing the gouges in the turf. Eventually they were split into two lines, running up to take pot-shots at Jehle and the Liechtenstein reserve keeper Martin Oehry, a huge barrel of a man who was surprisingly agile for such a big lad.

'It's funny, isn't it,' said Ralf as Oehry thumped away a piledriver from Patrik Hefti, 'goalkeepers get the most training but do the least work in a match.' He paused for a moment and then said, 'Actually, no. Liechtenstein strikers probably have the least work to do in a match. The goalkeeper is probably the busiest player in the team.'

The quality of the finishing varied between lashing the ball into the roof of the net, and lashing the ball into Switzerland. '*Jawohl!*' Loose would cry every time the net billowed. Ernst sat in a portable dugout with his laptop on his knees, cheering and clapping every goal, jeering every wild slice.

After training we wandered back to the changing rooms. I complimented Patrik on his finishing: more often than not his shots ended spinning and scratching around in the back of the net. 'I used to be a striker,' said the huge defender whose shoulders were so broad he almost had to turn sideways to go down the corridor. Hans-Peter Nigg, the jovial, white-haired kit-manager with a cigar clamped permanently between his teeth, pointed at Patrik, tugged an imaginary forelock and said, 'Sir Patrik!' before giving an elaborate bow. Hefti is evidently highly regarded in these parts.

Half an hour later I was outside Nexus again with Ralf, Patrik, Jürgen Ospelt, Freddie Gigon and Harry Zech, who had just climbed out of his snazzy four-wheel drive bearing the legend 'Harry Zech – Weinbau' (Winemaker) on the side, still clad in his training kit.

Real Madrid had just visited Gigon's club Stade Lausanne. They were the second team in the Swiss city behind the professional Lausanne Sports yet had managed to claim a pre-season friendly against the European giants thanks to connections with the International Olympic Committee. Once Real arrived though, Juan Antonio Samaranch stepped in and said that the professional club should really provide the opposition. Real still trained at Stade Lausanne, however. According to Gigon, every kid in the city converged on Figo and Zidane for autographs: Raul, Hierro, Roberto Carlos and the rest were ignored. Although the coach had told Gigon and his teammates not to hang around the stadium whilst Real were training, the Liechtenstein international had hidden in a locker in the dressing room in order to bag Zidane's autograph. He claimed it was for one of his pupils but this apparently selfless act was, I thought, beyond the call of duty for even the most dedicated of teachers.

Gigon was intrigued as to why I was following Liechtenstein and we started chatting. He's an irrepressibly cheerful character with a permanent smile and laughing brown eyes.

'I actually come from Switzerland,' he said in a French accent in contrast to the Germanic tones of his teammates. 'I always lived in Switzerland, but gained a Liechtenstein passport two years ago. I'd noticed that I qualified for a Liechtenstein passport when I was going to Berlin to study German and history. As a Swiss citizen I had to pay a lot of money in order to study there, but I learned that Liechtensteiners didn't have to pay. I have a Liechtensteiner grandmother and so I asked Liechtenstein if I could have a passport and they said sure, no problem. So I didn't have to pay for the course.

'Then Ralf Loose heard about this from my cousin; he knew I played for Stade Lausanne and so telephoned me in Berlin, told me that Liechtenstein were playing in a small friendly tournament in Germany and asked me to come down. I was convinced it was a joke, I was saying, "Sorry? Who are you? Ralf Loose? Who's that?" So I played in this tournament and we won it, even though we drew both games 0–0. My first full game was in a friendly with Bosnia that we also drew 0–0, and they told me, okay, you have to play because we don't often get 0–0 draws. Since then I think I've played every game, so I've been a lucky boy!

'I play for Stade Lausanne, but I'm a teacher by trade,

teaching kids between ten and fifteen. The children love it, they always watch me when I'm on TV, and then in my first class afterwards we have fifteen minutes when they tell me all the things I did wrong in the match. I've never been a professional footballer and now the reality is that I never will. I had the chance about ten years ago, and tried it for six months, but it wasn't my thing. Football's always been my hobby, that's how I have fun. I think if it was my work too, that really wouldn't suit me. I love my job, and I love to play football, so to play for Liechtenstein is really a dream. It might last for two more months, it might be two more years, but it's a wonderful experience and I'm trying to make the most of it.

'I do feel proud to be a Liechtensteiner and to represent the country. Spain was a real high point, as we played well and I was happy with my performance against Mendieta. If people came to that game not knowing who I was or who Mendieta was, I think that I would have come out of it quite well. Playing against these players is incredible; for the first few minutes you can feel your heart thumping. But then you think, okay, he's just another player, he's got two arms and two legs like me, so let's go. If he's playing much better than you, then it's normal, so you just do your best to show him you're not so bad as he thinks.

When you look at our team you can see that we're all happy and we're all friends; it's so enjoyable, it's like going on holiday for me, coming to play with the national team. I would love to win a match with Liechtenstein, but we have to be realistic. We can put on a super performance and lose 0–1 or 0–2 against a good team and we're happy. I think it also makes me a better player. I think I play ten times better when I play for Liechtenstein than when I play for Lausanne. I go back on such a high that people have to tell me, calm down, you're crazy! That lasts about two weeks, and then I'm back to being as bad as I was before I left . . .

'Ralf Loose is good for me too, because he gives me confidence. From the start he was telling me that I'm a good player, and I would think, okay, you're just being nice to me because

I'm a nice boy and always polite with you. But he'd tell me, you're playing against Mendieta and it's no problem. He has us all thinking positive, which gives us confidence. I would love us to get a point or score a goal.

'It would be great to win a game with Liechtenstein; the others won the game against Azerbaijan, and they're always talking about it. So I'd love to be there when we win another. My dream is to play against Switzerland, because that's where I'm from and also I think we could beat them. At the moment they have a poor team with a bad atmosphere, so we really have the possibility to beat them. It would be great to get them in the next qualifying group.

'I have had a few problems with work and playing for Liechtenstein. But I need football to keep the equilibrium in my life; without sport life would be bad. The school headmaster isn't really happy about me going away like this. I feel that that's because he's not really a sporty man, and if perhaps I told him that I was going to Bosnia to, say, sing with a choir or to act in a play he might say no problem. The president from the LFV always has to speak to him and there are long exchanges of letters. I'm sure he won't accept this for much longer, and will tell me I'm not allowed to go any more. I could go to another school, but I'm really happy there, I like the other teachers, so I don't want to change just because of the headmaster. I think he retires in the next few years but who knows, maybe I won't be in the team then!'

Once the players had departed, having shamed my beer and pizza by drinking mineral water and eating salad sandwiches, Ralf and I moved on to Bar Wolf, an establishment I hadn't tried in all my time in Vaduz. Stefanie joined us and, remarkably for Liechtenstein, her and Ralf didn't already know each other. They soon discovered something in common though – both had fallen asleep while driving and crashed into the central reservation of the motorway. They had a good old chuckle about this. After we had moved on to the Crash Bar, both offered me a lift home. I decided to walk.

The following morning, with nothing better to do, I went to hang out at the LFV offices to kill time before leaving for

the match in Lustenau. Ralf was in a panic. The Austrian club
had been trying to rearrange because their reserve team had a
cup match to play, and Lustenau had just realised they were
double booked. A compromise was reached: the cup game
would start earlier, the Liechtenstein game later.

Despite this last-minute hitch, coming as it did after the
training-ground fiasco, Ralf Loose was in the office and in
good spirits. We shook hands, his face creasing into a huge
smile as he stooped a little to speak to me, promising we'd sit
down and have a chat soon. He was really very tall. Also in
the office was Daniel Hasler, Liechtenstein's most capped
player. Despite having been sidelined for several months with
a cruciate ligament injury, he was in a good mood too, and
we had a three-way conversation with Ralf translating.

'I've just started learning English, but the course has only
been going for three weeks, so I'm not quite there yet,' interpreted Ralf.

Hasler is one of Liechtenstein's most highly regarded players.
A professional in his second season with the Swiss club FC
Wil, Hasler has been the linchpin of the national side, particularly in recent years. He scored Liechtenstein's first ever goal
in competitive football, in the 1–4 defeat in Northern Ireland
in 1994, and is also Ernst's favourite player, which was good
enough for me.

'Entering European competition was a big challenge and
opportunity for us to play on the big stage,' Hasler recalled
of the early days. 'We'd only seen the big teams and famous
players on television so it was incredible to think that we would
be on the same pitch as them.

'I didn't realise what was happening when I scored the first
goal. I think I'd only come on with about fifteen minutes to
go, and we were 0–4 down. Then I scored about seven minutes
later. Initially it was the normal joy at scoring a goal. We were
overjoyed that we had only lost 1–4 to a team as good as
Northern Ireland, and that was a great result for our first international match. It was only years later, when we realised just
how hard goals are to come by in international football, that
I started to realise what I'd actually done that night, and what

a great honour it was to have scored the first ever goal for my country in a qualifying game. It still makes me very proud.'

'That must be your greatest moment playing for Liechtenstein,' I said.

'No,' came back the answer straightaway. 'There have been lots of great moments, but the best for me was the 0–0 draw with Ireland in 1995. That was such an emotional game, because we were under so much pressure throughout. There were last-ditch tackles, great saves from the goalkeeper Martin Heeb and clearances off the line, and all of a sudden the crowd began to realise what was going on. They really responded, and there was singing and chanting; the support that day was incredible, like never before or since.

'Azerbaijan was another great moment, but Ireland was much more significant because the occasion was so emotional. Playing in Spain, in a sold out stadium, that was great too, but because we're more experienced now and have played a lot of good teams, we don't get so nervous and are less awed by the atmosphere than we used to be.

'Has playing against these teams made me a better player? It's a big challenge to play against people like Figo and Mendieta, and every game helps you to improve, and gives you more experience to take back to your club. I've learned a lot under Ralf Loose, but the younger players now will benefit even more than I have. When I started out, we didn't have the same organisation at youth level that we have now. Ralf Loose is great with the young players, and the advantage is that he can have them from youth level right up to the national team. When you think of the level the old guard has reached without the set up we have now, then the future must be better.

'Loose is not afraid to blood young players in the national team, and so far it's worked: none of them have cracked under pressure. He's good at putting the right people in the right positions, and that's some achievement for a coach at international level. This is definitely the best Liechtenstein team we've ever had, and it's the product of a steady improvement over a number of years.

'We're limited by the number of players we have to choose from, so we're never going to scale great heights in European football. We can, however, become a more solid team that can get results against the other smaller teams. We'll never have a chance of beating the top teams, but there are always surprises in football.'

I say that there are schools of thought, not least in Britain, that believe nations like Liechtenstein, San Marino and Andorra should not be in these qualifying tournaments. Or at least that they should play some kind of pre-qualifying tournament before the bigger countries allow them on to the same field. One well-respected British broadsheet columnist had railed against these teams just before I had left Britain, stating that countries like Liechtenstein were only in these tournaments for the money UEFA gives them. He even opined that the smaller nations 'stubbornly refuse to improve', a statement which even the most cursory of research would have disproved.

Yet the same writers are the ones who wax lyrical about the magic of the FA Cup, and how wonderful it is that non-league sides have the opportunity to pit themselves against Premiership opposition. Has a team from, say, the lower reaches of the Ryman League been 'stubbornly refusing to improve', or is it a question of resources? You decide.

So why, I ask Daniel, is it important for Liechtenstein to play in FIFA competitions?

'It's extremely important for a small nation to play against the bigger ones. We must ensure that we never reach the point where we have a pre-qualifiying round, because that would be so harmful for football here. After all, every member of UEFA is equal, regardless of their size.

'One thing that could improve though is the level of support. At every game the Liechtenstein people stand there with their hands in their pockets or their arms folded, and we have to play really, really well to get a response. Of course the team has to perform, but you sometimes wish when things aren't going well that the crowd would give us more encouragement. But we're aware that this is just the Liechtenstein mentality.

In the Ireland game, it took something like seventy-five minutes for the crowd to really get behind us.'

I ask him about the injury that has curtailed his participation in this World Cup.

'I'd only missed a few matches before this campaign, so it's a little frustrating for me. But I'm a realist and have to accept that things are the way they are. I've probably taken more from life than I've given back until now, what with training and working and playing. Now I have the time to take stock, spend time with my girlfriend and build myself up slowly again and get everything straight to make sure that I come back stronger than I was before. I still want to take my career at club level one or two steps higher and keep playing as long as possible and, of course, get back into the national team.

'I'm so proud to play for Liechtenstein. When I stand on the pitch and hear the national anthem it's very emotional. It sends a shiver down my spine even after thirty-plus internationals, and it's a great motivation. If a player doesn't feel that when representing his country, he shouldn't be on the field. I love Liechtenstein. I've travelled around a bit, but I always love to come home. That may sound old-fashioned, but I can't imagine it being any other way.'

Like most of the players, Hasler is intelligent, articulate, and has a refreshingly open-minded outlook on life. That's certainly something I noticed – they may have shared a football field with Figo, Mendieta, Hagi and, er, Niall Quinn, but they still have their feet firmly on the ground. There are no egos in Liechtenstein football and there wouldn't be room for them anyway, but there is a real sense of awareness that there is a life outside football that can often be missing in other countries' football teams.

Maybe that's one advantage of the lack of football culture in Liechtenstein; that the game is in its place. In Britain football is given a greater significance, hence the pressure becomes greater. In Liechtenstein, the players are aware of their limitations yet are also fanatically proud to represent their tiny country against some of the biggest in the world. It's certainly been a humbling experience following this team.

Later in the day, we set off in Ralf's car for Lustenau, about half an hour away at Ralf speed, carrying an LFV pennant big enough to propel a small yacht. The stadium was unlovely, a long, characterless concrete stand along one side and scaffold constructions on the other three. It was a depleted Liechtenstein team: not being a recognised full international, the professionals weren't there. Austria Lustenau, who were relegated from the Austrian top flight in 2000 and narrowly failed to return at the first attempt the following season, took the opportunity to look at a few triallists and reserve players. As I joined Ernst in the press box we agreed that it had all the makings of a really crap match.

It lived down to our expectations. A niggly affair with lots of needless fouls and misplaced passes, it was the home side who created most of the chances but proved incapable of taking them. A Brazilian triallist Edvaldo Oliveira stood out amongst the general mediocrity, but half-time seemed to take an age to arrive. During the break, the floodlights came on and the sun sank behind the mountains, which were a dusky blue against the pink sky. The lights also attracted every flying insect in the vicinity on a warm, sticky evening in western Austria.

In the second half Liechtenstein began to look more positive. The burly Fabio D'Elia headed a Thomas Beck cross over the bar shortly after the interval, and Beck crossed well for his namesake Matthias Beck to drag a shot across the face of goal shortly afterwards. Martin Oehry pulled off a couple of spectacular saves and I commented to Ernst that he's a good keeper.

'Yes, all round I think he's a better keeper than Jehle,' he said. 'But he's thirty-seven now and getting too old, especially as Loose prefers the young players.'

The match fizzled out into a wholly forgettable goalless draw, but Loose, resplendent on the touchline in pale blue short-sleeved shirt, beige shorts and sandals, at least had the opportunity to look at a few fringe players before choosing his squad for the Spain match, now only three weeks away.

I left the press box for a wander around as I waited for

Ralf. As Ernst tapped away at his keyboard, I wondered just what he was going to find to say to fill the necessary column inches in tomorrow's *Vaterland*. In the corner of the stadium a small bar had opened up, and a man was cooking sausages on a huge alfresco grill. Gradually the players arrived. Oehry, the bear-like goalkeeper who had been my man of the match, sucked frantically on a cigarette and gave his opinion of the game in a voice that sounded like coal trapped under a door on a stone floor.

Suddenly the floodlights went out. The entire ground was plunged into darkness save for the distant neon strip above the head of the still-typing Ernst Hasler. Momentarily disorientated, the flying insects soon spotted this, and converged on the only light in the vicinity. Within seconds I could see that Ernst was typing with one hand and flailing around at midges with the other. War correspondents have had to put up with less – what a pro.

Ralf had to head back to Vaduz for a post-match reception, so I drove back with Ernst. He said he'd been to London before, when he was fifteen in 1970. He'd gone with his father to an Arsenal v Tottenham game where Ray Kennedy had scored two goals. He thought it was fantastic, and has followed Arsenal ever since. What impressed him most, however, was that as he and his father queued for the tube station, there were people selling newspapers already carrying a report of the game he had just seen.

'That was real journalism,' he said. 'Now I have this laptop and it's easy. I can just format the page, e-mail it to the paper and it's done. I have a digital camera too. But then? Wow, that was impressive.'

He invited me for a beer and we took up residence outside Bar Wolf. A pretty girl walked past and Ernst whistled to himself. 'You see that guy she's with? He's been with the national team before, he's the goalkeeper from FC Balzers.' Shortly afterwards a corpulent man with silver hair strolled past our table and into the bar. Ernst leaned over conspiratorially and told me that he was the Liechtenstein chess champion. A few minutes later a stocky man in his forties, with a receding hairline and a thickening waistline, ambled past with his wife. 'That's Moser,' said Ernst admiringly. 'He was a great player. He played for FC Zurich when they played against Liverpool in the 1978 European Cup semi-final.'

I asked Ernst about his own playing career, having been told that the diminutive scribe had been quite a player in his day.

'I played for a few teams,' he said. 'Eschen-Mauren, Vaduz, Triesen, Triesenberg and Ruggell.' By a swift deduction I calculated that of all the Liechtenstein clubs the only ones Ernst hadn't turned out for were Balzers and Schaan.

'I still play now, even though I'm forty-six. Five-a-side. And I'm still better than most of the youngsters. I do a lot of coaching of junior teams too. I still coach the FC Vaduz junior teams, and was Daniel Hasler's coach for many years. I coached Mario Frick too.'

Albrecht, the owner of the bar, arrived, greeting Ernst as an old friend. He was a chubby, camp man with a waxed moustache and a gold bracelet that slid up and down his arm with every flamboyant gesture. He was in good spirits considering the imminent danger that his bar seemed to be in: the buildings either side had been demolished. When he learned that I'd come from London, he said, 'Okay, okay, name me any London Underground line, and I'll tell you which colour it is on the map.'

'Dark blue,' I said. 'Piccadilly,' he replied immediately. 'Red.' 'Central.' And so on. He even got the Hammersmith and City Line, which was particularly impressive considering he hadn't been to London for twenty-five years. I couldn't even defeat him with what Arsenal station was called before it was Arsenal station. 'Gillespie Road,' he squeaked, raising his arms in triumph, the lights flashing off his bracelet.

When it got to 2 a.m. (with the bar still open – what a civilised country Liechtenstein is), Albrecht realised that it was now officially Liechtenstein National Day, and ordered us a round of drinks on the house. It was on condition that we sang the national anthem, however, which he kicked off in an impressive *basso profundo* that belied the high-pitched squeak of his speaking voice. Ernst followed this with his customary rendition of 'Let It Be', but when the conversation turned to the barmaids' breasts, I knew it was time to hit the hay. There was a long National Day ahead.

Eighteen

The first thing I noticed was the buses. Every Liechtenstein bus had a little blue-and-red flag fluttering away at the front. Despite the previous late night, I was up early and keen not to miss the opportunity to 'mess on the field outside the castle'. The buses were full to bursting with people also keen to mess, and a slow procession of long yellow vehicles wound their way up towards the Prince's residence.

Now I'm a bit out of order here, because I knew exactly what 'mess' meant. Liechtenstein being the fiercely Catholic country that it is, I deduced that National Day was to begin with an open-air Catholic mass. Once we'd left the bus, I followed my fellow travellers the short way along the footpath to the castle, feeling distinctly underdressed. Amongst the men and women neatly turned out in their Sunday best, I did stand out a little in baggy green combats and a zip-up hooded top.

I feared that I would also stand out because of my complete lack of religion. I've never got Christianity, despite having been sent to a school whose founding purpose was to churn out spiritually devout young men who would then go to far-flung corners of the world and tell the local population where they'd been going wrong all these years.

To me the gospels are clearly nothing more than a prediction of the coming of Elvis Presley, an argument that bamboozles doorstepping Bible carriers every time. Especially as I have mastered telling them this with a completely straight face and reeling off a list of evidence in support of my theory (Jesus was the son of God, Elvis recorded for Sun Records, for example).

So there I was, a scruffy, non-believing foreigner gatecrashing Liechtenstein's very own private party. Although I had made enough friends now so as not to feel like a complete stranger, that morning made me realise once again that I didn't belong. For all my increasingly passionate support of the football team, for all the hours I'd spent in Vaduz drinking in the beauty of the scenery, it wasn't mine.

The field by the castle is a natural amphitheatre, and on that morning it was crammed with people. There was a small covered podium at the bottom, at the rear of which stood about a dozen priests in golden robes. A brass band stood to one side as the archbishop began mass by slowly and gravely intoning the words, '*Liechtenstein, Liechtenstein, mein einig schönes Liechtenstein*,' (Liechtenstein, Liechtenstein, my only beautiful Liechtenstein).

Liechtenstein did indeed look beautiful that morning. The sun was just rising above the mountain at our backs, bathing the castle to our left in golden light but leaving the field in cool morning shade. Colourful banners representing all eleven Liechtenstein communities hung from poles lining the road from the field to the castle gates.

It was a long, long service hosted by a short, fat, pink archbishop who intoned each syllable very slowly. As the sun crept around the mountain, the shade edged away to the right as if both were hoping the other wouldn't notice. Eventually the congregation was left standing in direct sunlight on a hot August morning. Even the most devout Catholics were beginning to sway, and a low hubbub of conversation was moving quietly around the field as the archbishop droned away at the front. He was accompanied by a tall, silver-haired priest wearing dark glasses, who looked very likely to have a machine gun concealed in a violin case under his robes. A few rows in front of me, a middle-aged man suddenly pulled out a white handkerchief and waved it above his head. Great, I thought, someone's offering to surrender. Alas he was merely trying to attract the attention of some late-arriving friends at the front.

Finally the archbishop wound down. '*Liechtenstein, Liechtenstein, mein einig, schönes Liechtenstein,*' he intoned again before the brass band struck up for a brief musical sting. There was a small 'thank goodness for that' commotion of leg stretching, minor stamping, a bit of turning-around-and-raising-the-eyebrows-at-the-person-behind and some puffing out of cheeks, before the Prince, recognisable from the countless photographs I'd seen in every building I'd been into, approached a lectern to give his annual speech. He was taller than I expected, and dressed in a sober blue suit. His hairline had receded about as far as it was possible to go without falling off the back. The speech was mercifully short, and delivered with a permanent benevolent smile. He might have been saying, 'Look, you're my subjects, I own the place, so if you don't do what I want then I'm going to sod off to Vienna. Then where would you be, eh?' for all I knew, but the warm, lengthy applause he received afterwards suggested he had adopted a less confrontational approach. A couple of politicians also spoke, presumably saying, 'Don't listen to him, he's just a power-crazed lunatic,' before the band struck up the national anthem.

And then I understood. Standing there in that field as the last of the morning dew disappeared into the atmosphere, I finally, truly understood. This was Liechtenstein. This was what it was all about. I watched as everyone in the field sang the Liechtenstein anthem, young and old, man and woman, fat and thin, rich and, um, rich. And I realised that what made Liechtenstein unique was not a prince, not a castle, not a football team, not even an impressive stamp collection. The true Liechtenstein lay in the collective consciousness of its people, most visibly demonstrated here as they stood, right arm upraised at the elbow, singing the words written by a German priest to a British tune a century and a half earlier. They did so in the shadow of the country's most identifiable landmark, which had stood since the fourteenth century, long before Liechtenstein even existed.

I could only stand open-mouthed in admiration. Liechtenstein is, after all, a false creation: named after a nobleman, brought into existence due to nothing more than the quest for influence and kudos. Yet here, in this sunny field on a hot August morning, the people were showing that they'd taken those fragile foundations and against the odds built a happy, successful and proud nation. This was not the skewed, aggressive jingoism taken abroad by English numbskulls, nor was it a deep-set sense of ethnic superiority of the sort that sparked war in the Balkans. This was simply the pride of a small group of people united by religion and residence in one of the smallest countries in the world.

The final cadence of the anthem died away, echoing around the mountain and down into the valley. The band led the priests the short way up the castle in a slow procession. Behind them walked the Prince and Princess, a Princess Michael of Kent-a-like with an immense sculptured hairdo topping a yellow Jackie Kennedy-style suit. As the people raced to line the route and applaud, the royals smiled and waved self-consciously, without the regal self-confidence of our Queen. The princely family strolled behind them, followed by the politicians and then the people in a tangible statement of Liechtensteiner hierarchy.

Now the fun could start. Inside the castle gates were stalls dispensing free beer, sandwiches and snacks. Although the circular beer stall I approached was lined three deep with people, rather than the pushing, shoving and swearing you'd expect, everyone was waiting patiently and indicating to the smiling staff when the person next to them was actually first. One man was flicking a V-sign at the girl serving him, but he was just indicating that he wanted two beers. The atmosphere was wonderful, and the weather fantastic. I eventually received a beer in a real glass with Fürstenberg (Prince's Castle) emblazoned on the outside, which I stole.

This being Liechtenstein, I bumped into someone I knew. Stefanie appeared out of the crowd and reminded me that I had agreed to walk the Fürstensteig with her and Ralf that afternoon. The Fürstensteig was a walking route through the mountains, and Ralf had thought it would be a great way to spend National Day.

'Are you afraid of heights?' he had asked. 'Of course not,' I replied, thinking of the leisurely walk to Triesenberg I had taken a few months earlier instead of the numerous occasions when Katie has had to talk me down from a stepladder.

I asked Stefanie if we were really going to abandon the free beer in favour of a hike through the mountains. 'Of course,' she said, looking at me strangely. Then I remembered how she had already told me of the many weekends she spends up in the mountains on her own or with her parents. I noted also her stout walking boots and thick socks from which protruded a sturdy pair of bronzed calves beneath some voluminous walker's shorts. I looked from my free beer to Stefanie's sturdy frame and back again. What had I let myself in for?

Ralf arrived shortly afterwards, also looking fiendishly fit and ready for a yomp through the mountains. I escaped into another part of the garden, following, bizarrely, a Scottish bagpipe band from southern Austria.

The Prince was standing nearby, talking to a group of smiling, fawning middle-aged people. The poor sod looked wholly ill at ease. His grin had become fixed and he was sweating profusely. It was turning into a scorchingly hot day, and his shirt was already darkened with damp around the collar and behind the tie-knot. Beads of sweat were forming on his cranium and running down to his chin. His eyes were fixed on whoever was talking to him, but occasionally they darted skyward, as if he was expecting a helicopter to come clattering over the castle dangling a rope ladder to whisk him away over the mountains.

I watched him for a while, as a choir of women in long, yellow, vaguely psychedelic dresses sang some gorgeous a capella music in the corner of the garden. The Prince was exceedingly pleasant to everybody, shaking hands with his right and nursing a glass of beer in his left. His only conversational gambit was listen to whatever was being said to him, dip his head slightly and say, '*Oh, ja?*' as yet another person told him how they'd met before, in 1978 at a business reception. I could only admire his patience and fortitude as the entire population crammed into his garden and drank his beer.

Eventually I decided to join the queue for an audience. Hans Adam II 'oh, ja-ed' his way through the queue, which was trying really hard not to look like a queue, before it was my turn to approach. I strode forward purposefully, smiled a winning smile and held out my hand. 'Hello,' I said, 'I'm from England.' He shook my hand, dipped his head, smiled and said, 'Oh, ja?'

And then I realised that I really didn't know what to say next. His Serene Highness Prince Hans Adam II *von und zu* Liechtenstein looked at me expectantly, while a rivulet of sweat ran down the side of his face to form a saline bulb at his chin. Our hands were still clasped together, and the droplet of sweat detached itself from his face and splashed on to my forearm. Later it struck me that if I'd been unwittingly developing any horrible diseases, I was probably now cured.

I still can't believe what I said next. I put it down to a combination of nerves at meeting royalty face to sweaty face, the blazing midday sunshine and the three glasses of free beer I had now consumed. So please bear this in mind when I tell you that I nodded over the Prince's shoulder at the castle and said, 'Nice house.' That's right, 'nice house'. A bit like nodding at the Statue of Liberty and saying to the President of the United States, 'I like your gnome.'

Prince Hans Adam II nodded again and said, '*Oh, ja?*' 'Um, *ja*,' I responded. 'Sank you,' he said, and released my hand. I backed away, a small voice in my head telling me that you should never turn your back on royalty, which was just making itself heard above another small voice telling me what a twat I was. Having thus backed into a bush, I went to find Ralf and Stefanie before the Prince set the Palace Guard on me.

'Did you speak to the Prince?' asked Ralf. 'Yep,' I admitted. 'What did you say?' 'Er, not much. Shall we go and walk up these mountains then?' Before I'm thrown out of the country for behaving like an arse in front of the reigning monarch.

As Ralf and Stefanie gathered together their sturdy hiking things (I'm sure I heard the clank of crampons from inside Ralf's duffel bag) I looked through the gate to the garden where the Prince was standing. I took heart from the fact that somebody else had clearly just made themselves look even more foolish than I had. A middle-aged woman was on her knees and the Prince was helping her up by the arm. Now either she had tried to show her devotion to her monarch by attempting to fellate the Prince, or she'd approached him for a chat and tripped over. How embarrassing, I thought, comforting myself that the Liechtenstein Berk of the Day award would not, after all, have my name on it.

Nineteen

The Fürstensteig is a long hike through the mountains of Liechtenstein, something that every Liechtensteiner does at least once in their life. You scale some of the country's tallest peaks, from where on a clear day you can see as far as Germany. Now I was expecting a similar walk to my Triesenberg expedition where I had congratulated myself on choosing such a safe place to explore. You know, a few gentle double backs, the odd open field to take in the scenery and a nice village at the end. Ralf reckoned the walk would take about four hours, quite long for a lazy bunter like me, but at least there'd still be plenty of time to get thoroughly stuck in to the evening's festivities.

So I wasn't too worried when we reached the start. I had wondered why Ralf had instructed me not to bring my bag, which accompanied me everywhere, but I was in good spirits and estimating totally incorrectly my personal level of fitness.

Whenever Katie comments on my parlous physical condition, I loftily inform her that I used to run half-marathons as a teenager, and you don't just lose that level of fitness. 'Oh yes?' she asks, 'and when did you last do one of those?' 'Um, 1986. No, 1987.'

So when we assembled at the start of the walk, my position at the pointy end of a direction sign reading SUCKA was not inappropriate. Another sign directed you to TOURISTLAGER, which I rather liked the sound of. Ralf, a bandana around his head, and Stefanie set off at breakneck speed and I was soon lagging behind, panting like a thirsty Doberman. And after about an hour of scrambling along chalky scree paths, I arrived at one of those life-defining moments.

Stefanie had told me that an average of one person a year dies on the Fürstensteig. I had presumed she was joking. No one had died in 2001, and now I was here. What faced me as we rounded a bend was the stuff that nightmares are made of. We had been walking along a path that snaked around the mountain, usually about six feet wide with the rockface to your right and a sheer drop to your left. That part I could just about handle, as long as I looked firmly at the ground two feet ahead of me. But here, the path tapered to a width that barely qualified as a ledge. For a length of about eight feet, the path was six inches wide. That's six inches between the side of the mountain, which at this point leant outwards at head height, and a sheer drop of hundreds of feet. There was a single black cord hammered into the rockface for you to hang on to and, given the protrusion of the rockface at that point, hanging was what you had to do, leaning right out into the abyss. Ralf and Stefanie both scampered across, dangling themselves from the cord out into the nothingness as if they hadn't even noticed the drop. They disappeared off around the corner and eventually noticed that I hadn't followed.

I was absolutely and completely terrified. Gingerly I toed a pebble over the edge and watched as it bounced down the scree a couple of times and then out into the air before vanishing completely from sight.

'It's easy,' said Ralf unhelpfully. 'You can't fall,' lied Stefanie. It took a good fifteen minutes of patient coaxing from my co-walkers before I even considered taking hold of the cord. Stefanie came back across and offered to follow behind me. They both gallantly offered to turn back with me and abandon the walk, but I couldn't let them down and spoil the day they had evidently been planning for some time by being such a drink of water. I thought of Katie sitting in her office at that moment completely unaware that I was in mortal fear of my life. I also thought how ridiculous it was that, should my number actually come up on the way across, the last thing I'd see as I hurtled to my death would be the face of the five times Liechtenstein national squash champion.

Eventually I grasped the wire. Then I put one foot on the ledge. I reached out with my other hand and held the wire further along and moved my other foot on to the ledge. 'Okay, take that hand off and cross it over,' said Ralf patiently. It occurred to me that I would rather just stay here for the rest of my life than take my hand off the cord, and I confess I may have used language wholly disrespectful to Liechtenstein National Day. Whimpering like a child I crossed my hands over and shuffled along a bit further. There was no turning back now. Gingerly I edged along the ledge, vowing to myself that I would never ever be scared of going up a ladder again. It seemed to take an hour, but must have been about five minutes. Finally I was across and leapt into Ralf's arms in a manner wholly unbefitting two chaps who barely know each other. Stefanie skipped lightly across again and I felt as relieved and exhilarated as at any time in my life. Endorphins coursed around my body, and I was now ready for anything. I laughed like a maniac.

I pulled out my notebook and scribbled illegible things that might well have been deep meditations on the meaning of life, but all I could read later was a shaky sentence recording 'the most terrifying experience of my entire life'.

Eventually the adrenalin wore off and I realised just how knackered I was. The good thing about being absolutely scared witless is that it rather takes your mind off other stuff, like how tired you are, your tax return, how close you are to your overdraft limit and how every sensible person in Liechtenstein was still at the castle necking free beer and not dicing with the grim reaper on the side of a mountain.

But tired I certainly was. We were at a considerable height, and Ralf apologised for forgetting that I wasn't used to altitude. We were a good few thousand feet above sea level and, whilst we weren't exactly needing breathing apparatus, the air was thinner than at ground level. At this point I should have apologised for being such a yellow-bellied scaredy-cat, but didn't. After a couple of hours more walking I was breathing hard and my legs were not responding. My eyes were in a permanent squint against the brightness of the chalky rock of the path, the mountainside and the steep slope to the left that was the quick way back to Vaduz. It was like being on a *Doctor Who* set.

Suddenly we discovered the land that time forgot. Rounding a bend, the dusty chalky rock gave way to a huge vista of lush green pasture in a valley between the mountains. I presumed I was hallucinating, but I was sure I saw a brontosaurus nibbling at the upper leaves of a tree far below. From the valley floor came the mass tinkling of what sounded like hundreds of cowbells. 'That's a lovely sound,' I gasped between forced breaths. Ralf and Stefanie both turned to look at me together, their expressions suddenly steely. 'Imagine if you could hear that non-stop, all day and all night,' said Ralf levelly. I took their point. My fellow walkers agreed to my pleading that we sit down and rest for a while before pressing on, so we sat on a handily placed bench and talked about Liechtenstein.

'The size of the country makes us special in some ways,' said Ralf. 'We are only thirty-two thousand in number, of which two-thirds are actually Liechtensteiners. I think that makes us more proud to be Liechtensteiners than other nationalities are, because it is something special to have a Liechtenstein passport. It gives us a strong national identity. That's fading away a bit now, but the former prince was highly regarded and highly respected because he made Liechtenstein into what it is now. Every Liechtensteiner respects that, and we'd have done anything for the old prince which we wouldn't do for the new Prince. He's not so popular. I think now that there are more Liechtensteiners who wouldn't mind giving up the monarchy than there were twenty years ago. I think the majority are still in favour, however, as that's what makes us special. We have nice mountains, but so do Switzerland and Austria. We have the same standard of living as Switzerland, and there's really nothing unique about Liechtenstein except the monarchy.

'The tax thing makes the country attractive, which is why we have so many foreign people here. We have around ninety-thousand letterbox companies, which is practically a Liechtenstein invention. That's the most famous aspect of Liechtenstein from a business point of view. Some people even say that Liechtenstein is the bank of the Swiss banks.

'In fact the royal family was losing money until a few years ago. Every now and then they would have to sell another picture from the collection to release some cash. Today's prince managed to stabilise the expenditure and now they don't have to sell pictures any more. He turned it all around. That's the thing with him: he doesn't want to be just a figurehead who shakes hands with people and says "welcome to Liechtenstein", he wants to have an influence over what goes on, hence these constitutional proposals.

'Everyone agrees that the constitution needs to be renewed, because it dates back to 1921. The Prince and parliament couldn't agree, and so they brought in four history professors who specialise in constitutional matters. Broadly they deduced that the Prince was out to get more power. We had a bad experience with the Prince back in, I think, 1993 when he dissolved parliament. That was a very unpopular move because people saw it as the behaviour of a dictator. He has a great deal of power already – the Prince appoints people to high office and parliament can only make suggestions. He also countersigns all the laws passed in the parliament – if he doesn't sign, the law doesn't go through. He's a bit like a shareholder with fifty-one per cent: he has the last word. But he's important because the Prince and the castle give Liechtenstein its image abroad.

'We are a member of many European organisations, such as the European Free Trade Agreement, and I think we are respected in these organisations. Sometimes there have been problems, like when we tried to join the European parliament in Strasbourg a few years ago. The Soviet representative said that they should not let Liechtenstein in until we had proved our independence. He said we have Swiss money and postal system, Swiss guards on the border with Austria; how are we an independent nation? And he had a point. It can be a problem that nobody knows Liechtenstein. You talk to people abroad and say, "I'm from Liechtenstein," and they say, "Oh yes, Luxembourg, I know." I've even had my nationality confused with Lithuania, people saying, "Oh yes, you had that revolution didn't you?"

'But we're fortunate. There's no real poverty, not absolute poverty, and the unemployment rate is very small, probably about three hundred people. A lot of people say that many of these could surely find a job, and I tend to agree. But there are also probably a lot who are ashamed to go and register as unemployed. The standard of living is as high as in Switzerland: low taxes, great landscape, no national service because there's no army, the weather's great most of the time, we get a lot of sun and the economy is working well. We have problems, but they are only small. When all is said and done, it's a pretty good place to live. Which is why we have to restrict the number of foreigners who want to live and work here.'

Stefanie's perspective was a little different, as she was one of these foreign workers. Indeed, it was fairly likely that she was about to be kicked out of the country.

'You have to re-apply for residency every year, although there are different types of residency. At first my job was only going to be six months, so they gave me a short permit. Usually, you only get this once. Then when the environment department asked me to stay on, I told them that I wouldn't have permission to be here. No problem, they said, we'll sort that out, and got me an extension until June this year. Then my boss said he'd extend my contract for another year, so I assumed it would be the same situation. However, when I asked for another short permit, they told me it wasn't possible. So I started getting worried, and eventually I got a phone call that told me I had to leave the country. And if I didn't go I wouldn't be allowed to return to Liechtenstein or Switzerland for ten years! They said I should wait for a letter to tell me I had three days to get out. The strange thing was that when I told them I'd rented a room in Balzers and had furniture and things there they said, oh, you can keep the apartment and your job, it's just that you're not allowed to sleep in Liechtenstein. You'll have to get out of the country overnight. Then they realised that it was a bit embarrassing that one section of the government wanted me to work here while another wanted me out of the country. So they said, okay, I can stay longer. And now I'm waiting to hear confirmation of that. It's the same for everyone: I met someone recently who has been here for twenty years and had to reapply for her residency every year.

'When I first arrived people were friendly. It's such a small place that the people have to make themselves different. I mean, look at the newspapers here. Where I come from you don't buy a newspaper, you might get a free one through the door once or twice a week. Yet here, they have two daily newspapers every day, that people buy! Everywhere in the world there are horrible things happening, but in Liechtenstein they put things like Status Quo coming to play on the front page.

'There are big environmental problems here though, which we're trying to sort out at the environmental department. I studied geography at university and wrote a thesis in ecology. My father acts as a consultant to the government here and knows people in the environment department, so he showed them my thesis and they offered me a job. Suddenly, I was in Liechtenstein, and I've been here now for a year and a half. I was a bit surprised by Vaduz: I'd been expecting a historical place, but it was just full of large ugly buildings. Vaduz tries to be a big city, but walk two hundred metres and you're out of town. At the moment they are trying to pass laws regarding spatial planning because of all the new buildings. Everyone's worried that they might be stopped from building. Everyone agrees that there's too much building work going on, but no one wants to be the one to stop. So they just talk about it and talk about it and the law doesn't get passed. But all the time the work is harming the environment by taking away the landscape. The intensity of farming grows as well, because the population is growing. Land is at a premium, so when people want to build, the land is very expensive. The economy is doing well, so people will always want to build new offices and houses for new employees, and it's hard to know when it's all going to stop.

'What have I noticed about Liechtensteiners? They all seem

to know each other. I was talking to someone at the office yesterday who had been to a business event the night before and was amazed that he only knew four people there. I noticed also that people don't gossip much, because then everyone would know everybody's secrets. Take my friend Claudia – there are probably people who know about her and Manfred, but would never let on because they might be seen with somebody they shouldn't be seen with themselves.'

Ralf was keen to press on. We'd conquered the first mountain despite the presence of a physically wrecked cowardy-custard in the trio, but my slow and terrified progress had put us well behind schedule. We ploughed on up the next peak, which was much more like what I'd expected – well-developed paths without a sheer drop to the side, for example. We were still at considerable altitude, and I was really starting to struggle. As we got near the top, I was finding it difficult to breathe at all, and was inhaling and exhaling in three gusts each way. The lack of oxygen was affecting my legs too, which felt like they'd been sliced open and the muscles placed on the outside for a group of small children to twang like rubber bands. Around twenty yards below the summit I saw what I thought was an illusion: there was a bench. I stumbled towards it and lay flat out, gasping and gulping. Ralf and Stefanie tried to persuade me to make it to the top, but I was having none of it. My language was deteriorating as quickly as my physical condition. 'You have to see the cross at the top,' implored Ralf, to which I may have responded, 'Bollocks to the cross,' but my recollection is hazy.

Eventually, they left me to it and I lay full-length on the bench, turning my head slightly so I could see Vaduz hundreds of feet below. I couldn't actually see the castle grounds from where I was, but in my mind's eye there were lots of happy, relaxed people, still drinking free beer while a tall, sweating man said 'Oh, ja?' a lot. I looked across towards Switzerland, noting that the Rheinpark Stadion was, from up here, smaller than a postage stamp. We were so high, I could see alps behind alps behind alps. It would have been breathtaking if my breath hadn't already been taken.

From above I suddenly heard a girlish giggle and what sounded like slurping. I swung my protesting legs to the ground and looked up. Yep, Ralf and Stefanie were getting it on, on top of the mountain. Oh great, I thought. Not only am I an unfit scaredy-cat who's holding back the whole expedition, I'm now also a gooseberry. There we were, three people at what seemed like the summit of the world, and two of them were snogging. I lay down again and tried to concentrate on making my breathing sound less like I was both hyperventilating and reaching orgasm at the same time. My heart was thumping away like a steamhammer, and I could feel the veins in my temples pulsing. My vision was almost black and white. Take my word for it, I had reached the outer limits of human endurance.

Clearly my word's not worth that much because at that point a couple old enough to be my grandparents trotted past the bench with a cheery '*Grüss Gott!*' I think I managed a feeble wave in response.

The arrival of the veteran hikers prompted Ralf and Stefanie to unfurl themselves from each other's grasp. We'd been gone four hours and weren't even halfway yet. Which was, of course, all my fault. Ralf suggested we turn back, and offered me the options of going back the way we'd come, i.e. along that fateful ledge, or a different way that might take longer. Guess which way I chose.

It was extraordinarily reasonable of them, considering I'd thoroughly ruined the walk by being a bad-tempered, sweary, good-for-nothing big-girl's-blouse who had moaned, complained and blasphemed his way across the roof of Liechtenstein. I had not shut up about being in need of a very large beer since we'd left, and now I must have been really getting on their nerves. The way back involved a series of steep double backs to a nearby summit, halfway up which I stopped, refusing to go any further. The sun was going down now, and the air was getting chilly. I could tell Ralf was starting to get worried about my physical condition, and how it might stop us getting back before nightfall which might not be particularly pleasant.

He told me that there was a restaurant just over the summit where we could stop for something to eat. And I believed him. He still had to propel me with one hand in the small of my back though, making my jellied legs whirl faster than was good for them. When we reached the top and I realised that the restaurant had been nothing more than a carrot in front of this wreck of a donkey, I crumpled to the ground and pleaded with them to let me die right there. It was then that I noticed that Ralf and Stefanie were not even out of breath.

A huge valley opened up in front of us and we began to descend. After an hour or so we saw lights – houses! There were houses!

Finally, as darkness fell, we reached Ralf's car, which he had left parked outside a restaurant. Ralf and Stefanie stopped at the car, but I kept going, straight through the gate, through the double doors, on to a chair and summoned the largest beer known to mankind. Ralf and Stefanie followed. And ordered mineral water.

Finally we were back in Vaduz some nine hours after our expedition had begun. Luckily we were just in time for the fireworks, and took up places in the car park opposite the Post Office.

What followed was the most extraordinary display of pyrotechnics I had ever seen. Huge fountains of colour appeared in the sky, enormous luminous tentacles that reached out towards you, followed a second later by an explosion that thumped you in the chest. For a full half an hour the sky over Liechtenstein was ablaze with bangers, rockets and blizzards of light that hurtled skyward from behind the castle. The climax of the display came when the phrase 'Für Gott, Fürst und Vaterland' ('For God, the Prince and the Fatherland') appeared in vast sparkling phosphorescent letters on the castle wall.

Then the fun could really begin. I had never seen Vaduz so busy. The streets were packed with people, inspecting stalls, buying beer and sausages, consuming beer and sausages, hailing friends and acquaintances. In the marquee next to the town hall, a band calling themselves Dr Schlager und die Kuschelbaren (which my dictionary translated as Dr Brawler and the Snuggle Bars) were in full swing, belting out a German-language version of 'Up Where We Belong'.

As I walked, or rather hobbled, past a table full of drinkers, there was a tug at my sleeve. At the table were Jürgen Ospelt and Harry Zech, a little the worse for wear. We called for more beer and speculated upon what a crap game it had been the night before. This time Harry didn't attempt to solicit my opinion of London's lap-dancing clubs. But then again he could hardly speak.

We sat and talked until the bar closed. Harry had heard that there was another open-air bar still open near the Post Office, to which we adjourned. As I waited to be served I became aware in the corner of my vision of a big beige thing moving towards me at great speed. I turned to look and was almost knocked flying by Patrik Hefti, clad in shorts, t-shirt and a natty pair of pink sunglasses. He was rather tipsy.

'My wife is still in America,' he confided, 'but she comes back tomorrow. Which is good because I have been drinking far too much beer this week.'

I asked if he wanted another one. 'Vodka and Red Bull,' he slurred. 'The coach of Schaan said we were not to drink today but he can . . .' Deciding that actions would speak louder than words, he turned around, bent over and slapped himself on the bottom.

It was a fine, fine night. As I stood, sharing a drink with the Liechtenstein national football team on Liechtenstein National Day, I decided that it really couldn't get much better than this. I got talking to somebody at the bar who, it turned out, used to play for the national team too. 'I played in a game in Ireland,' he said. 'I got booked and the whole crowd, about forty-thousand people, were boo-ing me. I felt like shit,' he said, before picking up his drinks and disappearing into the crowd.

In the interests of research, I stayed until the bitter end. Eventually everyone had gone home and I commenced the slow walk back to the Schäfle as the morning glow began to appear behind the mountains. The wind blew warm, moved empty plastic glasses around the streets and made the countless

Liechtenstein flags billow. A solitary lorry loaded up barriers, and a young woman walked alone in the same direction on the other side of the road. On hearing my footsteps, she turned around and waved with a cheerful '*Hoi*', the dialect greeting.

As I reached the Schäfle, a church chimed 5 a.m. It had been a long, occasionally terrifying, but fantastic Liechtenstein National Day.

I looked up towards Triesenberg and couldn't distinguish the village lights from the stars.

Twenty

Three weeks later I was sitting in the Adler restaurant with three Germans on the day after England had beaten Germany, and raising a froth-topped glass of beer. 'Cheers,' I said.

'Five times cheers,' came the tight-lipped reply.

I had arrived earlier in the day to be picked up at Sargans by Ralf. 'There's a German documentary crew in Liechtenstein,' he said as we drove at the speed of sound. 'They're making a film about our preparations for the match against Spain, and I told them about you. They're keen to meet you. Well, to be honest, they asked if they could meet some fans. No one could think of any, so I mentioned that we had this English writer coming to all the matches, was that any good? I think they want to speak to you.'

Hence that evening Ralf and I joined Peter, Stefan and Tim around a large wooden table in the same room that Playfair and Fitzgibbon had dined in half a century earlier. The contrast in documentary technique between their eschewing of the humble notebook and the equipment-laden German trio couldn't have been more marked. We agreed to meet the following day.

On Monday evening, forty-eight hours before the Spain game, I wandered down to training. A temporary stand had gone up behind the far goal, an extra 1,000 seats to take the capacity up to more than 4,500. The players jogged around the edge of the pitch. Patrik saw me and waved. It had been touch and go whether he'd make the game, as I had discovered two weeks earlier when he'd sent me an e-mail.

> Dear Charlie,
> How are you? I'm doing fine except I pulled my calf muscle last Monday at practice. We are not sure yet if I will be able to play against Spain. Loose thinks it won't be possible, but I told him you never know how long it will take to heal. It was a fun time on National Day but unfortunately I had a little too much alcohol.
> Best regards,
> Patrik

I felt terrible for him. The biggest game of his career, and he might miss it with something as trivial as a tweaked muscle. Just before I left for Vaduz, however, another e-mail arrived.

> Hi Charlie,
> My injury is getting better, slowly but surely, and I hope I will be able to play next week. Everybody in Liechtenstein is excited about the game and I'm sure it is going to be a great night. We'll practise on Saturday afternoon and on Sunday morning before we meet at Hotel Schaanerhof on Monday night. We will stay there until the match on Wednesday. Take care and talk to you soon!
> Greetings,
> Patrik

As he limbered up with the rest of the squad, it looked like the intensive physiotherapy had paid off, and Liechtenstein's burly defender would take his place against Raul and Morientes.

The TV crew showed up, sat me in the stand and asked me what I was doing in Liechtenstein. After ten minutes of flannel, I realised that I wasn't actually sure myself.

There were still forty-eight hours to go, and I was already nervous about the game. Spain needed a point to ensure their place in the World Cup finals, but the optimist in me was shouting about football being a funny old game. If they could get to half-time goalless, I thought, then something might happen. I mulled around the scoreline Liechtenstein 1 Spain 0 and decided that it had a nice ring to it. I imagined it flashing around the newswires of the world, one of the greatest upsets in world football since the USA beat England at the 1950 World Cup. And my team would have done it.

When I came down from the stand to the tunnel I was startled to find Patrik was standing there, showered and changed. The rest of the squad were still on the field playing attackers v defenders. I looked at him and raised an eyebrow. He shook his head and gave me a tight-lipped smile.

'I felt the muscle tighten while we were warming up,' he said, sadly. 'I knew straightaway that was it, I've got no chance of making the game.' He went quiet, watching the rest of the squad sprinting around the pitch and sighed. 'It didn't actually go, but I knew I had to do it for the team. It could have pulled at any minute. It would have been no good keeping quiet and then having to come off after ten minutes.'

Another pause. 'Plus I have to think of my club too. We have an important game on Saturday, and I can't let them down either.'

I made insufficient consoling noises. What could I say? That there was always next time? Because at nearly thirty-two, for Patrik there might not be a next time to play against a team like Spain. He was already mulling over whether to call it a day in favour of his banking career, and this game would have been the perfect occasion to make his last appearance for the team in Liechtenstein.

'The bank have given me the time off to play in this game. I guess I'll have to go back to work tomorrow now.' At his feet was a holdall, packed with kit and toiletries for three days with the squad. Now as the team headed off to the Schaanerhof to plan how they'd deal with Mendieta, Patrik would go back to his apartment, unpack everything, and lay his suit out ready for work the next day.

He was doing a good job of putting a brave face on the

situation, but it was clear that missing the game was hurting a lot more than a pulled calf muscle. The big defender picked up his bag, slung it over his shoulder and limped off into the night.

Later that evening in Bar Wolf I bumped into Ernst and his *Vaterland* colleague Fabio Corba, an earnest, quietly spoken young man with glasses on a cord around his neck. The conversation turned to Mario Frick, who during the close season had signed for Hellas Verona in Italy's Serie A to cap an eventful twelve months for the young striker from Balzers. A couple of weeks earlier he had made his debut as a late substitute in a 1–1 draw against the champions Roma. 'Liechtenstein will really miss him against Spain,' I said. 'I still can't believe what happened.'

'I knew there was something going on,' said Ernst. 'A few days before the Israel game I had to go to San Marino for the Games of the Small Nations. I called in on the way to see Mario just after Arezzo had lost the first leg of their play-off. Mario was asking about the games, and said maybe he'd come down for a day to support Liechtenstein.

'"But Mario," I said, "you'll be with the national team then, getting ready for the game against Israel." "We'll see," he had replied, "I have to speak to the President about that." I couldn't believe it. I tried to tell him that Arezzo's midfield was no good, that they had no chance against Livorno and he should come to Liechtenstein, but he wanted to play in this game. It's a terrible shame because I was once his coach, I know how good he is.'

It was another long night. Albrecht appeared late on, and started ranting about the European Union. 'The only way you'll get me to Brussels,' he said, prodding the table top with his finger, 'is by first class train, with the promise of a room at the most expensive hotel in the city, and Claudia Schiffer at my disposal.'

The following afternoon there was more training at the stadium. In the tunnel I found Martin Frommelt, the LFV press officer, happily putting press passes into little laminated pouches ready for the game the following night. There would be 120 journalists at the game, he told me proudly. He also said that the last tickets had been sold that morning, guaranteeing a 4,600 sell-out.

'That should be good for the atmosphere,' I said.

'Let's hope so,' he replied with a sigh. 'With Liechtenstein it's like we play every game abroad.'

After training I met Ernst at the *Vaterland* offices. For a newspaper with a circulation of around 10,000, the offices are highly salubrious. There are potplants and spotlights everywhere, and the walls are adorned with works of modern art. Everywhere you look computer terminals blink at you. It was a contrast to many British newspaper offices. Where were the mouldy coffee cups, I wondered? The stains on the carpets? The teetering piles of old newspapers?

Ernst was going through the photos he had just taken at training, trying to pick one for tomorrow's paper. Today's lead story had been the withdrawal of Patrik from the squad, but Ernst suspected that he would lead tomorrow with the Spanish training session for which we were shortly to depart. Much to the LFV's disappointment, the Spanish had chosen not to base themselves in Liechtenstein, but in St Gallen, over an hour away in Switzerland. It was a bit of a snub. Ralf had told me that the Spanish had been calling about the most ridiculous things – would there be hot water in the dressing-room showers after the game, for example? 'Where do they think they are coming to?' asked Ralf incredulously.

We drove to St Gallen as the sun set, eventually finding the Spanish squad training in a distant floodlit corner of a huge sports complex. We had paused on the way so that Ernst could load up his car with several boxes of aerosol horns. 'I think we might sell a few tomorrow night,' he said as he threw another box on to the back seat.

Around 300 Spanish fans lined the pitch, as Raul, Hierro and co. engaged in some light head tennis and two-touch matches. The players seemed relaxed, enjoying the session which finished with a full-scale practice match. Mendieta darted around, his mane of blond hair flopping behind him. Raul and Hierro indulged in practical jokes, pulling down players' shorts and wrestling them to the ground as they attempted to go past with the ball: it was almost like a Sunday league side having a kickabout. You almost felt you could join in, until you noticed the quality in the way they struck the ball, and the lightning speed of the passing movements. Even the goalkeepers could clearly land the ball on a sixpence from forty yards, as Casillas and Canizares demonstrated by belting a ball to each other. Camacho, the coach, looked on benignly, his hands clasped behind his back. A short, tubby man, Camacho's record number of caps for an outfield player would be equalled in the Rheinpark Stadion by his captain Hierro.

At the end of the session, the players tried to bolt for their coach before the fans reached them. To do so, however, they had to pass through the crowd and then along a 100-yard footpath. There was no escape. Spanish camera crews ran around, trying to grab players for interviews and dragging cables that flipped children over. The players were swamped by fans waving cameras and pieces of paper. Ernst was chasing Camacho, showing an impressive turn of speed as he waved his pad and pen, calling, 'Senor Camacho! Senor Camacho!' after him. Camacho waved his hand dismissively and ran up the steps on to the coach. I stood outside the team bus, watching the scene unfolding. Wide-eyed children high-fived each other, clutching precious autographs. Hierro came around the corner, waist deep in more children waving pens and paper. It was almost religious. Raul posed for a couple of pictures with little girls whose eyes sparkled with delight and disbelief.

Finally the coach pulled away followed by a cloud of exhaust and cries of 'viva Espana', and I inhaled a lungful of fumes. I felt almost anointed. And then it started to pour with rain.

On the way back to the office, Ernst expounded on what he saw as the arrogance of Camacho in not giving him an interview. He also proudly told me how he'd broken the news to Loose that Vicente and Xavi wouldn't be playing, staying instead with the under-twenty-ones. 'He'd been planning his defence around Vicente's runs down the left,' said Ernst.

Late in the evening, when the *Vaterland* had finally been put to bed, we repaired to the Nexus for a nightcap. An older man left with a voluptuous younger woman, whom Ernst had been eyeing up with little subtlety all evening. I asked if he was married.

'No,' he said. 'But I have a girlfriend.'

Then he fell silent. After a short while he spoke again, his eyes darker than usual. 'We had a son, but he was killed five years ago in a road accident. He was eight and a half.'

Another pause.

'He was . . . brilliant.'

Ernst's girlfriend Cornelia had taken it badly and now rarely left their house in Triesenberg. I thought I realised now why he led such a busy life, working late and starting early, travelling all over the world covering sporting events. He said that they talk about it a lot, and that the man who had just left the bar with the younger woman had also lost a son, two years earlier. 'The death of a child really affects a relationship,' he told me as he dropped me back at the Schäfle.

Katie was arriving the next day to watch the Spain game. We had been talking a lot about starting a family, and everything seemed ready out in front of us. We could pick and choose when and where we would be. Yet Ernst and poor Cornelia had had their family cruelly taken from them. Suddenly, I understood Ernst much better.

Twenty-one

It was the morning of the match, and I woke with butterflies. It was raining, as I'd come to expect, and all those David
v Goliath clichés ran through my mind. Heavy pitch. Won't
suit the Spanish passing game. Might bring them down to
Liechtenstein's level. Katie arrived in the afternoon and I
showed her around Vaduz, which took ten minutes. We went
for a meal before the game, in a restaurant full of Spaniards,
but my mind was on the match. As we left the restaurant, I
heard the distant parping of aerosol horns. Ernst was clearly
doing good business. In the *Vaterland* that day, he had made
several references to '*arroganter* Camacho'.

Outside the stadium, Spanish fans mingled happily, singing,
chanting and blasting their newly purchased horns. We found
our seats at the back of the main stand and my stomach was
in knots.

The loss of Hefti had been a major blow for Loose, given
that he was already missing long-term defensive casualties
Daniel Hasler and Christof Ritter. In front of Zech and hoping
to contain the threat of the Real Madrid pairing of Raul and
Fernando Morientes would be young Michael Stocklasa, more
comfortable in a midfield holding role, and the eighteen-year-
old FC Vaduz defender Andreas Gerster, winning only his third
full cap. Frick was absent, so was the bulldozer Fabio D'Elia
who had succumbed to a knee injury. Ronny Büchel and
Thomas Beck would be up front.

The teams took the field to a blast of aerosol horns. Meteorologists around the world leapt to their workstations as a miniature hole appeared in the ozone layer above Liechtenstein. As the teams stood for the national anthems I was like a jazz drummer on speed. I was drumming my fingers, tapping my pen and both feet were hammering the ground in a mixture of excitement and nerves. Bloody hell, I thought, I don't get this wound up when I watch Charlton play.

Loose emerged from the tunnel just as the team lined up to kick off. Some last-minute tactics to work out, I thought, or a curious personal superstition. I learnt afterwards that in fact the coach had gone to the toilet in the dressing room when the players had left for the field, only to be inadvertently locked in by an over-enthusiastic stadium attendant. Hollering and hammering on the door producing no response, it took a mobile-phone call for the Liechtenstein coach to be released from his unintentional incarceration and take his place in the dugout.

Predictably, Liechtenstein packed everyone behind the ball from the start. Spain immediately took up residence in the Liechtenstein half, stringing together short, quick passes, attempting to work an opening in the blanket rearguard. Inside the second minute a neat interchange of passes between Luis Enrique and Raul let in Fernando Morientes, but the Liechtenstein defence just stepped up in time to catch the Real Madrid striker offside. Shortly afterwards, Harry Zech slid in with a perfect tackle to win the ball from Morientes on the edge of the area. Gerster picked up the ball on the edge of the 'D', turned this way and that and laid a measured ball out to Ospelt on the right to clear the danger. Clearly the youngster was not overawed.

In the sixth minute Spain produced a wonderful passing movement that started with Hierro at the back, through three more players, and ended up with Raul again slipping the ball through to Morientes. This time there was no flag, and Jehle was out of his goal smartly to force the Real striker to slice a left-foot effort wide of the goal. It was beautiful football from Spain, who had moved the ball from deep in their own half to threaten the Liechtenstein goal with minimal running, just slick, two-touch passing that carved open the principality with worrying ease.

Realising the dangers posed by the Spaniards' neat passing, Liechtenstein buckled down, harassing their opponents before they had time to settle on the ball. Young players like Ronny Büchel and Thomas and Matthias Beck snapped away at the heels of the Spanish midfield, hoping to harry their cultured opponents into errors. Thomas Beck even managed to inflict an early shiner on Hierro, which darkened under his left eye as the match progressed. Gerster was showing an admirably calm head at the back, where the experienced Zech was talking him through the game.

Spain were committing players forward, and the edge of the Liechtenstein box was as congested as Oxford Circus on Christmas Eve. Spain's short passing game was being frustrated by the determination of Loose's side and, once again, Liechtenstein were denying more illustrious opponents clear scoring chances. Spain were building everything from Hierro at the back, but the big defender was finding it harder and harder to locate options for his subtle forward promptings.

Luis Enrique, who had missed the game in Alicante, received a stern lecture from the referee on the quarter-hour for an irritable hack at Telser's ankles, and you sensed that things weren't quite going as Spain had expected. They had been allowed far more space in the first game, and Liechtenstein's harrying tactics were frustrating their efforts to dictate the pace of the match. The home side were playing above themselves.

Two minutes later, Thomas Beck fouled Luis Enrique wide on the left. Gaizka Mendieta sent an inswinging ball into the area, which Raul nodded past Jehle and into the back of the net. As the Spanish fans celebrated, however, the referee called play back: as Mendieta had taken the free kick, he was still trying to ensure that the two-man Liechtenstein wall was ten yards from the ball.

Mendieta put the ball down again, floated exactly the same cross into the danger area, and Raul again applied the finish. It was an exact repeat of the first attempt only this one counted.

Mendieta's right-footed free kick swung over, Morientes jumped but couldn't get there, and Raul rose above Ospelt to nod the ball past Jehle. The horns blared and the Spanish trotted back to their own half with a couple of cursory handshakes. You couldn't help feeling that had the towering figure of Hefti been in there somewhere, neither cross would have got as far as the Real Madrid front man.

Nevertheless Liechtenstein regrouped and tried to put together an immediate response. Gigon sent a high ball into the area from inside his own half, Martin Stocklasa flicked it on, and Puyol just managed to get between Matthias Beck and the ball to allow Casillas to smother the danger. The ball moved swiftly to the other end, where Luis Enrique found himself in a rare patch of space on the edge of the area after skipping over Zech's challenge. The Barcelona midfielder looked up and sent a curling right-foot shot toward's Jehle's top left-hand corner. Somehow the Liechtenstein keeper, who had lost his place in the Grasshoppers team, managed to dive at full stretch and tip the ball around the post with a marvellous save. A minute later he was in action again, getting down low to smother a ball from Etxeberria to the near post as Morientes threatened.

Despite the constant pressure, where there were often twenty-one players in the Liechtenstein half, the young team remained unflustered, biding their time and hoping eventually to engage the visitors in their own half. When Thomas Beck was fouled forty yards from goal in the twenty-fifth minute, the home side had their first opportunity to mount a tangible effort on goal. Gigon and Matthias Beck stood over the ball, Gigon touched it to Beck and Martin Stocklasa thundered in a shot that flew over the crossbar. Normal service then resumed in the Liechtenstein half, with the Spanish patiently passing the ball around waiting for an opening. It rarely came and when it did, such as when Morientes threatened to shoot from close range just before the half-hour, Harry Zech was always there to slide in and clear the danger.

The captain was having another great night. Nothing was getting past him and he even saw fit to drop his shoulder in the penalty area and send Raul the wrong way on the half-hour. Winning his thirty-sixth cap, Zech was also using his experience to help his young colleagues through the game, chaperoning them in such a way that youngsters like Gerster were already playing with the calmness of veterans, and always making himself available for passes if they looked like they were in trouble.

There was only one defensive lapse in the entire half, when Morientes appeared unmarked at the far post for a Hierro free kick, but fortunately for Liechtenstein he sent a weak header straight into the arms of Jehle. Liechtenstein were playing out of their skins, and were neither overawed nor being outclassed. Shots from distance were charged down, and even Mendieta couldn't thread passes through the wall of blue shirts. Liechtenstein's solid defence had also virtually silenced the Spanish fans, most of whom sat glumly in the drizzle in the temporary stand behind Casillas' goal.

Spanish frustration was growing: on thirty-three minutes Luis Enrique went into the referee's book after leaving Martin Stocklasa prone and clutching his head on the edge of area, and shortly afterwards Gerster was left in a similar state by a clumsy Mendieta challenge. When Ospelt killed a forty-yard pass from Luis Enrique on his instep as Morientes hovered, the Spanish striker responded by hacking down Telser as he looked to escape down the right following Ospelt's pass. The Spanish were getting a bit niggly.

Nine minutes before the interval, Buchel turned Aranzabal and hared after a long ball from Ospelt. Casillas rushed from his area and hoofed the ball out of the ground as the Young Boys Berne striker closed in. Liechtenstein almost had the game in some sort of control.

The home side were reminded of their opponents' quality in the thirty-eighth minute, however. Hierro floated a high ball into the area, and suddenly Raul had it at his feet with just Jehle to beat. He skipped around the diving goalkeeper and slid the ball into the net past the covering Zech, only to see the linesman's flag raised for offside. It was either a lucky escape for Liechtenstein, or a brilliantly worked offside trap.

But the home side responded just as they had when they last picked the ball out of the net: by mounting an attack. Gigon found Thomas Beck thirty yards from goal. Beck, his socks at half mast as usual, moved inside, then darted between Luis Enrique and Augustin Aranzabal. With another touch he was past Oscar Tellez and free on the right side of the area. He hit a low shot across the face of the goal, and Casillas had to be at full stretch to prevent the ball going just inside the far post. It was a brilliant piece of work from the young Vaduz forward, and one that caused me to leap from my bench and send it to the floor with a crack like a gunshot.

Four minutes before the break, Jehle was in action again, smothering a shot from Etxeberria that he grabbed at the second attempt. As Spain swept forward again down the right, Telser, playing deeper than normal, robbed Aranzabal with a beautifully timed challenge. Thomas Beck nipped in and beat Luis Enrique with a delicate chip over the Barcelona star's challenge. Oscar Tellez moved in to clear, but Beck was too quick for him as well, and it needed Hierro to move across and halt the progress of the speedy FC Vaduz forward.

Liechtenstein finished the half with their best period of the game, knocking the ball around the midfield with increasing confidence. The enthusiastic Ronny Büchel and Thomas Beck continued to give Hierro a far from easy time, like two wasps buzzing around a sleepy lion. The only scare came late in the half when Michael Stocklasa missed a header, forcing Gigon into a fine saving tackle as Raul shaped to shoot from the corner of the six-yard box.

As the half-time whistle went I felt exhilarated. A team which contained five teenagers (plus Thomas Beck, just a few weeks into his twenties), and half a team of amateurs had restricted one of the greatest teams in the world to a single goal. I was beaming with pride. A girl sitting in front of me, who had enthusiastically celebrated the Spanish goal ('Why are there Spanish fans sitting here?' Katie had whispered as the girl cheered and clapped, used to the strict segregation of English grounds), turned and started talking to us. 'Spain, what a great team,' she was cooing. As she spoke, I suddenly placed her accent. 'You're from Liechtenstein, aren't you?' I asked. 'Of course,' she replied. 'Then, er, why are you supporting Spain?' I asked. 'Ach,' she said, wrinkling her nose, 'because the Liechtenstein team is rubbish, stupid, no good,' she said. 'Have you been watching the game?' I asked. 'They're playing well, they're only a goal behind.' 'Yes, but Spain have Raul, Mendieta,' she replied. 'Who do Liechtenstein have? No one. They are no good, they lose every game. Rubbish.'

Just what did this team have to do to please their public, I wondered? They had just played one of the best halves of football they had ever produced, had frustrated one of the world's best teams and gone in only a goal behind. Yet their own people were watching and criticising, writing off their super-human efforts. I was aghast.

The beginning of the second half was disjointed as Spain struggled to regain the territorial advantage they had enjoyed in the first half. At half-time, Camacho saw fit to withdraw two of his more influential players as Nadal replaced the captain Hierro and Jose Ignacio came on for Raul. Nadal's first contribution was to present the ball to Ronny Büchel in the centre circle. Büchel spread it wide to Thomas Beck, who hared down the right and sent a teasing cross into the box that Casillas had to snatch from Büchel's forehead. Without Hierro to kick off the slick passing movements, Spain were looking more to Mendieta for their creative impulse. Unfortunately for the visitors, the Lazio star was not having as successful a night as he had enjoyed in Alicante, and many passes were going astray. Just before the hour Mendieta cut inside and hoofed a wild shot high into crowd. Six months earlier he would have found the top corner.

Ten minutes into the half Luis Enrique broke inside the left of the area and chipped the ball across, only for Gigon to calmly chest it back to Jehle. Liechtenstein were looking more comfortable than they had in the entire game. Without the promptings of Hierro and the incisive runs of Raul, Spain were having trouble creating anything tangible and for the first time the cheery Spanish contingent began to whistle. When Morientes headed well over on the hour, it was only the fifth clear chance the Spanish had created, a fine tribute to Zech and his defence.

Just after the hour, the Spanish came as close to scoring as they had in the entire game. Puyol pushed the ball through to Luis Enrique on the left of the area. The Barcelona midfielder accelerated between Ospelt and Gerster and slipped it past Jehle. The goalkeeper had got a touch to the ball, but not enough to prevent it from heading inexorably for the back of the net. As the Spanish fans behind the goal leapt into the air, Michael Stocklasa appeared from nowhere to hook the ball off the line.

As Spain mounted another attack, Mendieta's miserable night continued. Luis Enrique's cross was flicked on by Morientes to find Mendieta between the corner of the six-yard box and the corner of the area. His right-foot shot thudded into the hoardings well wide of the goal. The Lazio midfielder looked thoroughly pissed off.

With just over twenty minutes remaining, as Ronny Büchel received treatment after being chopped down by Albelda, Loose brought off Matthias Beck and introduced Franz Burgmeier, the eighteen-year-old son of the Burgmeiers from the Schäfle, for his first full cap. Within a minute, Burgmeier had brought the crowd to its feet. Gigon intercepted a pass on the left and tapped the ball to the FC Vaduz youngster twenty yards inside the Liechtenstein half. Burgmeier beat Puyol, then slipped the ball past Jose Ignacio to Ronny Büchel, who gave it straight back to him with an impudent backheel. Evading Luis Enrique's challenge, Burgmeier then charged into the Spanish half, leaving both Aranzabal and Tellez on their backsides and headed for the penalty area. The crowd roared and I was on my feet. As he shaped to cut past Albelda, eight yards outside the box, the Valencia defender brought him down with a bodycheck, immediately raising both hands as an admission of guilt. He'd been on the field for sixty seconds, and Burgmeier had already upped the tempo of both the game and the crowd with a magnificent run. If Albelda hadn't illegally terminated the youngster's progress, Burgmeier would have been practically through on goal.

Clearly not lacking in confidence, the striker commandeered the free kick himself. A disappointing effort came back from the two-man wall, from where Mendieta passed right to Aranzabal. Burgmeier, keen to atone for his poorly taken place kick ran over, shoved Aranzabal to the ground with both hands right in front of the referee who waved play on, picked up the ball, cut inside and unleashed a twenty-five-yard daisy-cutter that flew just wide of Casillas' right-hand post with the keeper beaten.

Quite an introduction to international football. From somewhere away to my left a chant of 'Burgi! Burgi!' went up. In barely two minutes the teenage striker with dreams of turning professional had woken the crowd and demonstrated to the Spanish that the match wasn't over yet.

It was also a tribute to Loose's handling of his young players. Like Gerster, Büchel, the Becks and Jehle, Burgmeier was not in the slightest bit overawed by his illustrious opponents, something further demonstrated shortly afterwards when he attempted to nutmeg Gaizka Mendieta – with a back-heel. Conscious of the new threat, Camacho withdrew Luis Enrique and brought on another striker, Diego Tristan of Deportivo La Coruna who had bagged two goals in his three previous games for the national side. It appeared that Camacho had twigged that he needed to finish off the plucky principality.

Burgmeier was everywhere, even winning tackles against Mendieta close to Liechtenstein's left corner flag, and the crowd was starting to respond. Just as Daniel Hasler had recalled of the 0–0 draw with Ireland, it wasn't until the final minutes of the match that the home crowd really started to get behind Liechtenstein. The atmosphere had picked up substantially since Burgmeier's introduction, and Liechtenstein had visibly stepped up a gear. Spain had two good chances, with Tristan shooting over and Mendieta sending another shot horribly wide, but Liechtenstein's tails were up. The match was being beamed live to seventeen countries in Europe and South America, and my chest swelled as I thought of the millions watching this extraordinary team take the game to their opponents.

With ten minutes remaining it was clear that the baby-faced Ronny Büchel was struggling. As well as having run himself into the ground for eighty minutes, he'd had some harsh treatment from the Spanish defence, irked at his tireless impudent running, and a nasty kick from Tellez in the centre circle finally ended his part in the game. As Büchel limped off to warm applause with his arm around the physio, Loose introduced another teenager, Marco Büchel from FC Balzers, for his third cap.

With eight minutes remaining, a tiring Gigon brought down Mendieta wide on the right. The Lazio midfielder picked up the ball and sent it curling into the area where Real Mallorca's Miguel Angel Nadal got above Ospelt on the penalty spot and powered a thunderous header past Jehle and into the top corner for the decisive goal.

Any optimistic thoughts I'd had of the principality saving the game thus disappeared. But no one had told Burgmeier. As Liechtenstein kicked off again, the youngster scrapped for and won the ball and set off towards the goal. Nadal, the goalscorer, hurtled across and chopped him down. Despite having run into what must have felt like a concrete slab in a Spanish shirt, Burgmeier picked himself up, dusted himself off, and sent a dangerous curling free kick into the Spanish area that Puyol was forced to head over his own crossbar for Liechtenstein's first corner of the game.

Nadal headed the ball clear of Michael Stocklasa, and Marco Büchel sent a sidefooted volley just wide of the post. Despite their tireless running Liechtenstein seemed actually to be getting stronger. With two minutes left Loose withdrew Thomas Beck, whose relentless legwork had so unsettled the Spanish throughout the game. The bright-eyed young forward was given a huge ovation as he left the field, even by the Spanish fans. In his place came another teenager, Marco Nigg of St Gallen, a defender for a forward as Loose sought to protect the two-goal deficit.

There was still time for Puyol to hack down Burgmeier, possibly in retribution for the substitute's nerve in skinning him with his first touch, and for Mendieta to thread a dangerous ball into the area that Tristan couldn't quite reach with only Jehle to beat, but it was clear that Liechtenstein had pulled off a great result with arguably their best ever performance.

At the whistle the Liechtenstein crowd rose as one, cheering their heroic team. I spotted the tall figure of the LFV President Otto Biedermann at the front of the VIP section, punching the air and turning to embrace his wife. The players applauded the supporters, embraced each other and deservedly milked a standing ovation. Zech was grinning broadly, Thomas Beck was waving both fists in the air, wearing Aranzabal's shirt. Burgmeier trotted off the field with Mendieta's shirt draped over his shoulder. 'We Are The Champions' thundered from the PA system. It had been a wonderful performance, and remarkably I could feel tears of pride welling up. The difference between the two teams and the two nations was incredible: Barcelona alone have three times as many season-ticket holders as Liechtenstein has people, yet this tiny nation and its team of small-time professionals, bank workers, a winemaker and a schoolteacher had all but matched one of the world's greatest sides for ninety minutes.

I grinned maniacally at everyone as we made our way to the lounge. Markus Schaper said, 'We can be very proud,' as I gushed praise upon the team. There was laughter and cheering, and the clink of glasses as everyone toasted the magnificent performance by the home side. Patrik was there, grinning and clapping me on the shoulder. His wife Shannon was also there and in the spirit of bonhomie invited us to dinner the following night. The blue flashing lights of an ambulance cruised past the window, and the Spain coach pulled away in the other direction virtually unnoticed. Ralf Loose moved through the bar, a huge beaming smile fixed to his face. Everyone shook his hand as he passed, his expression one of pure elation. You'd have thought Liechtenstein had won. The players began to drift in, wearing fixed smiles of joy and disbelief.

Then Ralf Wenaweser appeared looking ashen and drained. He beckoned me over. 'You know Tommy, the guy that runs the catering units in the stadium?' I'd seen him around, but didn't know him as such. The TV crew had interviewed him before me at training earlier in the week. 'He's dead,' said Ralf.

'What?' I spluttered.

'He's dead. Massive heart attack. He went to a storeroom at half-time and no one saw him after that. His assistant was ringing his mobile but getting no answer, so he went to look for him. He found Tommy flat on his back, dead. I was the second person on the scene.'

As the news spread through the bar, the atmosphere became suddenly muted. This being Liechtenstein, everyone had known Tommy. He had an ice-cream parlour in the centre of Vaduz and was a popular local character. From the post-match euphoria, everyone was suddenly quiet. Eventually a small group of us adjourned to the Schwefel for a reflective drink. This was nothing like the party after the Israel game. Ralf turned up, looking drawn. 'Have you ever closed someone's eyes when they're dead?' he asked. 'I just did that. It was like shutting off the lights of somebody's life.'

Inevitably, the mood lightened when the greatest sports writer in the world arrived, dishing out page proofs from the following day's *Vaterland*. Jürgen Ospelt had been sitting with us, but moved to another table.

'He hates me,' said Ernst with a chuckle. 'I only gave him two out of five in Alicante, because he was too slow. All the Spanish papers praised him, gave him five out of five and called him The Terminator after he put Munitis out of the game. But I could see that he had a bad game, and marked him so. Shows what Spanish journalists know. He's not forgiven me yet.'

It turned into a long night. Patrik and Shannon left early, and we were left with the hardcore of Katie, me, Ernst, Ralf, Stefanie and a serious, sharp-faced young man with lank hair called Helge. Helge was putting together a book, the complete statistical record of Liechtenstein football. A work in progress, it currently weighed in at 800 pages, and he'd only got as far as 1960. In his spare time, Helge watched Faroe Islands' matches.

What a weirdo, I thought. Fancy following an obscure

national football team with whom you had no connection.

Ernst was soon in full flow, still on a high from the extraordinary match. He was relating the tale of FC Vaduz's promotion party of four months previously. They'd been in the Schwefel until 5.30 a.m., at which point someone had the bright idea of driving to Malbun for a pizza. Ernst rang one of the hotels, got the chef out of bed and instructed him to fire up the pizza oven, FC Vaduz were coming up the hill and they were hungry. He then told us a long story about combining watching a Liechtenstein training session with going to see the Rolling Stones in Zurich, before launching into his traditional closing time rendition of 'Let It Be', a song I will never listen to in the same way again.

As dawn began to break Katie and I went back to the Schäfle. Somewhere in the same building, Franz Burgmeier was sleeping, Mendieta's shirt draped over a chair. Whatever he was dreaming about, it couldn't surely have matched his extraordinary debut for the national team.

On our last day in Liechtenstein, we decided to call in on Ernst in Triesenberg. We'd enjoyed the hospitality of the Hefti household the previous evening, now it was the turn of the Hasler house. Cornelia looked drawn, but made us welcome with warm smiles, coffee and biscuits. A picture of Fabian, their late son, stood in a frame on the table. Ernst drove us to the bus stop by the church with the onion-shaped bell tower, and offered to show us Fabian's grave. 'I go there every day,' he said, 'except when I'm working abroad.'

It was at the end of a row, furthest from the church. A marble stone depicted a small boy looking up at a rainbow as the sun shone above. There was an oval photograph of Fabian cuddling a dog.

'He loved to have his picture taken,' said Ernst proudly. 'If ever I brought the camera home from the newspaper, he'd demand I get it out and take pictures of him.'

I comment on what a nice stone it is.

'Yes,' said Ernst, his voice suddenly fragile, 'we chose that because he always loved to look at rainbows . . . ' He broke off, and suddenly his whole body racked with an enormous sob. He fished frantically in his coat pocket for a handkerchief, but it was too late, the tears were already rolling down his cheeks. He pressed the handkerchief to his face as his shoulders shook with barely controlled grief. I put my arm around him, patting his shoulder and feeling utterly, utterly inadequate.

'We'd better go,' he sniffed eventually, dabbing his red-rimmed eyes with the handkerchief. 'Your bus will be here soon.'

Katie and I passed the journey back to the Schäfle in silence. The death of Tommy the ice-cream man, and Ernst's undiminished grief for his son made my quest to follow the Liechtenstein football team seem so ridiculous. The euphoria and emotion I'd felt in the immediate aftermath of the Spain match felt embarrassingly trite.

That evening, Ernst joined us in the bar of the Schäfle for a farewell drink. He was running late, having just taken a coaching session for the FC Vaduz under-eleven team. He was back to his old self, telling stories and jokes, even whisking Katie around the dancefloor at such a tempo that she lost both her shoes. It was as if the scene in the cemetery hadn't happened, as if Ernst had learned over the years to compartmentalise the grief that underpins his life.

Another of the footballing Burgmeier clan joined us. He'd been looking after the Spanish team during their stay. They were great, he said, easier than some. Apparently, one well-known international squad expect ladies of the night to be provided after matches, with two players in particular enjoying getting together with five girls to while away the hours. Only after matches, mind.

It was another night of warmth, hospitality and bonhomie that finished far too late. I was really going to miss Liechtenstein.

Twenty-two

If Liechtenstein football had reached its peak on 5 September, the carefully planned ascent was about to descend into chaos. It emerged shortly after the match that plans were afoot among a group of club chairmen to elect a new president of the LFV at the forthcoming annual general meeting, despite the continuing popularity of the current chief Otto Biedermann.

Liechtenstein's seven clubs all vote bi-annually to elect or re-elect a president, and, given the remarkable progress made in Liechtenstein football during the five years of his presidency, Biedermann's re-election was widely believed to be a straightforward formality. Biedermann, a board member for sixteen years, was a popular boss whom many credited as the main reason for the turnaround in the Liechtenstein game over the previous decade. Popular with the players, Loose, the public (such as it was) and the press alike, it was surely no coincidence that the national team had enjoyed its best years ever with Biedermann at the helm. His emotional reaction to the final whistle against Spain showed his passion and commitment and, at that moment, the bright future of Liechtenstein football opened out in front of him. Those ninety minutes in the Rheinpark Stadion represented the pinnacle of sixteen years of tireless endeavour for him personally, and Liechtenstein football as a whole.

But five club chairmen didn't like Otto Biedermann. Without

questioning the excellent work he'd done in his time on the board, the five clubs announced in mid-September that they would not be voting for his re-election at the end of the month. 'That's how it is in Liechtenstein,' someone told me. 'Whenever a person enjoys a bit of success, then other people get jealous and want to knock them down.'

Two weeks after the Spain game, and a fortnight before Liechtenstein's quest for the World Cup would come to an end in Bosnia, I received an e-mail from Patrik.

Hi Charlie,

How are you doing? I'm doing fine beside a few phone calls. Daniel Hasler, Harry Zech and myself gave an interview to the newspaper regarding the election of the football president. We told the paper that if the teams are not going to vote for Otto Biedermann we will take some action. So many people in Liechtenstein were quite angry about that. They said that players shouldn't get involved in this kind of matter. But we wanted to express our opinions and support Otto Biedermann. Since then my phone rings all the time.

Best regards,
Patrik

The meeting at the end of September was farcical because the original presidential candidate withdrew just before it, leaving the LFV rudderless for several days before a replacement was found and another meeting called to elect him. Soon afterwards another e-mail appeared in my inbox, this time from a clearly furious Martin Frommelt, the LFV Press Officer. Questioning whether there was any good reason to unseat Biedermann, his blisteringly angry message informed me that the entire board of the LFV had resigned in support of the erstwhile president with the exception of General Secretary Markus Schaper. It was clear that Frommelt, other board members and a number of the players were not particularly impressed by Schaper's non-action. Indeed, Frommelt wrote that in his opinion Schaper was a 'Judas' figure and he even wondered whether he had been in contact with members of the new board, an opinion that he believed other board members and some of the players shared. He went on to question whether the new president actually knew anything at all about football.

We feel that fifteen years of work by the LFV has been completely destroyed [Frommelt fumed], and I doubt very much whether national coach Ralf Loose will renew his contract in June. Most of the national players are completely shocked, and I wonder if they can concentrate on the next game in Bosnia. From my side, I finished as Press Officer and I sure will never do anything for the LFV again.

So, not only had Biedermann gone, but everybody except Schaper had quit too, from the vice president to Hans-Peter Nigg, the jolly kit-manager. Whilst Schaper plummeted in my estimation, I tried hard to understand his actions. As the only board member to be employed full time by the LFV, his resignation would have been far more than a simple point of principle. During our meetings I'd been struck by his enthusiasm for football in Liechtenstein. But had he been in cahoots with the new board, cheerfully working with Biedermann until the axe fell? Bosnia, whence I would leave for Liechtenstein's final qualifying match on 7 October, might, as it turned out, be far from the anti-climax to the campaign that I'd anticipated.

The Austrian Airlines plane came in low over the hills on its approach to Sarajevo. The undulating landscape was scattered with terracotta roofs, interspersed with grey, scorched buildings open to the elements, still in disrepair from the war that had ended six years earlier. I hardly recognised the airport since my last visit two years previously. The cattle shed of three check-in desks and one interminable passport queue had gone, replaced by a swanky new building of glass and steel, crammed with passport kiosks and other amenities. Even the burnt-out planes either side of the runway had gone. Sarajevo was clearly bouncing back from the horrific three year siege it had endured during the Bosnian war.

Like the players, I was staying at the Holiday Inn. The hotel, a bizarre bright yellow cube that was constructed for the 1984 Winter Olympics, had played an unwitting but major part in the war. It was when Serbian marksmen opened fire from its upper floors on a peaceful demonstration outside the Bosnian parliament across the road in 1992 that the conflict started in earnest. During the subsequent siege of the city, in which 10,000 people died, the war correspondents were holed up in the Holiday Inn, its western side shot to pieces but its restaurant still fully-stocked. Looking out of my window at the shattered hulk of the tower block across the street that was once the Bosnian parliament helped to put the shenanigans at the LFV into perspective. All the same I was both apprehensive and eager to hear the latest when the Liechtenstein party arrived a few hours after me.

The match had been moved from Sarajevo to the town of Zenica, an hour's drive away. However, that evening the team would train at the Bosnian national stadium, the Kosevo, not far from the Holiday Inn. I waited in the lobby, a sumptuous affair of leather armchairs, greenery, lamp-posts and bow-tied waiters bringing beer and coffee. I knew that the stadium was only twenty minutes' walk from the hotel, but I was hoping to cadge a lift from somebody. The players began to drift out of the lifts, from where Ralf Loose emerged in stockinged feet with his boots in his hand. He had a few defensive selection issues to ponder – as well as long-term-injury victims Daniel Hasler and Christof Ritter, he would also be without Harry Zech. Thankfully Patrik Hefti's calf strain had healed and he would definitely play. Also on Loose's mind was his new baby daughter, born just four days earlier. Who knows, if she'd shown enough early tenacity in the tackle maybe he would have brought her along to help ease his defensive crisis.

It was hard to know what to expect from the game, but I was optimistic. Bosnia were certain to finish in fourth place and had nothing to play for. Barbarez was missing with an injury. Austria and Israel had been due to play in Tel Aviv on the same day to decide which nation would go into the play-offs, but the match had been postponed due to the unstable situation in the Middle East. Liechtenstein's superb showing against Spain would have instilled confidence in the squad, but how much would the political shenanigans at the LFV have affected the mental state of the players? In most countries they would have just concentrated on playing football. In Liechtenstein, however, it wasn't that simple as nearly everyone was personally involved with the situation. Otto Biedermann, for example, was Patrik Hefti's boss at the LGT Bank, whilst Hefti's club FC Schaan had been one of those to vote against Biedermann in the presidential election.

I was reasonably confident that Liechtenstein were capable of gaining a point from their last match, and certain that they would break their scoring duck. The way Franz Burgmeier had got amongst the Spanish and careered goalward at every opportunity suggested that he might play a significant role, and I was sure that Liechtenstein would create more chances against Bosnia than they had against Spain a month earlier. And anyway, they had to score to avoid the ignominy of being the only nation in Europe to go through the entire campaign without a single goal.

The lift pinged again and Patrik strolled out into the lobby. He was pleased to see me and gripped my hand firmly in an iron handshake. We spoke briefly about the LFV coup, but soon began chatting about the game. 'Without Harry at libero, I think we might even play a flat back four,' he said. It was a tactic that might open the game up a little, I thought. I was becoming increasingly certain that Liechtenstein would at least score, maybe grab a point and, who knows, possibly even sneak a win. Or was I getting carried away?

Outside the hotel, Patrik bundled me on to the back of the coach with the team, and we headed for the Kosevo. It was in complete darkness when we got there, but as the coach came to a halt with a hiss of hydraulics the floodlights clunked on and the bowl-shaped arena was suddenly bathed in misty white light on a cool October evening. The pitch was covered with a dewy sheen, through which the dark green footsteps of the players gradually spread as they set off on their warm-up jog, clouds of breath trailing behind them. The word 'Sarajevo' was picked out in the seats along one side of the stadium, defiantly facing the hills from where the Bosnian Serbs had relentlessly shelled the beleaguered city but failed to break its spirit.

Schaper and two new board members appeared in a taxi soon after we had arrived – one of the party had told me that when the General Secretary had arrived at the airport ready to depart he had been ignored. Not one person shook his hand which, to someone to whom ceremony is so important, must have been a significant gesture. The squad were in good spirits though. A large, full, yellow moon hung between the flood-lights as the blue-and-black clad players went through their paces. It was a productive session, easily the most keenly contested that I had seen. Indeed so committed were the players that the groundsman later complained about the damage their exertions had caused to the pitch. The players were clearly up for it, and we returned to the hotel optimistic about the match two days hence.

The next morning Ralf and I explored Sarajevo, where I already knew my way around a little. I pointed out the white obelisk gravestones in the public parks, tragic evidence of how every piece of grassy ground except the Kosevo had been commandeered as a cemetery. We also stepped around the 'Sarajevo roses', star-shaped gouges in the pavement where shells had landed. It couldn't really have been a bigger contrast to Vaduz. When we returned, I found some of the players lounging in the lobby watching Yugoslavia play Luxembourg on television. Many of them were clearly bored, counting the hours before leaving for a light workout at the stadium in Zenica later that evening. Martin Stocklasa wandered over with Patrik, and we began chatting.

The elder of the Stocklasa brothers plays professionally in the Swiss top-flight for FC Zurich. He's a mature, intelligent man, whom I was startled to discover was still only twenty-two years old.

'I turned professional with Zurich when I was nineteen,' he said, 'but soon afterwards the coach who'd signed me left. The replacement coach couldn't work with young players, he just wanted to use older, experienced ones. So I dropped down a division last season to play for SC Kriens, which was in hindsight the best thing that could have happened to me. I grew and developed both as a player and a person, improving myself on and off the pitch. Some of the players looked up to me, because I'd played in the top league in Switzerland even though I was still young, so I had possibilities to show my ability and potential at Kriens. But then the coach at Zurich changed again and the new one brought me back, which was another lucky break. And now I'm a regular in the team.

'I first played for the national team when I was seventeen, in a friendly against Germany just before Euro 96. We lost 1–9, but played pretty well. There were thirty thousand people there in Mannheim, so it was a great feeling, and a nice way to start my career. From then on I've played nearly all of the games. In Liechtenstein it's easier to get into the national team than it is in other countries because the population is so small, so we can play five or six times a year against great teams like Spain and Germany and you can learn from them. When you play against people like Oliver Bierhoff or Raul, you can absorb aspects of their game into your own in a way you couldn't just by watching them on television. Obviously results are hard to come by, and it can be a little bit difficult playing for Liechtenstein because many people don't seem to appreciate that we are a very small country and it's impossible to compare us to great football nations. But when you see what we're doing at the moment, and the young players who are coming through now, I think we have a big future. In football, anything is possible, and I think we're proving that.

'The coaching is a big part of it. Ralf Loose has been in Liechtenstein now for five years or so, and he knows all the players very well. He knows the strengths and weaknesses of each player, which are their best positions, and I think that's been the secret of our success. The average age of this team is about twenty-two or twenty-three, so we'll probably all play together for another seven or eight years. That would be great, because we'd hopefully be able to take more points from bigger nations by virtue of all having played together for so long.

'We know our people in Liechtenstein, so the lack of interest doesn't really bother us. We're used to travelling to countries like, say, Spain where we'll play in front of thirty thousand, out of which there will be maybe ten or twenty people shouting for us. And it's the same at home. Against Spain last month, there were about four thousand fans shouting for Spain and about five hundred for us! It was the same against Bosnia, Austria and Israel too. Many countries can say that their supporters are like a twelfth man on the field, but we can't. But as a team we function well enough on the pitch that I think we have learned to manage without big support.'

I ask whether it's true that with Liechtensteiners being so successful in their jobs and personal lives, they find it hard to appreciate that the team enjoys a different kind of success, despite its record of defeats.

'The first thing you think about when you're at school in Liechtenstein is your career, what you're going to do when you leave. Football is just a hobby, nothing more. People don't see it as a serious thing. That perception has changed a little in the past two or three seasons because people like Mario Frick, Peter Jehle and I have turned professional. Maybe in another three or four years the whole team will be professional and the perception of football might change more. At the moment we have players who have to take three or four days off work for matches, which means they're not focussed only on football.

'It's important for me as a Liechtensteiner to represent my country abroad. To arrive here as a team, all dressed the same with 'Liechtenstein' on our clothes, it makes me so proud to be part of all this. Going out on to the field in a full stadium and hearing the national anthem, it's such a great feeling, you can't compare it to anything else. I play football every week for a living, and it becomes a usual thing for me. But when you're playing for your national team six or seven times a year, it remains a very special feeling.

'We're a small country in the heart of Europe, surrounded by powerful countries like Germany, Austria and Switzerland. Now though, we are starting to take part in big organisations like the European Economic Area, and every part of Liechtenstein life is starting to move into these bigger arenas. We want to be someone, to prove to ourselves that we can change things and have an influence. It's the same in our football, it's the same in our business and government. In football we have players playing in Switzerland and now in Italy too, which can only help Liechtenstein to become better known. Five years ago people would ask where I was from, and say, "Liechtenstein? Where's that?" Now it's different. Almost everyone I meet now knows where Liechtenstein is, whether it's because of football, banking or whatever. It doesn't matter how it happens, as long as we can find and assert our position in the world.

'Take the last time we played Germany, in Freiburg. When the referee blew his whistle after about seventy minutes, I looked up at the scoreboard and it said Germany 2 Liechtenstein 2, and I thought, that's incredible, look at that; now people will take us seriously. We had conceded a goal after about fifty seconds, but we came back and I scored, then they scored and we equalised again and for a few minutes it really was like playing in a dream We faded towards the end, however, particularly the semi-professional players, and had no power left, but that was still a great moment. We had the feeling that we could make them a little bit angry by playing so well. Before the game they'd been expecting to win seven or eight nil and expected to just brush us aside. But after the game they had to admit that they didn't play very well, and that we put on a great performance. To hear players who play regularly in the Champions' League say things like that was just incredible.

'I think we're starting to earn more respect from the bigger teams. In the past when countries like Liechtenstein, Luxembourg and San Marino went to countries like Spain and Germany, they would expect to score five, six or seven every time. Now they have to pay more attention to us because every year the smaller nations improve and pull off unexpected results. A couple of years back we drew 0–0 with Hungary, and a few years ago against Ireland. It doesn't happen very often, but as we improve a result like that is possible every time. The bigger nations are starting to realise that now, and they're not so sure of us any more.

'If other teams had conceded eighteen goals in seven games they would consider that a lot. But for us it was always our aim to concede less than about twenty-three goals. We haven't scored any ourselves, which isn't so good, but people must remember that our aims are different to most countries. We try to get some points, and in the Euro 2000 qualification we earned four. We've come close to winning a point in some games, such as Austria at home, and we are definitely very happy with this qualification campaign. Okay, our aims are not exactly high, but we've achieved what we really set out to do, and we aim to get better every year. We no longer lose 0–7 or 0–8 – if we did, we'd consider it a disaster, whereas in the past we might have been happy to concede that many against the really good teams.

'It's important for us to play in these qualifications because it helps us improve as players, and our results prove that this is working. If we had to play a pre-qualifying tournament with countries like Andorra it would be a disaster, not least because there would be no money. We played a friendly with the Faroe Islands a year ago, and there were only about five hundred spectators instead of the capacity crowds we've had for most of our games in the World Cup. Also if we had to get through a qualification round, playing teams like that would be really difficult for us, because we're not a team who is used to forcing the game. We're a reactive team, not a proactive one. To take the game in our own hands would be so difficult, and would take us years to achieve.

'The money the association receives as a result of playing in these games filters down to the clubs, who can then improve their facilities and coaching staff, and then have more opportunity to allow young players to reach their full potential. There is so much opportunity for footballers in Liechtenstein

– if you're in the team that wins the cup, for example, you go on to play in the UEFA Cup. In Switzerland, to do that you have to succeed in the highest league, which is much more difficult to achieve. Then the cycle of improvement continues – look at Vaduz, they're now in the second league in Switzerland, the highest any Liechtenstein club has ever been. And this can only help the national team as well. We obviously know that our potential is limited, but I think we have another five or six years' worth of improvement, then we'll see where we are.

'The problem with having such a small, close-knit squad is that when somebody drops out for whatever reason, like Mario or Harry for example, they're difficult to replace. Especially when we've all played together for so long. We only have about two hundred or so players even vaguely capable of playing at a reasonable level, so it's difficult for us, even when people are only injured or suspended. We'll have a lot of young players on the field tomorrow, so we hope that they'll benefit from the experience and get better, and hopefully have the opportunity to turn professional.

'When we play well, it's easier to present ourselves as representing our country. When we started out in world football, everyone laughed at us. Now they're starting to understand how and why we're doing this, and what we can do for Liechtenstein as a whole. I hope that we can stay together like this as friends and as a team, and that after every game we can say that we gave everything and look forward to doing more in the next. Who knows, in the next round of qualifications there might be a team in our group whom we can beat, but all we can do is take things one step at a time. We can say to ourselves, okay, this time we finished with no points, next time we have to earn one, two, maybe three points. But it's important not to get carried away – if we start deciding, we will win a match, that's when you lose 0–8. That's what happened in the 1–11 against Macedonia. Everyone's aware of that, even the young players.

'Who were the best players I've played against? Alan Shearer when Zurich played Newcastle United in the UEFA Cup. Also

Oliver Bierhoff. I'm aware that I'm very lucky – I'm still only twenty-two, I've played twenty-seven internationals, sixteen UEFA Cup matches and I've played against some of the best players in the world. These are experiences that no one can take away from me and, who knows, maybe when I'm thirty-five or so and have stopped playing, some of that experience will help me in life.

'Playing at Newcastle was incredible. When we were warming up there were a few people there but not that many, and we thought, okay, there won't be much of a crowd tonight, maybe fifteen thousand, that will suit us. We went into the dressing room and when we came out ten minutes later the place was full of people yelling and screaming. It was incredible, and the fans were so near the pitch. Extraordinary. It's always been a dream of mine to play in the Premier League in England. I used to tell people that I wanted to be a professional footballer and they'd say, oh yes, let him speak, he'll come back down to earth soon enough. But I proved them wrong and have now been a professional for three years. So when I say I dream of playing in England I know that perhaps it is possible. Look at Shaun Bartlett, he was at Zurich for four years and is a good friend of mine. He did well for the first couple of seasons but after that things didn't go so well and everyone started to write him off. Then he moved to England to play for Charlton and scored two goals against Manchester United in his first game.

'Playing in the national team raises your profile. Other clubs won't come and watch a team like Zurich. They might hear about you and think, ah, he's playing for Liechtenstein against Spain, one of the best teams in Europe, let's see how he does in that game. When you see how many coaches and trainers are sitting in the stand at national games, it's incredible. The Spain game was amazing though. The whole team gave one hundred and twenty per cent, and we even had a couple of chances to score. And it's not even as if Spain put out a weakened team: they played with every star. The result and performance was probably the best thing that ever happened to soccer in Liechtenstein.

'One of our strong points is that everyone is aware of his own ability and everyone else's. That way everyone helps each other – when someone makes a mistake, no one makes a big deal out of it. The coach won't dwell on mistakes or errors, he doesn't say, if you make another bad pass I'm taking you off. We know what we can do, we know that our defence is strong, so we get on with it. Loose doesn't have to shout and scream and tell us we have to fight. In the dressing room before a match he is quiet, he looks into your eyes to tell if you're ready or not. After the Spain game he was so happy and proud of us. Everyone was so tired, but it was just the greatest feeling to know we gave a hundred per cent, and the game really couldn't have gone much better.'

At that Loose called the players into a room for a team meeting, from which they emerged just as news came through that David Beckham had scored an injury-time equaliser against Greece to send England through to the World Cup finals and condemn Germany to the play-offs. This caused much delight among the Liechtensteiners, who huddled around my mobile phone as the text messages came in. Germany's football team seems to be as unpopular in its own backyard as it is in England. I felt a huge hand thump down on my shoulder from behind. Patrik leaned over me and said, 'I am the captain tomorrow.'

'Brilliant,' I replied, 'congratulations.'

'Oh, I don't know,' he said, laughing. 'Look at my predecessors. Mario doesn't play any more, Daniel Hasler's got a really bad injury and Harry doesn't play either. What next for Hefti?'

I was smuggled on to the coach again as we departed for Zenica for training. Patrik and Ralf weren't sure what Loose, sitting at the front, would think about my presence, and advised me to keep my head down. Later it transpired that I had been noticed and my presence disapproved of. 'What's the Englishman doing on the bus?' Loose was heard to ask his assistant Sepp Weikl. Weikl shrugged and Loose lapsed into a long, brooding silence. The coach doesn't like his players being distracted before matches, and he had already seen me hanging around with them in the lobby. I resolved to keep out of his way.

The journey took over an hour, enough time for the sun to sink behind the mountains in a dramatic blood-red sunset and ensure that we arrived in darkness. On the way we passed innumerable houses that were either half built or half destroyed. Some residents had improvised their roofs, and houses were covered with tarpaulins and plastic sheeting rather than slates. The poverty was obvious, and surprised the Liechtensteiners.

When we arrived, the stadium was locked and in darkness. Eventually somebody located a key to the stadium, but the dressing rooms were locked. The Bosnian FA had sent Milan, a scruffy man with a moustache as saggy as the arse of his jeans, to look after the Liechtenstein team. Milan was utterly, utterly useless. The more Ralf tried to gee him up to let the players into the dressing room and get the floodlights switched on, the less inclined he seemed to do anything vaguely useful. Ralf, conscious of Loose's thunder-faced, arms-folded presence nearby, flapped around him like a mother hen, squawking, 'We need dressing rooms and lights immediately! Immediately!' Almost oblivious to this, Milan leafed slowly through an ancient, dog-eared address book, apparently looking for the phone number of anyone who might know someone who would possibly have a key. At that point, three other Bosnians showed up, a tiny man in thick glasses, an elderly man and a huge fat guy with a bald head horribly scarred at the rear by what appeared to be buckshot. Milan was delighted to see them, and Ralf hopped from foot to foot as they all kissed each other on each cheek, shook hands and exchanged pleasantries. 'Can we have the key and the lights on, please?' said Ralf weakly, having given up on his previous Mr Angry stance and resorted to pleading.

'Of course,' said Milan in a voice that said 'why didn't you ask before?' A short debate then began among the four Bosnians over ownership of the keys. After a couple of minutes it transpired that Milan had had them all along. Ralf rolled his eyes as he passed me, and stage-whispered, 'That guy's a fucking wanker,' in perfect English vernacular.

From the dressing room to the pitch was a long walk along the length of the stand, down two flights of stairs and out of the tunnel by a corner flag. A huge mesh fence surrounded the tunnel, presumably to keep the crowd from the players, or vice-versa. A group of children had gathered behind one goal, hooting and jeering as the players began their warm up. Ernst was sitting pitchside on a metal box with his laptop atop his lap, bashing away. He looked up, gestured in the direction of the kids behind the goal and announced, 'The quality of the spectators here is the same as the quality of the Bosnian supporters in Vaduz. Very rough, very abusive.' He carried on typing.

'Have you seen the dressing room?' asked Freddie Hilti, the affable new vice president. I went to have a look. Dirty and cramped, with a broken toilet seeping water over the floor in the light of a dim bare bulb and streetlights shining through a couple of cracked windows; this was hardly the glamorous side of the World Cup. I returned to the pitch and raised my eyebrows at Hilti. 'We are very lucky in Liechtenstein,' he said.

Later that evening, once we had returned from Zenica, I was waiting in the lobby for Ralf and Ernst in order to head out for a drink at a bar I knew from my previous visit to Sarajevo. As I lingered by reception, Ralf Loose strode through the hotel door. He spotted me and started walking in my direction. Ulp, I thought, here it comes. I was about to launch into a long-winded apology for distracting his players when his face broke into a beaming smile and his hand thrust out to shake mine.

'Hello,' he said, 'I am sorry about last time in Liechtenstein.' I had arranged to meet him two days after the Spain match at the LFV offices, only to discover when I arrived that he had gone to Switzerland on a training course.

'Er, that's okay,' I spluttered, disarmed by his friendliness.

'I would like very much to talk with you,' he said. 'How about after breakfast in the morning, down here?'

'Great,' I said, 'thanks very much. Oh, and congratulations on the new baby.'

'Oh,' he said with an embarrassed chuckle, 'thank you very much.' And with that he disappeared into a lift and was gone.

Twenty-three

After breakfast the next day Ralf Loose was already in the lobby waiting for me, dressed, as ever, in a blue Liechtenstein warm-up suit. He jumped up, shook my hand, and gestured at me to sit down. He looked at me expectantly as I fumbled in my bag for notebook and tape recorder. I was all fingers and thumbs, nervous about meeting properly the man responsible for Liechtenstein's tremendous improvement in recent years. His English was excellent, something that surprised some of the players when I told them later, and he answered my questions thoughtfully and patiently, leaning forward in his chair with his hands clasped together.

'I had to stop my professional career because I was injured,' he told me. 'I tried for a year and a half to come back, but finally decided to study for a coaching licence in Cologne. When I passed I became the assistant coach at FSV Mainz 05, who are now top of the second league in Germany. After that I came to Liechtenstein as coach to the junior national team and assistant to Dietrich Weise. And now, for the past three and a half years, I've coached both the full national team and all the junior teams.

'It's always a problem for a player when he stops playing for whatever reason. He has to work out what he wants to do next, and for me the decision was to stay in football. That meant my next move was to get a coaching licence. Even then you need a slice of luck to find a job straightaway, and fortunately I had that luck with Mainz and then with Liechtenstein. I've been reasonably successful here, and so I am very happy. It was in the winter of 1996 that Dietrich Weise contacted me. He had been the national coach of the German national junior teams when I was playing, and I had been his captain when Germany won the World and European junior championships in 1981. He remembered me, knew that I'd stopped playing and had earned my coaching licence and invited me to Liechtenstein, which is how I ended up there.'

'It can't have crossed your mind that you'd end up as coach of a national team,' I said. 'You must have expected a career at club level?'

'Well, yes,' he replied, 'but although my title is national coach, I don't really work like other national coaches. I am out on the pitch with the juniors every day of the week, with matches in the Swiss junior championships every weekend, and then every few weeks there is a game for the full national team. So in a way I am like a club coach who coaches the national team on the side. I am a young coach, and I enjoy working with the players and being on the pitch every day.

'Liechtenstein is certainly different from Dortmund. It's a richer place, and the lifestyle is very nice with the mountains and the rivers. You don't have to go far for skiing, so it was no problem for my wife and I to go to Liechtenstein. I like it very much there.'

In only his third match, Loose masterminded Liechtenstein's first ever victory, the 2–1 against Azerbaijan. That must have been a good feeling, I ventured, having seen a video of the game and the mass love-in of the entire bench at the final whistle.

'Yes,' he said with a chuckle. 'The feeling was unbelievable. It was a big surprise too, because Peter Jehle was playing his first game and he was only sixteen years old and we had a very young team. I think this match was the start of the progress that we are seeing today. Many players are professional now, and hopefully there will be many more following that path. That way the national team can get stronger. That's what we're aiming for in the long term, and I think that everything is going well at the moment.

'The first change I made was to play a zonal marking system rather than the man-to-man tactics of Dietrich Weise. It wasn't easy at first because most of the players didn't play that way for their clubs; I think it is a tribute to them that they adapted so well and so quickly. Each game is different, but I think Azerbaijan was a great performance because we won, obviously, and scored two goals. It was a great day for Liechtenstein. Then we drew 0–0 with Hungary and have had games that have finished just 0–1 or 0–2, which isn't really all that different from drawing 0–0. But you need luck to get these results.

'One problem for me as a national coach is that I don't know in what condition the players will arrive when they report for matches. I hope that the best players will come, and that no one is injured, and then maybe we are able to get a good result. The best game in my time, however, must be the game against Spain in Vaduz last month. We had a very young team playing against one of the top ten teams in the world and we played very, very well. In those matches, it's not necessary to win or get a point to regard it as a great game.

'All the results in this qualification round have been good, even though we have lost every game. No one who knows anything about football can say that we have done badly. Unfortunately there have been some problems of a political nature between some of the clubs and the Association – although everyone recognises the good performance we have put up in this qualification group, there are some who speak out in another way. It's a problem. If all the people who are interested in football worked together rather than against each other, then things would be much better at this moment.'

I ask him about the level of support for the national team from the Liechtenstein people.

'Well, you come from England and I come from Germany, where we have an atmosphere at matches that you wouldn't get in Liechtenstein, and a lot of noise in the stadium. I can't believe the lack of atmosphere at our matches. It's a problem for us because when we play at home, such as against Bosnia and Spain, it's like an away match for us.

'In Freiburg for the match against Germany there was a great atmosphere, and it was fantastic for me as a German to coach a team against my native country. The stadium was full, and it was Germany's last match before the European Championships so they were keen to do well. But our team was in a good condition that day and we played with big hearts. We also attacked well and scored two goals. Only in the last ten minutes did the Germans get on top and scored five goals. They'd changed their team completely at half-time and the players were fresh, and I think that's the reason the score ended up the way it did. For me it was a special game, but it was hard to take all those goals at the death and the result was a disappointment to us in the end. The problem is that people will look in the newspaper and just see the result 8–2, and if they haven't seen the match they won't realise how close it actually was.

'Through performances like that I think we have started to earn much more respect from other coaches and other teams. In a way though that's a problem, because then they come out very focussed and concentrated against us. It was better for us when the teams would come out expecting to win easily – their concentration levels wouldn't be as high as they should have been, and that would sometimes give us opportunities to exploit this.

'It's important for us to play against the big countries. Not just in terms of money, although that is important. The LFV has a deal with a TV company, and Bosnia versus Liechtenstein isn't going to bring in much money from that. But from the players' point of view it's good for them to play against great teams, and be able to exchange shirts with famous players – it's a great motivation for them.'

Does he mix much with other national coaches, I wonder, exchanging ideas and thoughts on tactics. I had a sudden vision of Eriksson, Trapattoni and Loose hunkered down over a late-night coffee, talking tactics long into the night.

'No, not really,' he says. 'I am friendly with a few coaches in Germany, and I get on well with Atli Edvaldsson, the national coach of Iceland. We discuss some things, but a coach is always a man alone. If you win then everyone comes up and congratulates you and everything is okay, but if you lose and lose badly, then you are alone.

'When I arrived the plan was to make the LFV a more professional organisation, and I think we have achieved this. Last season my under-seventeen team won the Swiss championship, so we are in good condition at that level and have established ourselves as a strong force in the league with the top Swiss clubs. I said in 1999 that by 2005 we need to have a national team comprised entirely of professional players. Now we have six full professionals and five semi-professionals and it's only 2001, so Liechtenstein football has developed rapidly in a short time, which means everybody should be happy. But as you know we have new people in charge, so we will have to wait and see what happens. Five clubs were able to change the president when they were the only ones against him. It had nothing to do with sport, just political issues, and it's not good for Liechtenstein.'

I asked him his thoughts about the current World Cup qualifying campaign.

'I was very happy with the draw, because against Spain, Austria and Bosnia we had full stadiums. The only disappointment for me was that we were in a group of five teams instead of six. In a group of six we would get another team out of our pot at the draw and then maybe it's possible to win or earn a point. I would love to be in a group with England or Italy, and also Switzerland, because they would be good games for us.

'I'm giving a lot of thought to the future at the moment because I have just become a father for the first time. My current contract is up in June, so I need to hear the ideas of the new board and then decide what to do. At the moment I think anything's possible, maybe I'll stay in Liechtenstein for the next qualification or maybe I'll change and join a club somewhere. I'm not sure at this moment.

'A few clubs from Switzerland have shown interest in me, because they see results like my under-seventeen team winning the championship. German clubs have noticed the results I've had with the national team, like against Spain and Austria, but they don't take it any further. But I'm happy with the way things are going now. We have many young players who I think will get better and better. I think it's important that they go away from Liechtenstein and carve a professional career at foreign clubs; that's the main issue at the moment, helping the players to find good clubs. There are many players in the junior teams who will do very well in the future for the Liechtenstein national team.

'Take Franz Burgmeier for example. Two years ago he couldn't even get into the under-seventeen team because there were better players ahead of him. He was quite small then, but now he's filled out considerably and has become very good. I've now lost Harry Zech, who has retired from the national team because of the political situation. He was my captain and a very important player for me, so it's disappointing that he won't play any more.'

Finally, I ask him about the Mario Frick situation. Will he play again?

'Mario Frick is a player who has a great deal of talent, but talent is not always enough to make a really good player. He was captain of our team, and I think he should be living, working and thinking for and about the team, but he doesn't do that. As you know, coming from England, your heart has to be in wearing the shirt or you should stay at home. I'm sure that if a player did this in your country the press and the fans would be very hard on him. But in Liechtenstein everything happens another way. Everyone knows everyone else; people in the press know the Frick family so they are easier on him than I think they would be elsewhere.

'He was only thinking about himself and his club, and he didn't want to be here. When I speak with the team, they say, well, if he doesn't want to be here then we don't want him here either. Maybe Mario will think another way in the future and come back, but at this moment I don't think it would be right for him to play for Liechtenstein. It's up to him. I tried phoning him, but now he'll have to approach me.'

In the late afternoon we prepared to leave for the game. The players, looking relaxed and confident, boarded the coach. Schaper and the board members followed behind in a swanky, air-conditioned Space Cruiser with leather seats. Ernst, Heinz Zöchbauer from the *Volksblatt* and I were put in a battered old Mercedes taxi. This strange convoy was topped and tailed by a police escort that our car managed to lose within minutes.

We drove through the countryside, past games of football being played on scrubby pitches with warped goalposts. One game went on while a horse grazed in one of the goalmouths, employed by the kids as a goalie. The sun set behind the ghosts of mountains barely visible in the haze. About half an hour into the journey there was a sudden rattling noise beneath the gearbox, followed by a resounding, unhealthy clunk. Something bounced under the chassis a couple of times, there was a horrific wrenching sound and the car began to slow. 'Ohhhh,' said the driver sadly as he pulled off the road.

We climbed out of the car as he opened the bonnet and examined the engine forlornly. So there we were, an hour and a half before kick off, stuck somewhere in the middle of the Bosnian countryside with a taxi that was going nowhere in the foreseeable future. Thinking quickly Ernst called Schaper on his mobile, and within five minutes we were on our way again, wedged up against the new board members in the back of the Space Cruiser.

Finally we arrived in Zenica, a town we were destined not to see in daylight. Which from what I could gather was no great loss. Making our way up through the stand, a young woman behind a desk told us that she had given our press passes to Milan. Oh great, I thought, she might as well have given them to the goalkeeping horse. Having tracked Milan down to a bar beneath the stand we claimed our passes. We had to cross the pitch to get to the press box on the other side of the ground, from where Ernst spotted the only Liechtenstein supporter in the stadium, an elderly Croat living in Balzers who had driven down for the game. The temperature cooled and the floodlights created ghostly sails of mist in each corner.

The teams came out with Liechtenstein all in red, the anthems were played, Patrik performed a captain's duty with the pennants and then Liechtenstein's final qualifying game was underway.

To my delight Loose had opted to play Burgmeier from the start. Jürgen Ospelt would play at sweeper, with Hefti and Andi Gerster in the centre of defence. Excitement welled up inside me as the match kicked off. This was the last time I'd see them play and I was certain that they'd not only score a goal but claim a point too.

Bosnia attacked from the kick-off, with Vedin Music creating havoc down the left and, but for Jehle and some poor finishing, Liechtenstein could have been two or three down in the opening five minutes. Somehow though, they survived. It was clear that the absence of Zech meant that the back line was not as impenetrable as before. As usual the lack of an early goal subdued the crowd, a game plan that had worked well for the principality during the campaign. On a quarter of an hour, striker Dzehaludin Muharehovic thumped a header into the ground with such force the ball flew up over the crossbar from barely five yards out. The crowd whistled its disapproval.

Liechtenstein were giving away free kicks in some dangerous positions, but a combination of poor shooting and good defending prevented the deadlock from being broken. In the twenty-third minute, the principality had their first shot on goal when Freddie Gigon touched a free kick to Martin Stocklasa, who drilled a thirty-yard effort just wide of Piplica's goal. It was positive stuff, and Martin Telser was making some aggressive moves down the right. My hunch that Liechtenstein would score looked promising. Worryingly though, Bosnia were creating a number of clear chances, and after Hefti had been booked for an innocuous foul on Baljic, Bosnia broke the deadlock just after the half-hour. For the second time in the space of five minutes, Coventry City's Muhammad Konjic was allowed to rise unchallenged for a corner. His first effort had been saved, but this time he made it count, thundering a header past Jehle for the opening goal.

Liechtenstein tried to probe forward, with Thomas Beck and Ronny Büchel chasing everything with their customary enthusiasm. It was looking good for Liechtenstein as half-time approached – to go in only a goal behind boded well for the second half. But just before the break, disaster struck. A cross came over from the right. Muharehovic got his head to it, the ball bounced in front of and over the diving Jehle, and would have gone in just under the bar had Gerster not leapt athletically to push it over the top with his left hand.

The young defender was trudging towards the dressing room before the referee pulled out the red card, disappearing into the gloom in the corner and away up the tunnel. I thumped the table in frustration. Not only would Liechtenstein have to play the rest of the game with ten men, Elvir Baljic had placed the ball on the spot and was standing at the end of a short run up. The whistle blew, Baljic stepped up, Jehle went left, the ball went right and Liechtenstein were two down.

Almost immediately the referee blew for half-time and the team traipsed dejectedly back to the dressing room. Buggering bollocks, I thought. From expecting to go in in a good position, only a goal behind and having created problems for the home defence despite not playing particularly well, Loose now faced a major damage-limitation exercise. The sending off and the penalty had woken the crowd, and you felt that the Bosnian players smelt blood and would be looking for goals in the second half against their depleted opponents.

Not surprisingly Loose took off Thomas Beck and replaced him with a defender, young Marco Nigg. Immediately after the interval though, Bosnia were carving through the defence. On forty-seven minutes Music, a constant threat down the left, cut inside and lashed a shot into the side netting by Jehle's left-hand post. Two minutes later, the diminutive Nemin Sabic burst through the rearguard and, with Martin Stocklasa in pursuit, dragged his shot wide. Bosnia had now created more chances in this game than Spain and Israel combined in the previous two matches.

Just before the hour, however, Liechtenstein reminded the Bosnians that they were still in the game. First Burgmeier thumped a first-time effort wide after a Freddie Gigon free kick was headed clear, then Telser burst through the centre to find Büchel on the right, but the baby-faced striker found little in the way of support and the chance was gone.

Despite some dogged defending from the ten men, they fell further behind on sixty-eight minutes when after a neat passing move Sabic speared the ball past Jehle for the third goal. And then, for the first time in the entire campaign, Liechtenstein heads started to drop. As the team regrouped for the kick-off, shoulders sagged and heavy feet dragged up the field. Loose withdrew Burgmeier, who'd had a disappointing game, in favour of Matthias Beck, but the third goal had extinguished the spark and fight from the side like someone snuffing out a candle. With eight minutes left Marco Nigg tripped Baljic on the left side of the area to concede another penalty. Jehle got a hand to Baljic's spot kick but couldn't prevent the fourth goal. Three minutes later it was five. Sabic broke down the right and rolled the ball into the centre where an unattended Mario Dodik turned it past Jehle. 5–0. I couldn't believe what I was seeing. It was the most extraordinary end to a wonderful campaign. Liechtenstein chins were on chests and hands on hips. None of the fight that had secured the superb result against Spain and recovered the disastrous start against Israel was visible. With three minutes left, Baljic almost added a sixth when Jehle did well to save a twenty-five-yard free kick, and for me as well as the team the final whistle couldn't come quickly enough.

When it sounded, and the team trudged dejectedly from the field, I sat for several minutes with my chin in my hands, looking glumly across the pitch as the stadium emptied and reflecting on an inglorious end to the campaign. Although Liechtenstein had defended well for most of the game, the irre-spressible, tails-up, previously unquenchable determination had gone. Had the LFV coup affected the team's performance? Or had they fallen victim to the over-confidence that Martin Stocklasa had referred to the previous day? Eventually I managed to drag myself across the pitch to the press conference. Which, helpfully, was in English.

'It was an easy game for Bosnia,' said Loose, looking wearier than I'd ever seen him. 'Our preparations were not so good, and it didn't help that we had to drive for more than one hour to get here. For ninety minutes my team as I know them were not on the field. I always say that football is about fifty per cent talent, and fifty per cent character. We don't have a lot of talent in Liechtenstein, but tonight we showed no character whatsoever. It's not easy to pinpoint why either. My professional players lacked character tonight, and that's why we lost five nil. I think in the future I'll have to see if it's possible to change things in the heads of some players.'

Bosnia's coach Drago Smajlovic was understandably happy with the result. 'We played well,' he said, 'and didn't underestimate Liechtenstein. We agreed in the dressing room beforehand to treat Liechtenstein in exactly the same way we would a top team, and I'm satisfied with the approach of the players. We still have some problems in converting chances, but this is a precious victory because no one has beaten Liechtenstein so heavily in this competition. They are a good team, and I wish them well in future tournaments.'

It was a long and sombre drive back to Sarajevo. In the lobby of the Holiday Inn Freddie Gigon came over. 'That game was no fun,' he said, the sparkle in his brown eyes missing for the first time in a year. 'At half-time Loose said that if he could substitute seven players, he would. It's frustrating because Bosnia are not a particularly good team and they didn't play particularly well.'

The usual suspects were starting to gather. I'd envisioned some kind of farewell bash, an end-of-qualifying knees-up, but unsurprisingly no one seemed to be in the mood. I'd never seen the players so glum. Ernst arrived in the lobby, followed by Patrik and Jürgen. It was way past one o'clock in the morning, but I hoped that a bar I knew would still be open. It had fast become my favourite watering hole in Europe, not least because of the people. The previous evening we had got talking to a large, bleached-blond girl, half Swedish and half

Turkish, who claimed to have twenty-six body-piercings, of which six were immediately visible. She had also just got out of a Turkish prison after shooting her philandering husband in the leg.

It seemed a good place to wash away the grimy memories of the game, and we also wanted to escape the gloomy atmosphere in the lobby. After a fifteen-minute walk, however, the four of us arrived to find the gates closed and padlocked with an enormous chain. We set off back to the hotel – the lobby would be littered with dejected players and officials but at least we'd be able to get a drink there. When we approached reception though, it turned out that the man with the keys to the bar had just gone home. Valiantly Ralf gathered all our room keys together and raided the minibars. So there we sat, the captain, the full-back, the journalist, the national team secretary and the Englishman, at the end of a memorable World Cup qualifying campaign. It was two o'clock in the morning, and we were in a Bosnian hotel lobby drinking warm cans of beer that were six months out of date. Somehow it seemed a fittingly depressing conclusion to a dreadful evening.

Twenty-four

The next morning everyone was itching to go home. The team was due to leave at nine, and although I wasn't going until lunchtime, I got up early to go and say goodbye. Patrik was one of the first people I saw. 'The plane is delayed by three hours,' he said glumly. 'It hasn't even left Zurich yet.'

Everyone had packed their bags and checked out, and there was little alternative but to lounge around in the lobby. I went to have a chat with Peter Jehle. The young goalkeeper, still only nineteen, had been one of the stars of the qualifying campaign, and would be returning to Zurich to try and regain his place in the side.

'I have two older brothers who played football,' he said, 'and so from about three and a half I was playing with them in the street. We lived in a cul-de-sac in Schaan, and there were about a dozen kids who would be out all the time playing football. So the game was pretty important in my life from an early age. It's funny, in the street games I was always in goal because I was the youngest, but when I started playing properly I was an outfield player. After last night, maybe I should have stayed an outfield player.

'But eventually I joined FC Schaan as a goalkeeper, did quite well and so when I was sixteen I played my first game for the national team, in the 2–1 win over Azerbaijan in 1998. I remember being really nervous before the game, but as soon as we kicked off the nerves disappeared. I felt proud that I had been given the opportunity and was determined to take it. The whole team played well that night and it was just the perfect start to my international career. At the same time I was also goalkeeper for the under-seventeen and the under-nineteen national teams, which was great because it meant I was getting a lot of games which was important for my career and development at that time. That's when the professional clubs started getting interested. Crystal Palace and Liverpool called me at home, and so I went over to England for about a month. Karl-Heinz Riedle was at Liverpool then, and they had got him to phone me. I wasn't in at the time. Then they sent me a letter, which was good because otherwise I'd have thought it was a practical joke! I spent three weeks at Palace and ten days at Liverpool. The trip began well – Crystal Palace tried to sign me on the very first day I was there, but I said no because I was still only sixteen and was too young to leave Liechtenstein and move to England.

'The main thing I noticed was the passion and the fire in the heart of everyone in England. Liverpool was just incredible; the supporters create an unbelievable atmosphere at the matches. They offered me a contract as well, but I didn't sign because I was afraid to move away from home when I was still so young. I said to them maybe in a couple of years when I'm a little older. When I got home I just started praying that I'd get another chance to be a professional footballer!

'Looking back even now though, I still think I made the right decision. I needed those two years at home to complete my education and my business apprenticeship, because I wanted to make sure that part of my life was okay before I committed myself to professional football. When I was in England I saw with my own eyes young players who had come over from Northern Ireland, for example. Football was their whole life, they didn't have anything else and they weren't interested in anything else. They were devastated when they were told they wouldn't make it, and I was determined not to end up in that situation.

'Soon after I came back from England Bayer Leverkusen

tried to sign me. That was a really tough decision for me because they were so interested. They completely understood about my wanting to finish my education and even offered me a business apprenticeship at one of the Bayer pharmaceutical factories. They did so much for me, but I still felt it was a little bit too early. I thought long and hard, but had to turn them down as well. And then Juventus called!'

The young keeper's bird-like features opened out into a chuckle as he related the latest on the list of big European clubs who had sought his services. It was almost as though he could hardly believe it himself. He was conscious that he might sound like he was boasting, but there was no question of that. Indeed I marvelled at his maturity: how many sixteen year olds, when offered contracts by some of the biggest names in world football would turn around and say, sorry, I'm not ready for this yet?

'Juventus also offered me a contract, but I had a bad feeling about the situation. I felt that Juventus at the time were trading players more like stocks and shares than footballers. They knew that they could sell you on to a lower division club and make money out of you because of the Juventus connection. It wasn't actually Juventus people who gave me this impression, rather it was an agent acting as a middle man. I didn't have an agent myself, I made all my own decisions, and this guy I just had a bad feeling about. For him I was just an investment on which he hoped to make a profit. But again it was a difficult decision because Juventus offered me a lot of money to join them. But I had a good life in Liechtenstein and money wasn't the issue. As with all the other offers, I listened to my heart and said no thank you.

'I knew that there were some Swiss clubs interested in me too, and I had to figure out which offered me the best chance. I spoke to quite a few and decided that Grasshoppers was the best option. Zurich is not too far from home: I didn't really think about that at the time, but with hindsight I now realise that that was important.

'My first team debut was quite eventful. I'd been on the bench a few times, but obviously a substitute goalkeeper has very few opportunities unless something drastic happens. We were playing against Basel and the regular goalkeeper Stefan Hüber gave away a penalty and was sent off. It was injury time, the match was 0–1 and I had to go on and face a penalty on my first appearance. Now I didn't realise at the time but the penalty taker was Massimo Ceccaroni, who had been at Basel for fifteen years and never scored a goal. He was a legend at the club who had stayed with them through good times and bad, this was his last season before retiring and they'd let him take this penalty just so he could score his first goal. The whole crowd was chanting, 'Massimo! Massimo!' I knew nothing about this and assumed he was the regular penalty taker. The referee had said, look, this is the last kick of the game, no rebounds or anything, I'm blowing the whistle straightaway. Anyway I saved the kick. It wasn't till afterwards when a reporter asked me if I knew what I'd done that I realised! I was in all the newspapers because of this duel: my first game and his last chance. We were even on chat shows together.

'Anyway, I played the next game and we won 4–0, but then the regular keeper came back from suspension. He was injured towards the end of last season so I came in with about ten games to go. In my next game I saved another penalty to ensure a 0–0 draw as Grasshoppers went for the title. Our last game was away to St Gallen and we had to win to be champions. The only trouble was St Gallen were unbeaten at home in thirty-four matches. It was like Fort Knox there. We played a perfect game and beat them 4–0. So there I was, nineteen years old and winning my first title. That was quite a thrill.

'The Spain game last month was another highlight. I'd seen players like Raul on television and suddenly there he was, two yards away from me. I thought, what the hell am I doing here? I almost felt like asking for his autograph! In Alicante I could see he was getting frustrated because he'd missed a couple of chances, and I was thinking, wow, we're making him angry!

'I played my first Champions' League game this season, against Porto. Going there was incredible. Their badge is a dragon, and you walk on to the pitch out of this dragon's mouth, with fire spitting everywhere and everything. There were fifty thousand people in the stadium and the noise was incredible. We played well, but I made a big mistake for the first goal. We drew 2–2, lost 2–3 at home and then I was dropped. The newspapers really got on my back, and *Bild* blamed me for Grasshoppers missing out on £10million from the Champions' League.

'Yesterday was a disaster though. For some reason we had found it difficult to prepare, and I felt it because I've been on the bench at Grasshoppers for the last month and not had any games. I'd lost the feeling to sense and anticipate passes and crosses, I really noticed that last night. But the whole team was poor, and it was definitely a low point for me. Sometimes shit just happens, but last night was a big shit. Maybe we expected too much having played some really good games recently. It was terrible. We've made some really good progress during this campaign, but that was definitely a step backwards.'

I asked how much of an influence Ralf Loose has been, the coach who blooded him in international football at just sixteen.

'Oh, he's a great influence,' said Jehle. 'He was brave enough to throw me in at sixteen years old when other coaches might have waited until I was twenty or twenty-one. But I'm nineteen now and have more than twenty caps. He also taught me how to live for football, to eat, sleep and breathe the game and to concentrate on the right things, even in my diet. That's the German way. In England I think it's different; they can go out and have a few beers but play with such fire and passion that it doesn't matter so much. When I was sixteen I found it difficult to be disciplined because football in Liechtenstein was more of a hobby, something you did aside from your job. Now though, it's my job and it gives me a good wage, so it's not so difficult, and I'm grateful to have been given the opportunities I have received.

'Playing for Liechtenstein is so important to me, but all we can do is try as hard as we can for the best result. Usually when I go back to Grasshoppers they tease me about the national side, but after the Spain game they were forced to think a little bit more. It's sad that we'll never play in the

World Cup finals, but that's the way it is. I'll still keep trying to improve my game. I need to improve my aggressiveness. I think at the moment I'm a little bit too shy on the pitch, too nice. When I go up for crosses I never hurt other players, it's always me who gets hurt!'

With the wealth of experience he has already gained, I wondered what ambitions he has, given that most of his career is still ahead of him.

'I'd love to play in England,' he replied. 'I like the mentality of the players there. But my first priority is to win back my place at Grasshoppers. That's the first step, then I can think beyond that about going to England. I'm nineteen now and have grown up a lot in the last couple of years. A good friend of mine, Bernd Haas from Grasshoppers, is playing at Sunderland. He says that it's not a particularly nice city, but every guy in town goes to watch the match and the atmosphere is amazing. And they want to see honest football – if you lose but give your best then the supporters don't mind so much.

'I think I'd need to toughen up a bit to play in England though. I remember when I was first at Crystal Palace and going up for crosses – the strikers would just crash into me which was a big surprise.

'Looking back over the World Cup campaign, I think we can be very satisfied. We've had some good chances and played some good games. I think with a little more self-belief we might have scored some goals and maybe got a couple of points.'

By the time the coach was ready to take the players to the airport, it was time for me to leave as well. Patrik offered me a lift on the team coach, reckoning that now the game was over Loose wouldn't mind. Freddie Gigon spotted me on the bus and pretended to grass me up to Loose, who was sitting as usual at the front. 'Excuse me, head coach,' he called with a grin, waving his finger in the air, 'this person shouldn't be on here!'

Having passed through the tight security at the airport, in the immediate wake of the World Trade Centre disaster, we sat in the airport café over coffee. Suddenly the Liechtenstein plane was called and everyone leapt up in a flurry of activity and pulling on of coats. After a few handshakes they were through passport control and away, and I was left alone amidst the half-empty coffee cups and half-drunk fruit juices.

And that was the end of Liechtenstein's quest for the World Cup.

Twenty-five

Four weeks later I returned to Liechtenstein for the last time to say goodbye. When I reached Vaduz the trees on the mountainside that overlooked the capital had changed from a uniform dark green to the warm browns and yellows of autumn. There were more new buildings, of course, and the foundations were already being laid for the next wave of development.

Harry Zech, so sorely missed in Bosnia, had agreed to show me around his winery, and Patrik joined me on the walk up the steep road to the rear of Vaduz's enormous church. We pushed open the door and descended some steps into a cool, dim cellar where the smell of grapes mingled with the sharper tang of disinfectant. 'Zech!' boomed Patrik into the gloom, his voice bouncing around the vaulted ceilings. A familiar head popped out from around a distant corner and Harry emerged and gave us a tour of his subterranean refuge. Huge silver vats filled with fermenting wine dominated the enclaves, while in another room racks of bottles lay maturing, ready for distribution.

Harry had served a one-year apprenticeship as a winemaker at the Prince's vineyard, the Hofkellerei, followed by another year in Switzerland. A three-year oenology course followed before he was fully qualified. As luck would have it, the premises he now occupied had become available just after he had graduated in 1998, and he took the considerable risk of striking out on his own straightaway. Fortunately Harry made excellent wine and won the contracts to supply Liechtenstein's two most exclusive restaurants. He also caters for the weddings that take place in the church above, and these three clients alone provide him with a good enough living that he doesn't need to open a shop.

'Although I didn't like what went on at the association,' he said, 'I couldn't have gone to Bosnia anyway because this year's vintage was at a critical stage and I couldn't leave it. Normally it's not a problem as being self-employed I can usually organise my time, but the end of September and October are so important, and I work alone so can't leave the wine unattended. Late September is vital for harvesting the white grapes, and October is the month for the reds, so it's my busiest period and I just can't take the time off to play for the national team.

'I have just over two hectares of vines,' he continued, 'mostly in Vaduz. The Föhn means that we can grow good grapes here and produce good wine. In the late summer and early autumn I have to check the sugar levels in the grapes and pick them at just the right time. The whites I have to leave as long as possible, and the timing is crucial because if they start going rotten they're useless. Then I harvest them, and most of the national team come and help with this. I sort the good grapes from the bad, put them in the wine press, add yeast for fermentation and leave it to mature. The whites are usually ready in April, the reds in June.

'I'm lucky to be self-employed, not least because what I do is a dream job for me, but also because it means I can still devote enough time to playing football. My job is so much more than a job to me, and football will always come second. That's why I play for Eschen-Mauren in a lower league, because the demands on my time aren't so great and I can play for enjoyment. When Austria Lustenau were in the top league in Austria they offered me a semi-professional contract, but I turned it down because I was still studying. Vaduz and Chur in Switzerland both wanted to sign me last season, but if I had joined them I would have had to employ someone here, which

I didn't really want to do. Obviously though, I'm proud to play for my country and have some great memories. I played in the first game against Northern Ireland and in the 0–0 with Ireland at Eschen. Both Spain matches as well, they'll leave me with special memories. Being made captain was a great honour too, especially against a great team like Spain.

'The advantage of having played international football for so long now is that we aren't overawed any more. Obviously we still have great respect for these teams, but we're not afraid of them. Some of the big teams have been a disappointment, refusing to swap shirts with us after we played them, for example. Salihamidzic of Bayern Munich, he was disappointing too when we played against Bosnia. He made so many fouls and I didn't like his attitude; I expected more from a top-flight professional like that. Spain were great though. I swapped shirts with Sergi at the end, and I had to ask who he was! He just laughed and told me his name.

'I'm glad that I'm not a professional footballer. I did have ambitions when I was younger, but I suffered quite a lot with muscle pulls early in my career and it never happened. In hindsight I'm so glad things turned out the way they did. My whole life is set up, with a nice job, a good income and being my own boss. It's a dream for me to be where I am now. It was a bit of a risk to start up on my own – as the pressure is on to produce top quality wine. Fortunately I'm lucky enough to have really good clients. Thinking about it I guess it is a bit strange for a national team to have a captain who makes wine for a living. What do you think David Beckham's wine is like? I remember once that we had a friendly match with Switzerland in Basel a few years ago. I had an examination in the morning which involved wine tasting: I had to rush straight from the tasting and play in an international, which is probably a bit unconventional.

'Having played for Liechtenstein from the beginning, however, I can say that this is the best team there has ever been. I'm going to miss being with them. There's such a good atmosphere in the squad and I'm good friends with many of the players. It's more than likely that I won't play again; it's not definite yet, but I didn't like how Biedermann was removed. The new board approached me and asked me to reconsider and I said I would. As things stand at the moment though, the answer is still no. After all, Spain was such a good game that it would be a nice way to finish.

'I think we have to give the new board a chance. They are in a difficult position because they have such a tough act to follow. I just hope that football in Liechtenstein can continue to develop the way it has.'

That evening Ralf and I went to watch a Liechtenstein Cup quarter-final, the last game I'd see in the principality. FC Schaan Azzurri, an amateur team founded by Italian ex-pats, were facing the might of FC Vaduz, with the team from the capital winning 14–2 in the drizzle and providing almost as many goals in one match as I'd seen watching the national team for more than a year. My new hero, Franz Burgmeier, scored four.

The next day huge snowflakes fluttered down on the valley. The trees on the mountainside looked like they'd been dusted with icing sugar, among which the castle looked even more enchanting. I'd been invited to lunch by Otto Biedermann, the ousted president, and Martin Frommelt, the former press officer now editor-in-chief of the *Volksblatt*. I trudged through the snow to the Gasthof Löwen, arguably Liechtenstein's best restaurant. One of the oldest buildings in the principality, the Löwen is a sturdy stone construction with huge thick wooden doors. As I stamped the snow from my shoes, I discovered that I was early and was shown into the private room that Biedermann had booked. A few minutes later he came bounding into the room, filling it immediately with his presence. He was a tall, bespectacled man in his forties with a booming voice and I was almost knocked off my feet by the warmth of his welcome. Martin would be late he said, but we should start without him. I heaved open the enormous leather-bound menu and noticed straightaway that at the top of the wine list was 'Vaduzer Blauburgunden Harry Zech '99'.

Biedermann was coming to terms with suddenly not being involved with Liechtenstein football any more, but he was clearly hurt by Markus Schaper's role in the change at the top of the association. 'I was a little surprised,' he said. 'I thought it was strange that the whole board had resigned except the General Secretary, who would now be working for the new regime. As far as I am concerned, it's as if Markus had been playing for Celtic and then suddenly moved to Rangers. You just don't do that. Now he's very important for the federation because the new people have a lot of things to sort out and they don't have the experience. We're hosting the 2003 European Under-Eighteen Championships, Loose's contract will be up for renewal soon and there's a lot of work to be done and money at stake. But it was a democratic decision and we have to abide by it. One thing that does disappoint me is that since the vote was taken at the meeting, I have not heard a thing from any of the new board. Not a letter saying thank you for my work, or even telling me officially that I'm not the president any more.'

Martin Frommelt arrived as we were talking about the role of Schaper. 'Huh,' he said as he sat down, 'I think that if you mention the name Judas, everyone in Liechtenstein will know immediately who you are talking about.'

As Frommelt grumpily assaulted his starter, Biedermann smiled across the table, shrugged slightly and said, 'This is a very small country . . .'

'When he calls me at the *Volksblatt*, I'm always busy,' responded Frommelt. 'And I'm pretty sure I'm not the only one who's not talking to him.'

'The whole situation was poor,' said Biedermann sadly. 'All the annual reports were passed by the meeting. Everything was passed, everyone was saying "very good". Which proves to me that they weren't upset with my work, it was just me, my personality they didn't like.'

'The only criticisms they made were over an interview that Otto gave to radio after we beat Azerbaijan,' said Frommelt. 'He was very euphoric, and the radio station turned it into a jingle that was played very often. The five clubs were saying, listen to him, he's obnoxious, egotistical. The other criticism they made was that the LFV website wasn't updated often enough, that communications weren't so good. And then they couldn't even give the press a manifesto, setting out anything they would change. And the man who was supposed to be the new president withdrew two days before the meeting. To me it was a complete farce.'

'I'm disappointed in Markus,' said Biedermann. 'You only have to look at the situation. When I was removed all the other board members said, well, if Biedermann is not the president, we are part of his board, then we will go too. All of them said that, except one person. They were all people who lived for football twenty-four hours a day. Even though I have a very responsible job at the bank, I'm thinking about football from the moment I wake up in the morning until I go to bed at night. I don't think you can say that about the new board.'

The following morning, I took a final walk around Vaduz. It looked different in the snow, but as I made the circular perambulation for the last time, the familiar landmarks were all still there. I passed the enormous church, behind which Harry Zech continued to bottle his 2001 vintage whilst mulling over whether to play for Liechtenstein again. The raised car park opposite the Post Office, from where I'd watched agape as the National Day fireworks lit up the sky, and where I'd caroused the night away with the team that hot summer night, was covered in a film of snow. I passed the supermarket, where I'd purchased the sickly rosé wine during my first stay, before going on to the funfair nearby and unwittingly trying to pick a fight with a Hell's Angel. The Old Castle Inn, where I learned never to ask for a large beer, the tables and chairs stacked in a corner of its snowy terrace. When I reached the roundabout I looked across to the Adler and Vanini's, the historic establishment frequented by those pioneers of Liechtenstein travel writing, Playfair and Fitzgibbon, and its modern upstart neighbour. I passed the Baron's souvenir shop, where I'd bought my postcards over the past year, the old Town Hall, the open area next to it where I'd swayed to the brass band a year before and grooved to Liechtenstein rock on National Day beneath canvas: now it was open, snow-covered and criss-crossed with footprints. Off to the left was the staircase I'd climbed as the prelude to my walk to Triesenberg. There was the old art museum and the new, the postage-stamp museum, and then down to the Town Hall, into which I'd blundered out of the rain a year earlier.

I paused and looked up at the castle, the ancient building that had overlooked most of my journey into perennial defeat, its roofs and battlements topped with snow. I tried to drink it all in for the last time. I passed the Schwefel on the bus on the way to Sargans, where Claudia had unburdened herself and where I had first met the extraordinary players of this wonderful football team, and whooshed past the Grünesholz as its '*Zimmer Frei*' sign spun in the wind.

And before I knew it, I was past the Gutenberg Castle, over the Rhine and in Switzerland.

Twenty-six

The stadium was packed and a riot of colour, blue and yellow at one end, black and white at the other. The two teams emerged from a subterranean tunnel at the pitchside and the place exploded. The Juventus team was announced, each player's picture appearing on the big screen at one end of the ground. Edgar Davids, David Trezeguet, the away fans cheered each one, just audible above the whistles of the home supporters.

The announcer moved on to the home side, each of whom was welcomed with a full-throated roar. '*Numero sette*,' boomed the voice from the speakers reaching number seven, 'Super Mario Frick!' A familiar face appeared on the board, with an eager smile and his hair slicked down over his ears. The crowd roared even louder.

Ernst turned to me and grinned proudly. In front of him was the Verona v Juventus match programme, the cover of which showed Liechtenstein's greatest player celebrating his first ever goal in Serie A, scored at Parma the previous week. Ernst's expression said it all. The boy's done good.

The previous evening I'd arrived in reception at the Hotel San Marco, close to the stadium, where Mario Frick had suggested we meet. As I arrived a dozen young men in matching blue-and-yellow tracksuits had just got up from the dining room and were milling around, some heading back to their rooms, others going into the lounge where city rivals Chievo were live on television away to Venezia.

Mario wasn't among them. I asked at reception, where the young woman picked up a telephone, tapped in some numbers and said something in Italian. 'He'll be down in five minutes,' she said.

I was nervous. Frick's presence loomed so large over Liechtenstein football that he had become almost mythical to me, especially now that he was a regular in Serie A, one of the best leagues in the world. On his Verona debut against Roma he had shared a pitch with Gabriel Batistuta, Francesco Totti and the other players who had helped the team from the capital to win the title the previous season. Seven days earlier he had thumped a header into the back of the Parma net for his first goal for his new club in a 2–2 draw. Tomorrow, he'd be playing against the 'Old Lady', Juventus, a team packed with stars. Not bad for a skinny kid from Balzers.

A tall, familiar figure bounded down the last flight of stairs. Dressed like the others in the pale blue-and-yellow tracksuit of Hellas Verona, Mario loped over and shook my hand, directing me to a sofa in a small enclave beyond reception. He was friendly, open and spoke excellent English despite his reticence. 'Sorry,' he apologised with an embarrassed smile, 'for the last year I have been thinking in Italian, now I suddenly have to speak English.'

He was in a good mood. A fortnight earlier his girlfriend had given birth to their second son, Noah Zinedine Frick. As well as naming his new addition in tribute to the French World Cup star, Mario is clearly a tennis fan too: his sons are called Yannick and Noah. When he scored against Parma, he lifted his shirt to reveal a t-shirt emblazoned with a picture of baby Noah. And tomorrow he was taking on one of the best teams in the world. 'So things aren't going too badly, then?' I asked.

'Life in Italy is wonderful,' he said, 'and to play in Serie A was always a dream for me. The standard of football in Serie A is so much higher than anything I've ever known before. Against Roma, my first game, I played only twenty minutes but it was amazing, the quality of the players around me. I had played in Switzerland for seven years, then after some problems with the coaches there I moved to Arezzo in Serie C. I had a good year, scoring sixteen goals, and then came to Verona. There were two or three clubs from Serie A and another seven or eight from Serie B interested in me, but I thought Verona, it's a great place, it's Serie A and the fans, they are just wonderful. It's very different from Liechtenstein where the fans are so quiet. It's difficult to play there because there is no atmosphere, but here the atmosphere is incredible, and it's a beautiful place to play football. I have a villa that overlooks Lake Garda, so life away from football is good too. I am so happy, it's like living a dream.'

Noting the reason behind my visit, he broaches the subject of the national side almost immediately.

'As you know, I don't play for the national team any more,' he said.

'And will you ever play for Liechtenstein again?' I asked.

'Yes, sure,' he replied immediately to my relief, before adding, 'As long as the trainer is changed.' He laughed nervously.

'Is that what it would take to see you in a Liechtenstein shirt again?' I asked.

'Maybe, I don't know. It's hard to say, but as things are right now, if there was a change of trainer I would play for Liechtenstein again. I don't like Loose. The problem was that there were two matches going on in the same weekend, one for my club and one for Liechtenstein. First Loose told me I could play with my club Arezzo, but then he said I had to come to Liechtenstein instead, which was very bad of him. I went to Liechtenstein, but there were some problems when I got there and so I went home and played for Arezzo. I don't like the way he treats the younger players; he's very hard on them. It's difficult for me to play for Liechtenstein, because I rarely touch the ball. Maybe four or five times a game, which is not enough. It's so different here, we play with three strikers and that's much better for me. I'm sure that I'm already a better player having come to Verona even though I've only been here a short time.

'The national team has improved. Defensively it's the best ever, but in terms of attack it's not so good. I don't like the system we have. We must play a more attacking game – look, we didn't score a single goal in this qualification. When I think back to the win over Azerbaijan, that was the best match ever because we played so aggressively and so well. And we won, so it clearly worked. Yet that was the last time we scored in a qualifying game.

'I know that I have a responsibility to Liechtenstein as my national team but, given the trouble there has been, I have to wait to see if there will be a change. There's nothing else I can do. If Loose phoned and said, Mario, I'm sorry for all that's happened, will you come back to the national team, then I would probably say yes. He's doing a good job for Liechtenstein but he does nothing to attack. If I was the coach I would change a few things around, I'd play with three strikers and try to attack teams. We have some good young attacking players now, like Fabio D'Elia, he's very strong and probably our best prospect, and Thomas Beck is very good. Franz Burgmeier I like very much – he reminds me of how I used to be when I was his age. I was small and fast, but luckily I grew quickly as I got older.

'Away from the national team I still have many ambitions. My first is to score against Juventus tomorrow. I'm looking forward to the game so much – it's amazing to think that one year ago I was playing in the third league in Italy, and tomorrow I'll be playing against Davids and Trezeguet in Serie A. To come from Liechtenstein, a country of just thirty-two thousand people, and end up playing in the best league in Europe is just a dream come true for me. The people here are wonderful, much more open than in Liechtenstein, and the football press is thousands of times bigger. When I walk around the city, I can hear people saying, look, there's Mario Frick, and they're happy to see you, which is really nice. In Vaduz everyone would say, oh, look there's Frick, the arrogant footballer. It's not easy in Liechtenstein: when somebody earns a bit of success, people become jealous very easily. I hope that I can help people change their attitude. But for the moment,

I am concentrating on my life here and the game tomorrow.'

As the teams lined up in Verona's Bentegodi stadium, a huge bowl to the west of the historic city, I was immediately struck by how much stronger and fitter he looked than when I'd last seen him in action in Innsbruck seven months earlier. His shoulders were broader and his legs chunkier: clearly the Serie A training regime had helped him develop even further from the short, skinny kid of his teenage years. As the players stood over the ball waiting to kick off, the Verona fans took up a deafening chant that they would keep up for most of the game, one which Ernst helpfully translated for me as 'Juve, Juve, arseholes'.

The game opened at a frantic pace, and in the fourth minute Mario broke away down the left. He'd got faster over the intervening months as well, and his pace took him inside Lilian Thuram before laying a visionary pass to Oddo on the right flank. The move, alas, came to nothing.

Six minutes later, Verona took the lead. Juventus goalkeeper Buffon spilled a header from Verona's Romanian international Adrian Mutu and Leonardo Colucci speared the ball into the back of the net. The stadium erupted in an explosion of blue and yellow. The game was being played at a phenomenal pace, with Mario chasing everything and running hard. The tall Liechtensteiner was playing furthest forward, a target man for fellow strikers Mutu and Camoranesi, who were succeeding in pushing the Juve full backs towards their own goal and preventing them getting forward to create chances from the flanks.

Verona were deservedly holding their lead. On the hour Mutu threaded the ball beyond Thuram and Mario was away and running. As he bore down on Buffon, Juve's Croatian international defender Igor Tudor produced a brilliant tackle to deny the Liechtensteiner as he was about to slide the ball beyond the keeper and into the far corner. Five minutes later though, the home side doubled their lead. Mutu broke down the left and sent a low cross along the six-yard line. Frick slid in but couldn't quite make contact; fortunately Camoranesi was at the far post to tuck the ball away. The noise was deafening. Suddenly the

Rheinpark Stadion could have been on the other side of the world.

With eight minutes remaining Igor Tudor pulled a goal back for the visitors when he headed home a corner. Deciding to sacrifice his attacking policy to preserve Verona's slender lead, coach Alberto Malesani decided to take off the Liechtenstein striker. Mario's number seven flashed up, and the former FC Balzers player trotted to the touchline as the stadium rose as one – he'd had a fantastic game. As Mario left the pitch, a huge blue-and-white banner appeared along the front of the upper tier behind the goal where the Verona fans had gathered. '*Copa la Vecia con Frick*', it read: 'Destroy the Old Lady with Frick.'

In injury time, David Trezeguet lashed home a brilliant equaliser and Verona were denied an historic win. No matter. Mario Frick had now truly established himself at the pinnacle of the European game. Not only that, he looked fitter, stronger, faster and hungrier than ever before. Surely Liechtenstein cannot do without him any longer.

The plane that took me from Verona back to England passed almost directly over Liechtenstein. As we soared above the clouds I knew my journey was coming to an end, but life in the principality thousands of feet below went on without me. It had been a wonderful experience following this national team with a winemaker for a captain, a bank manager at centre half and a schoolteacher at full back, and I felt I understood both Liechtenstein and football a little better after my year hanging on to the coattails of the national team.

A few months later the World Cup finals would begin in Japan and South Korea in an orgy of glamour and publicity. As my plane passed over the mountainous principality I reflected that regardless of who picked up the golden trophy at the end of the tournament, a little piece of it would always belong to Liechtenstein.

Afterword

Exactly eleven months after the disappointing Bosnian conclusion to Liechtenstein's World Cup odyssey, a knot of blue-shirted players stood over a football amid lengthening shadows at the end of a hot, sticky alpine day at the Rheinpark Stadion. The 2002 World Cup had been and gone in a blaze of glory, despair and intrusive sponsorship and Liechtenstein were coming to the end of their opening Euro 2004 qualifying tie against Macedonia.

The game was following the usual pattern. Liechtenstein were fighting hard and creating a few half-chances, but Macedonia had scored early and had settled back to see the rest of the match out with minimum exertion on an energy-sapping day. It was just three weeks shy of four years since Liechtenstein had last scored a competitive goal, so the visitors felt, justifiably, that their work in Vaduz was done. After all, it wasn't so long since they'd travelled to the Rheinpark Stadion and plundered eleven goals – surely this time one would suffice.

As the Liechtenstein team tired, the match had petered towards its inevitable conclusion. By the third minute of injury time many people in the disappointing crowd of 1,500 were beginning to make their way out of the ground. Then Martin Stocklasa was fouled twenty-five yards from goal, which sparked the knot of players discussing their options over the ball.

I shielded my eyes from the low sun to see that every Macedonian player had placed himself between the ball and the goal as the Liechtensteiners debated their plan of attack. When you spend most games stoutly defending your own eighteen-yard line, clever free-kick routines tend to be fairly low on the list of training priorities. What was to be done?

The visitors tried to delay things by refusing to retreat ten yards, knowing that the longer they took the greater likelihood there was of this being the last kick of the game. Every Liechtenstein player, bar Peter Jehle and the three standing over the ball, was in the penalty area. One of the burlier Macedonians – which, believe me, is saying something – went into the book for timewasting. Eventually the Ukrainian referee was happy enough with the eighteen players jostling 'twixt ball and goal to allow the kick to be taken. Twenty-one-year-old Michael Stocklasa puffed out his cheeks, looked from the ball to the goal, took three steps and thundered in a low, scudding shot that barely left the turf. The ball disappeared into a thicket of legs, flashed past the Macedonian goalkeeper and billowed the bottom-right-hand corner of the net.

There was a brief silence, then the little stadium erupted. I jumped higher out of my seat than should have been humanly possible, while on the pitch the younger Stocklasa's blond head disappeared under a pile of jubilant blue-shirted players. The roar of delight echoed around the Rhine Valley, its reverberations probably still startling cows even today. Hats, programmes and paper cups were launched skywards and yelping strangers embraced. I found myself being struck repeatedly on the head by the rolled-up programme of the joyful Liechtensteiner behind me. Suddenly 1,500 people sounded like 15,000.

The final whistle went as soon as the Macedonians rolled the ball off the centre-spot, and pandemonium broke out. To a man, the Liechtenstein team punched the air and ran to each other in delight. Strung along the pitch, hand in hand, the players saluted the crowd again and again, raw exhilaration subduing fatigue. I all but shed a tear – it was not only a goal, the first goal I had seen them score in my three years of following this extraordinary collection of players, it was a point. A palpable, perceptible, perspicuous point – only the sixth in Liechtenstein football history – and I'd been there to see it won. Four years without any tangible reward for dogged determination and steady improvement from a young team for whom the odds were always firmly in the opposition's favour. Four years of 'Liechtenstein nil'. Finally, gloriously, breath-takingly, some reward for all the huffing, puffing, optimism and soul-searching of the previous years.

In the bar afterwards I realised that Liechtenstein were sitting a proud second in the group seven table – two places above England. Okay, England hadn't actually played any games yet, but when I pointed this out to Ralf Loose, it didn't stop him vowing 'I'm going to frame that table'. In Vaduz later I sat outside the Old Castle Inn with Patrik and Shannon Hefti, so dazed with delight we could hardly speak.

If ever there was one moment that could be classed as a turning point in Liechtenstein's football progress, Michael Stocklasa's screamer of a free-kick was it. At last, all the patient development, the progress of the Loose era that had hitherto been measured only in gallant defeat, had produced something tangible. A goal, and one appropriately from a young man who, having emerged through the youth ranks, was the epitome of the Loose regime. Not only that, it was a goal that had prevented another customary defeat.

A 5–0 reverse in Turkey followed, in the dying moments of which the prodigal son Mario Frick, who had by then patched up his differences with Loose, missed a penalty. Then the principality prepared for the arrival of England at the end of March 2003. Although this was to be unquestionably the biggest game ever staged in Liechtenstein, there was another issue dominating the agenda: the referendum to decide whether Hans-Adam II should be awarded the increased powers he desired.

The prince, who remains universally popular throughout the country, had made it clear that if he didn't get these new powers, including the right to dissolve the government and appoint judges himself, he would be ringing up a bloke in the local paper with a van who calls himself 'Mr Move-It' and leaving Liechtenstein altogether for Vienna. Actually, come to think of it, I don't think he mentioned Mr Move-It, but that was certainly the gist.

The referendum process was keenly contested. So much so, in fact, that the former prime minister, Mario Frick, (no, not that one), an outspoken critic of the prince's proposals, awoke one morning to find a pig's snout nailed to his gatepost, while another leading campaigner had a skinned cat tossed into his garden. Whether such tactics had an effect will never be known, but the result of the referendum saw two-thirds of voters making Hans-Adam the closest thing we have to an absolute monarch since Louis XVI's head was still attached.

In the aftermath of the referendum, the English football team arrived. Liechtenstein had never seen anything like it in terms of security – Swiss soldiers were on Liechtenstein soil for the first time since the Second World War and a series of fences was erected around the stadium to cope with the influx of ticketless England fans who were converging on the principality. Only 950 tickets had been issued to the English FA, but several thousand people were travelling.

Security worries couldn't detract from the game, however, and Liechtenstein more than rose to the occasion. When, on the morning of the game, I'd told a BBC radio programme that England should count on no more than a 2–0 win, the presenter had burst out laughing. So the fact that the score was exactly that shows how it was a moral victory for the home side, as Liechtenstein's collection of part-timers, semi-pros and small time professionals matched the finest England could offer.

Emile Heskey, memorably named 'Emily' by the stadium announcer, managed to look like a barely mobile piece of industrial plant. Steven Gerrard was practically anonymous, failing spectacularly to take advantage of the space afforded him by the short-of-match-fitness winemaker Harry Zech, who was playing his first game in three months after injury. Daniel Hasler had an almost flawless game, missing only one tackle in the entire ninety minutes but that was only against Kieron Dyer so it didn't matter. Granted he gave away the free-kick that led to England's second goal, but, given the fact he doesn't get to see much Premiership football, he might have been forgiven for thinking that Heskey posed some kind of threat on the edge of the box.

The atmosphere in Vaduz was friendly, on the whole. It was bizarre seeing so many people on the streets in the Liechtenstein capital, and there were few signs of trouble – most of the England fans intent on causing aggravation had done so in Zurich the previous evening.

On the day of the game it seemed that every bus arriving in Vaduz was disgorging England fans. There seemed to be two distinct types: beer-bellied replica-shirt wearers with shaved heads and the Burberry brigade, all of whom were of a pallor that suggested they wouldn't recognise a vegetable if they saw one. Whereas on previous strolls to the Rheinpark Stadion I've only had a couple of tethered goats for company, it took the best part of an hour to enter the ground through two security checkpoints and the turnstiles.

Ten minutes before kick-off, around two hundred England fans tore down a fence and gained illegal entry to the game. It was a slightly less imaginative approach than those of the two Barnsley supporters who had climbed into the ground during the night and hid in a shed until it was safe to emerge and the man whose attempt to paraglide over the fences fell about two hundred yards short and into the waiting arms of the Swiss police.

The rest of the campaign passed solidly and unspectacularly. In the return leg of the England game at Old Trafford, watched by a crowd twice the size of the population of Liechtenstein, the team excelled themselves again – reaching half-time at 0–0 for the first time in nearly five years. Again, England were restricted to a 2–0 win by a dogged performance by the visitors. By the time this game came around, however, Liechtenstein had a new coach. Ralf Loose had never seen eye-to-eye with the new regime at the FA, and had been dismissed prior to the Old Trafford game after a series of disagreements. It brought to an end the most successful era Liechtenstein football had ever seen, and the name of Ralf Loose should be written large in the history of the game in the principality.

His replacement, the former Austria Vienna player Walter Hörmann, combined his day job as FC Vaduz coach with the national team role, a logical decision given that he was already working with most of the national team day-in, day-out. Although Loose's dismissal was deeply unpopular with the players, they soon took to Hörmann who employed more of an attacking philosophy than Loose. The performance at Old Trafford boded well for the new era, but Hörmann didn't stay long, leaving in November 2003 to take over at Austria Salzburg.

As I write this, Liechtenstein are enjoying their most successful qualifying campaign ever under their latest coach, the former Eintracht Frankfurt boss Martin Andermatt. In fact for one extraordinary week in October 2004, Liechtenstein football was in dreamland. On Saturday 9 October 2004 Portugal arrived in the principality for a 2006 World Cup qualifier and the match seemed to be following the usual pattern of Liechtenstein's encounters with the big teams. Midway through the first half Pauleta headed home a Cristiano Ronaldo cross, and six minutes before the interval Daniel Hasler inadvertently turned the ball into his own net.

Three minutes into the second half, however, a terrific run by Thomas Beck and a fortuitous rebound from a Portuguese defender set up Franz Burgmeier to drill a shot past Ricardo in the Portuguese goal. Then, fifteen minutes from time, a Beck free kick eluded everyone in the penalty area, bamboozled Ricardo and drifted into the net to complete possibly the unlikeliest comeback in football history. Liechtenstein had equalised. For the first time in six years they had scored twice in a competitive game; enough to earn them a draw with one of the world's greatest football nations. It was an extraordinary result, one on a par with the great upsets in world football like the Faroe Islands defeating Austria in 1990 and the US beating England at the 1950 World Cup, and one that earned the principality its first ever World Cup point.

But Liechtenstein weren't finished yet. Four days later they took to the field at the Stade Josy Barthel in Luxembourg, the scene of a 3–3 draw in a 2002 friendly in which Martin

Stocklasa scored a hat-trick. That game was the only occasion in thirty-three matches that Liechtenstein had avoided defeat away from home.

This time there were World Cup points at stake – and all three would leave Luxembourg with the Liechtenstein team. By half-time Liechtenstein were two up thanks to Martin Stocklasa and Franz Burgmeier, and with an hour gone Mario Frick had made it three. 'Burgi' added another before the end, and Liechtenstein's miracle was complete.

'When you play at home against one of the biggest and best teams in Europe then you have nothing to lose, have you?' Martin Stocklasa told me afterwards. 'I mean, Portugal came to Liechtenstein with all the star footballers they had and we knew that it would be very tough but we weren't afraid. We'd learned from the past and we said we just have to have fun. And that's exactly what we did. We were quite lucky to get the first goal, but then we saw that they were nervous and so we tried to do the impossible – which worked. Sometimes you get what you earn, and we'd worked, fought and believed in ourselves.

'In Luxembourg, for the first time in our history, we were favourites to win; a new and dangerous situation for us. Our biggest opponents were ourselves! But we knew we deserved to win, and we did. That gave us self-confidence, and for me it was very special too. I'd already scored a hat-trick against Luxembourg in the friendly, and then I scored against them in the World Cup. Quite impressive for me!

'The future looks bright in Liechtenstein. We're redeveloping the stadium to take the capacity up to 6,000, and we're still developing as a team as well. We've had the opportunity to play against England. The main difference between the old Liechtenstein and the new is that we are not just peanuts for the big teams any more, as we proved in the games against England and Portugal. I think nowadays we are able to surprise anybody.'

One man who has missed out on these latest developments is Patrik Hefti. The game in Bosnia, for which he captained the side, turned out to be his last in the blue jersey.

'I stopped playing for the national team after the 2002 World Cup campaign mainly because of my studies,' he told me. 'I realised that I was getting older because after a tough game or training session my body hurt more then ever before. Additionally, I had neither the drive nor the time to practise as much as I used to, so I'm going to retire from football altogether in the near future.

'The bank offered me a position as Head of Settlements in Singapore after I completed my business administration degree. I'd finished top of my class which surprised nobody more than me, but I guess my ambition changed places from the football pitch to the classroom, and I've accepted the position.

'We have to see what the future holds. Football is not going to be a part of my life for a while. However, I would like to be a youth coach one day because football has taught me so much. I would love to show kids that it's a great sport that helps them to develop their personality and much more. I'm very thankful to God for the opportunities I've been blessed with and for the future to come.'

London, August 2005